donation

War, Lies & Videotape

how media monopoly stifles truth

D0733637

International Action Center
New York, NY

2000

International Action Center
39 W. 14th St, Suite 206
New York, NY 10011
212 633-6646

ISBN: 0-9656916-5-9

Library of Congress Cataloging-in-Publication Data

Aristide, Jean-Bertrand.
    War, Lies & Videotape : how media monopoly stiffes truth /
    Lenora Foerstel (ed.) ;
    Jean-Bertand Aristide, Ben Bagdikian and others.
      p. cm.
    Includes index.
    ISBN 0-9656916-5-9 (alk. paper)
      1.Mass media—Ownership. 2.Mass media—Censorship.
    3.Journalism—Objectivity. 4.Press and propaganda. 5.Mass
    media—Political aspects. I. Foerstel, Lenora, 1929- II.
    Bagdikian, Ben H. III. Title.

P96.E25 A75 1999
302.23—dc21
                                                99-052468

visit the IAC web page at http://www.iacenter.org

ACKNOWLEDGMENTS

Women for Mutual Security (WMS) and its International Coordinator, Margarita Papandreou, would like to thank the organizations and individuals who helped to make the Media's Dark Age conference, held in Athens, Greece on May 24-28, 1998, a great success. The following organizations played a major role in making the conference possible: the Andreas Papandreou Foundation; the Institute for Strategic Development Studies (ISTAME-Andreas Papandreou); and the International Action Center (IAC).

The IAC was created by former U.S. Attorney General Ramsey Clark. Sara Flounders, a co-director of the IAC, provided helpful direction and staff support in the preparation of the conference. Support for the conference was provided by the Piraeous Bank, Attika Bank, Ethiki Insurance, Astir Palace-Viouliagment, DFI and Micromedia-Sharp. We wish to acknowledge the sponsorship of OTE (Hellenic Telecommunications) and KTIMATIKIBANK (Mortgage Bank). We are also grateful to the General Board of Global Ministries, and especially Elizabeth Calvin, Executive Secretary of the Ministries of Women and Children, for their financial support.

The success of any project depends on the work and dedication of many individuals. To Annita Kontoyianni, Dina Vardarmatou, Evelyn Seegers, Frank Alexander, Deirdre Sinnott, Ellen Andors, Susan Harris and Peter Brock we owe a special thanks. We also wish to thank our communication sponsors: Express and Lambrakis' Institution; Mr Dimitri Chryssikopoulos, Director of Olympic Airways for North and South America; John Keissanis, Manager of Support Services, and Maria Vicenti, Group Sales Assistant, for Olympic Airways.

We thank them for their patience and cooperation in bringing participants to the conference.

The editor of this book would like to thank her husband, Herbert Foerstel, as well as Gregory Dunkel and Paddy Colligan, for their editorial assistance.

Lol Rook found time working a very busy schedule to design the cover of this book. We greatly appreciate her efforts.

We would also like to thank the International Action Center (IAC), and specially Sara Flounders, for making the publication of this book possible. The People's Rights Fund is acknowledged and thanked for supporting the publication of this book.

Table of Contents

IV: Cultural Imperialism: Third World Perspective

V: International Alternatives to the Media Monopoly

INTRODUCTION

LENORA FOERSTEL

In 1998, over a hundred international journalists and activists met in Athens, Greece, for the "Media's Dark Age" conference, a gathering that would critically assess the world's beleaguered media. Participants from around the world expressed deep concern about the newly developing global media system, which is dominated by powerful corporations seeking to control the news and world markets.

Media and its corporate owners act as patronizing advisors to the American public on world events, orchestrating public opinion on issues of war and peace. That manipulative power grows as media companies merge and centralize. In 1961, Edward R. Murrow, a vice president of CBS News, was instrumental in mobilizing consent for the Vietnam War. At that time, NBC was owned by RCA, which carried out military contracts through the RCA laboratories at Princeton, New Jersey. In 1986, General Electric acquired RCA and became owner of NBC, maintaining its heavy investment in military research and weapons manufacturing. CBS was subsequently bought by Westinghouse, another defense contractor involved in nuclear production.

As a handful of giant corporations takes over the media, news is merged with entertainment and traditional standards for reporting the news are discarded. Disney/Cap Cities, current owner of ABC, and Time Warner, a major U.S. cable owner, are the backbone of world entertainment. The myth that entertainment is value-free is easily dispelled when one examines how motion pictures and television are permeated with class, racial, gender and political biases. Xenophobic stereotypes abound, encouraging aggressive chauvinism and militarism.

The media drumbeat for war often provokes the government into military adventures. On Sunday, September 20, 1998, the *New York Times* editorial page encouraged the Clinton administration to intervene in Kosovo. "If American diplomacy can not persuade all other NATO leaders to press ahead, Washington should assemble a coalition of those willing to act," said the editorial. "If necessary, America should act on its own."

The great media conglomerates often work in concert with the U.S. government to influence public opinion abroad. The U.S. has spent millions of dollars influencing the beliefs and actions of foreign citizens in an effort to ensure the election of government officials who will support U.S. policies. In 1997, the U.S. sent troops to seize television transmission towers in the Bosnian Serb area of Pale in order to clear the airwaves for a "pro-West" voice, former Bosnian Serb President Biljan Plavic. Plavic was running against a candidate considered unfriendly to the U.S., yet despite heavy U.S. financing of her campaign, she lost the election.

With U.S. support, Russia's Robber Barons applied the American model of news control and took over their mass media. "Almost all of the major financiers and business magnates jumped into the news business, which they considered vital for defending their empire. Millionaire Vladim Gusinsky of Media-Most and Boris Berezovsky of Logovaz invested heavily in television and controlled two of Russia's largest channels as well as a small Moscow daily newspaper." (*Washington Post*, Sept.19, 1998). The rise of the American-style Robber Barons marked the beginning of the "Dark Age" for Russia's media, during which money controls the news. As in the United States, the newspapers print the views from the boardrooms rather than from the streets.

In the United States, public relations firms play a major role in packaging and disseminating propaganda in the mass media. Indeed, the 150,000 PR practitioners in the U.S. outnumber the 130,000 American reporters. What the PR firms feed the media is slanted and unconfirmed material, yet it is used by many editors and journalists because it is convenient and cost effective. Hill and Knowlton (H&K) and Burson-Marsteller together represent a third of the most quotable sources in the country, an enticement the media cannot resist.

In 1990, shortly after the Iraqi invasion of Kuwait, Hill and Knowlton formed Citizens for a Free Kuwait, a front organization intended to lobby Congress and the media on behalf of Kuwait. The propaganda created by H&K and its front group quickly became a major source of information on TV networks. Citizens for a Free Kuwait set out to convince the American public that it was necessary for the U.S. to intervene in the Persian Gulf in order to protect Kuwait. Selling the war was a difficult task, since it meant supporting a notorious oligarchy in Kuwait which suppressed any form of democracy, censored and intimidated journalists, hired foreigners to carry out the nation's physical work under slave conditions, and withheld both human and civil rights from women. H&K's effective propaganda helped to bring the U.S. into a war that cost the American public billions of dollars and devastated the nation of Iraq.

Ruder Finn Global Public Affairs is a less prominent PR firm than H&K, but its international influence is unparalleled. They were hired by the Bosnian Muslim and Croatian governments, each paying thirty thousand dollars a month for the firm to tell their story to the world. Like H&K, they falsified stories in order to move the United States into war, this time in the Balkans.

Reports were circulated of massive numbers of rapes of Muslim women by the Serbs, an alleged 50,000 by late 1992. The 50,000 figure had been provided by Bosnian leaders and reached the United States and Europe through the offices of Ruder Finn, which made no effort to check out the improbable numbers. Such reports were passed on in the American media on a daily basis, and the contrary evidence emerged too late to reverse the demonization of the Serbs. In July 1999, the UN reported that their investigation had documented a total of 800 rapes in Bosnia committed by Serbs, Croatians, and Bosnian Muslims combined. The report was ignored by the media, which found the bogus figure much more appealing.

Because Ruder Finn's project to demonize the Serbs made heavy use of Holocaust images, it could only gain public credibility if prominent elements of the Jewish community signed on to it. When James Harff, director of Ruder Finn Global Public Affairs, was asked to describe his proudest public relations achievement during his work in the Balkans he responded without hesitation, "To have managed to put Jewish opinion on our side."

Harff explained that this process was extremely sensitive, since the dossiers of his clients, the Croatians and Bosnian Muslims, were notoriously anti-Semitic. Harff said President Tudjman of Croatia had been "very careless" in his book *Wastelands of Historical Reality.* "Reading this book, one could accuse him of anti-Semitism," admitted Harff.

Harff also acknowledged that President Izetbegovic of Bosnia was no better than Tudjman, because his book *The Islamic Declaration* strongly supported the creation of a fundamentalist Islamic state.

"Besides, the Croatian and Bosnian past was marked by a real and cruel anti-Semitism," admitted Harff. "Tens of thousands of Jews perished in Croatian camps. So there was every reason for intellectuals and Jewish organizations to be hostile towards the Croats and Bosnians. Our challenge was to reverse this attitude. And we succeeded masterfully. . . .We outwitted three big Jewish organizations—B'nai B'rith Anti-Defamation League, the Jewish Committee, and the American Jewish Congress."

Ruder Finn convinced the Jewish organizations to publish an advertisement in the *New York Times* and to organize demonstrations outside the UN. "This was a tremendous coup," said Harff. "When the Jewish organizations entered the game on the side of the [Muslim] Bosnians, we could promptly equate the Serbs with the Nazis in the public mind."

Harff said his task was made somewhat easier by the fact that most Americans had no understanding of what was happening in Yugoslavia. "But, by a single move," he said, "we were able to present a simple story of good guys and bad guys, which would thereafter play itself. We won by targeting the Jewish audience. Almost immediately there was a clear change of language in the press, with the use of words with high emotional content, such as 'ethnic cleansing,' 'concentration camps,' etc., which evoked images of Nazi Germany and the gas chambers of Auschwitz. The emotional charge was so powerful that nobody could go against it."

When an interviewer asked Harff about the morality of peddling stories about the Serbs for which he had no proof, Harff responded, "Our work is not to verify information. We are not equipped for that. Our work is to accelerate the circulation of information favorable to us, to aim at judiciously chosen targets. . . .We are professionals. We had a job to do and we did it. We are not paid to be moral."

It was the task of the participants at the Media's Dark Age conference to suggest ways to free news reporting from "professionals" like James Harff. The papers assembled in this book describe how the U.S. government and media shape the news in ways that leave the public powerless. Notable among the distinguished speakers was the former President of Haiti, Jean-Bertrand Aristide, who revealed the human suffering being caused by the structural adjustment policies imposed on the Third World by international lending institutions. That suffering is ignored by the media monopolies that measure progress by profits.

Former U.S. Attorney General Ramsey Clark told the Athens conference of the "enormous artificial culture" being built by the U.S. media in the hands of a small number of mega-corporations. Scott Armstrong, who worked for the Senate Watergate Committee as a senior investigator for Sen. Sam Irvin, points out that even though the media helped to expose Watergate, it also withheld vital information surrounding that scandal. Among the things the public did not learn was that after Nixon's resignation, a full investigation involving many more issues was suppressed with the complicity of the media.

The American government's censorship of the news extends beyond the United States and includes everything from secret CIA newspapers and radio stations to open interference with the airwaves of sovereign nations. Early in the Cold War, Radio Free Europe was created as a CIA front, and even after its nominal "privatization," it resorted to dirty tricks, disinformation and election frauds.

Several papers in this book, including those by Ben Bagdikian, Peter Phillips and Michael Parenti, describe how the new corporate ethics compromise the reporting of foreign events by the U.S. media. "Little wonder," states Phillips, "that the U.S. news is so biased against democratic liberation struggles all over the world and so favorable to multi-national capital flow."

Parenti's paper, "Media Evasion," covers the deliberate omission of news as well as the arbitrary labeling of people and events. Such terms as the "Free Market," states Parenti, are pet labels "evoking images of economic plentitude and democracy," when in reality "free-market policies undermine the markets of local producers. . .and create greater gaps between the wealthy few and the underprivileged many."

The media's increasing use of "technical terms" in conveying the news is particularly disturbing. By technical terms we do not mean scientific jargon. Quite the contrary. We mean terms with arbitrary meaning, assigned by government bureaucrats, editors or publishers. The best current example is "weapons of mass destruction," defined to be chemical, biological or nuclear weapons. Note that mass destruction itself is not the concern here. After all, 24 million people, mostly civilians, were killed in one country alone during World War II, and conventional weapons were more than adequate to do the job.

The media have not used the issue of weapons of mass destruction to address killing. Their concern is simply to demonize a handful of Third World countries by guilt through association. If the press really wished to address the dangers of weapons of mass destruction, it would have approached the story quite simply: Who has them? Who has used them? That straight-forward journalistic approach has one major problem. The United States and its allies would appear to represent the major threat. After all, the United States is the only nation in the world that has all three weapons of mass destruction, and has used them all in war: Biological weapons in the Indian wars, chemical weapons in World War I, and of course, nuclear weapons in World War II.

Ramsey Clark's paper, "Media Power," expresses his concern with the use of misinformation and lies in the popular media. He states, "Struggle as we may and must, the greatest challenge in the struggle for democracy is the search for truth. The question of human survival and, if successful, of human nature, will depend largely on whether we can see the truth in time." Clark sees the willingness of the media to demonize entire nations and their leaders as "its most dangerous and vicious power."

Ben Dupuy also discusses the demonization of progressive international leaders. As former Ambassador-at-large for Haiti, he closely observed the smear campaign against Jean-Bertrand Aristide, a liberation theologian who assumed the presidency in Haiti on February 7, 1991, after receiving 67 percent of the vote. Predictably, many American political leaders regarded Haiti's first democratically elected leader as a threat to entrenched business interests. Henry Kissinger called Aristide "a psychopath," and Patrick Buchanan labeled him "a bloodthirsty little socialist."

The former governing junta in Haiti hired lobbyists and PR representatives to discredit Aristide and defend U.S. interests there. The junta's most aggressive lobbyist was Robert McCandless, who also represented a U.S. company in Haiti.

McCandless, a good friend of syndicated columnist Robert Novak, was able to get Novak to write a series of columns in support of the junta.

Danny Schechter and Laura Flanders examine the impact of media conglomerates, their policies and the interconnections which allow them to operate globally with little regulation or social responsibility. Flanders, a freelance journalist formerly featured in *FAIR* magazine, points to a 1990 study of the mass media which revealed that 89% of the guests invited to interpret world news on radio and television were males and 92% of them were white. The most frequent guest news interpreters were Henry Kissinger, Al Haig, Elliott Abrams and Jerry Falwell. In short, says Flanders, a war criminal, a Watergate co-conspirator, a man who lied to Congress, and an evangelist for white Christian supremacy.

Sara Flounders and Brian Becker, also representative of the alternative media, focus on the relationship of capitalism to contemporary communication. "Every ruling class imposes on society as a whole the lies, deceits and biases that justify their existence," writes Flounders. "This has always been true. But historically this control of ideas and information has not been able to stop great change from breaking through."

Aiding such changes are journalists like Zoran Pirocanac, Michel Collon, Diana Johnstone, Thomas Deichmann and Brian Becker, whose papers describe the manipulative strategies used by the Western media in covering the Balkan Wars. Mr. Pirocanac characterizes the modern media as the fourth branch of NATO's army, "acting rather like an additional task force." His view is reminiscent of a similar analysis by Ben Bagdikian, former editor of the *Washington Post*, and John MacArthur, publisher of *Harper's Magazine*, who described the media as "a second front" for the U.S. military during the Gulf War.

"It's interesting to note," writes Pirocanac, "that the so-called 'aggression from Serbia' was successfully marketed, though Serbia never sent troops to Bosnia. Even today, a key military fact in the war is still concealed—that between 30,000-50,000 regular Croatian Army troops have continually been in operation on the territory of Bosnia-Herzegovina from the outbreak of the war in 1992."

Michel Collon points out the dangerous effect of the silence maintained by the press with respect to the activities of Germany and the United States in the Balkans. Since the beginning of the '90s, writes Collon, NATO has been geared up to carry out interventions in several strategic regions, including the Balkans, Turkey and Eastern Europe. Eventually, Russia and Eurasia will be targeted. Control of the Balkans and the sea routes to Eurasia will help the U.S. to gain access to the vast mineral resources and oil located in the Caspian Sea area.

Zbigniew Brzezinski, in his book *The Grand Chessboard*, states that the Eurasian Balkans (regions with many small contending nationalities) are extremely important economic prizes because of their enormous concentration of natural gas and oil reserves. He anticipates the use of NATO as an arm of American political influence and military power on the Eurasian mainland.

The *Washington Post* has recently described the Caspian Sea region as the target for the last great oil rush of the twentieth century—a potential $4 trillion prize. The oil rush lured a group of prospectors who just happened to be former high-ranking U.S. officials bent on winning a stake in the bonanza for themselves and the companies they represent. Included in this effort were two former national security advisors, Brent Scowcroft and Zbigniew Brzezinski.

During 1999, as NATO troops move southward in the Balkans, the Western media described the war in Kosovo as a struggle by ethnic Albanians for their human rights, a view at odds with the realities of the separatist war. As early as July 12, 1982, an article in the *New York Times* revealed the agenda of the armed struggle by the small group of Albanian secessionists: "An ethnically clean Kosovo, and merging Kosovo into a greater Albania." This openly acknowledged basis for the conflict in Kosovo has been buried in news coverage since the U.S. developed an economic interest in the area.

The breaking up of the Balkans has become a test case for a new form of colonization. Germany's sponsorship of Croatian independence in 1991 and the U.S. backing of Bosnia-Herzegovina's independence in 1992 initiated the dismemberment of Yugoslavia. European and American citizens were told that NATO was there to protect one part of the population (humans with rights) from another part of the population (humans without rights). "Nineteen months after German unification," writes Diana Johnstone, "and for the first time since Hitler's defeat in 1945, German media resounded with condemnation of an entire ethnic group reminiscent of the pre-war propaganda against the Jews."

While demonizing the Serbian people and accusing them of "ethnic cleansing," the media rarely mentioned how many Serbs have been ethnically cleansed, a quarter million in the Krajina alone, more than any other group in the Balkans. Yet ethnic cleansing has become a term of opprobrium directed against the Serbs.

Media attention to the conflict in Yugoslavia, says Johnstone, is dictated by threats, power interests, lobbies, and the institutional ambitions of "non-governmental organizations," which are often linked to powerful governments "whose competition with each other for financial support provides motivation for exaggerating the abuses they specialize in denouncing."

Joining the ranks of the demonizers, says Pirocanac, are the "journalists of attachment," who specialize in a form of reporting which no longer pretends to be objective, but takes on a position of advocacy without investigation.

Thomas Deichmann's paper, "The Pulitzer Prize and Croatian Propaganda," documents the lowered standards of reporting so common in today's media, including the use of biased and bogus sources to support a preconceived political agenda. Deichmann had earlier published the definitive expose on "journalism of attachment" in which he revealed the contrived and misleading "Picture That Fooled the World."

Independent Television News (ITN) had sent a crew to the Trnopolje refugee camp located in the Prijedor region of northern Bosnia. ITN returned with footage and commentary that described Trnopolje as a "concentration camp." Deichmann returned to the location that the ITN crew had filmed and found that the camp was in fact a voluntary refugee facility that had been misrepresented by filming it from *inside* a nearby section of barbed wire fence. In this way, a group of Bosnian refugees were made to look like prisoners. Yet even after the fraud had been exposed, U.S. TV stations continued to show the misleading ITN footage.

BBC television anchor Nick Gowing has described such practices as a "secret shame" for the journalist community. "I think there is a cancer which is affecting journalism," said Gowing. "It is the unspoken issue of partiality and bias in foreign reporting." (*The Nation*, Sept. 22, 1997, p24)

Several of the papers presented at the Athens conference offered a Third World perspective on the media. India's Manik Mukherjee describes Western journalism as "smeared with a self-centered careerist outlook of life, an apathy to social problems, a fascination with sex, violence and commodities that sell well, but rob people of morality, ethics, zeal and the determination to fight against injustice and exploitation."

Nawal El Saadawi provides an interesting view of the transnational advertising agencies which are increasingly active in the Southern hemisphere, where poor men and women obey the messages of western advertisements, even when those messages are detrimental to their health. She concludes that the media "has developed an ideology of individualism based on destroying the resistance of the individual" while discouraging "any idea of collective resistance."

Palestinian author and journalist Adel Samara describes the frightening Israeli control and censorship of Palestinian newspapers. "Since its beginning in June 1967, the Israeli colonial regime has imposed military control over all aspects of life in the West Bank and the Gaza Strip," says Samara. "All local radio stations, newspapers and publishing houses were closed or transferred to Amman, Jordan." In addition, the Israeli occupation forces produce an annual list of prohibited books, any one of which is immediately confiscated if found.

Without a democratic media there can never be a true democracy. At the Athens conference, Jean-Bertrand Aristide, former president of Haiti, encouraged the assembled journalists to make a giant leap forward. "We must democratize democracy," he declared, and he offered a grassroots example from Haiti, the opening of a center for street children in Port-au Prince. The children were given the opportunity to open a radio station, Radyo Timoun (Little People's Radio). They broadcast their music, their news and their commentaries 14 hours a day. When asked for their definition of democracy, the children said it must begin with "food, school, and health care for everyone."

Barbara Nimri Aziz, Louis Hiken, Manse Jacobi, David Barsamian and Charles Levendosky told the Athens conference of alternatives to the media monopoly. Aziz, an anthropologist and free lance journalist, has spent a great deal of time working in the Middle East. "A lot of news," she observed, "can and does travel by word of mouth. From the center of power, the military councils, and the diplomatic corps, news travels through family and school networks and beyond to the wider public." Aziz says information also crosses the borders of neighboring countries via newspapers. From Rabat to Baghdad, Jerusalem to Dubai, all use the Arabic language and read the international Arabic dailies.

Communication of news by word of mouth is also common in African countries, but without modern technology, many Africans find it difficult to keep up with world events. Brian Murphy, an attendee at the conference, has proposed a strategy for bringing computer technology to Africa. Murphy had earlier worked with a group of Canadian NGOs to set up an alternative news agency in Southern Africa that could combat apartheid censorship. With the help of some intrepid engineers and some smuggled modems, cables and portable computers, Murphy and his colleagues built a virtual micro-telecommunications system inside the existing telephone network of Zimbabwe.

Having the most current technology does not, of course, guarantee a broad spectrum of news and opinions. This was clearly demonstrated in the news reporting during the Balkan Wars. Louis Hiken, an American attorney representing micro-radio broadcasters, notes that the present media does not accommodate the needs and interests of the American population. Hiken defends the rights of microradio broadcasters to operate micropower stations, extending the right of U.S. citizens to receive information suppressed by government and corporate channels.

Manse Jacobi is the technical director for Free Speech Internet Television, and, like Louis Hiken, he warns that the Telecommunications Act of 1996 has left the communications industry with few protections against the arbitrary power of great corporations. Jacobi reminds us that "Vice-President Al Gore's adaptation of the term 'information superhighway' serves as a useful analogy to his grandfather's initiative in the 1950s to build a national highway system which would serve the military-industrial complex." He warns that those who now benefit most from the new media technologies are the military and its associated corporations.

David Barsamian, founder and director of "alternative radio," calls himself a "radio interventionist" doing combat on the airwaves. In his paper he lays out a model of how truly democratic radio programming can be realized.

Charles Levendosky told the Athens conference of good news and bad news. He declared, "There are over a thousand small newspapers across America with circulations of 25,000 to 75,000, whose aggregate circulation far exceeds that of the *Washington Post, New York Times, LA Times,* and even the number of viewers of major television network news programs." The bad news, he said, was that there are a number of forces trying to control and censor the media, and the U.S. government is a major force among them.

The papers here assembled are a testimony to the wisdom and commitment of the progressive journalists and activists at the Athens conference. But these individuals were intent on building a process that would continue long after their words. They left Athens with an agreement to form the Progressive International Media Exchange (PRIME), a computer list-service to exchange frequently suppressed news stories from around the world. In the year since the conference ended, PRIME has flourished, and it was particularly important as a source of accurate news during NATO's 1999 bombing of Yugoslavia. Information never published by the mass media was sent to journalists in nations from Europe to Africa to the Middle East. Alternative newspapers around the world have in turn sent their stories to PRIME.

PART ONE

MEDIA CENSORSHIP

AND

MANAGEMENT OF THE NEWS

The Subtleties of Censorship

Censorship and control of the media, as Charles Levendosky has pointed out in his paper, can no longer be described in terms of prescribed subjects, editorial guidelines or dictates. We're not talking about cut and paste, snip-snip with scissors, burning copy or reading over someone's shoulder. That's no longer needed. Government and media shape news together, censoring and self-censoring sensitive subjects. By referring to this form of information control, I don't mean to downplay in any way the more overt censorship in those oppressive regimes in which it exists. It can be fearsome and I stand second to no person in addressing those issues.

I was the first person to invite Salmon Rushdie to the U.S. after his fatwa [death sentence for blasphemy]. I was the only person to testify during this nation's first criminal prosecution of leaks by a government official who had provided information to the press. But at the same time, I think the issues of self-censorship, though more subtle, are no less pernicious. I spend my days and nights concerned with this more subtle form of censorship, rather than the classic forms of repression. I am concerned more with the established media's increasing homogeneity and loss of independence than with the notion of the press manufacturing crises or dictating support or dissent.

I consider myself a product of established media. The *Washington Post* or National Public TV cannot be regarded as anything other than established media. Indeed, my book publisher, Alfred Knopf, always esteemed for its independence, has been gobbled up by Random House, which is soon to be swallowed by Bertelsmann, no doubt one of the five media conglomerates that Ben Bagdikian suggests will survive by the year 2000. But we're stuck in this environment, in the web of government and dominant media influence, and if we choose to play in the field of public opinion, if we choose to educate, organize and move people, we must begin to learn how to manipulate these organizations, how to keep them honest, how to demand accountability.

The question is often asked whether the media serves the ruling class. Absolutely. The media shares with the government that ruling class role. What we must not mistake, however, is the form in which that role, that manipulation occurs. It requires a popular consensus, one that's not too difficult to achieve at present, one that can ignore the facts much of the time. So, I'm offering at least an alternate view within the established media towards some of these subjects and I welcome debate about those relationships.

I have a permanent naivete that comes from the roles I've played in these establishments. On Friday the 13th, July 1973, I sat in an underground room interviewing Alexander Butterfield, an obscure Air Force colonel. I worked as a senior investigator for the Senate Watergate Committee, and we were concerned about establishing the bona fides of John Dean who was testifying that President Nixon, as you recall, was involved in a cover-up. It's difficult to roll things back to that point, but at the time it didn't look likely that we were going to be able to prove the president's involvement. The attorney general of the U.S., John Mitchell, was testifying upstairs while we were doing our interviews downstairs, and he was kicking the Watergate Committee around quite fiercely. Mitchell had become the president's campaign manager, and this was an era before attorney generals were assumed to be liars, that form becoming more regular after the fact.

We proceeded to question Colonel Butterfield, who referred to a very detailed account of the president's meetings with John Dean, information that he said had come from the White House. We asked what source this account could have come from. After some hemming and hawing, Butterfield said, "I guess you know that the president has an automatic secret tap-ing device in each of his offices." I said, "Of course we know." Of course we didn't know. He then began to tell us about it in increasingly painful detail, painful for him because he recognized that he was giving away a major secret. I re-member thinking that, with this revelation, the hearings would likely come to a very rapid conclusion. They didn't. It took an-other year. It took a Supreme Court decision. It took essentially a Nixon resignation, a resignation that preempted the report of the Watergate Committee, which would have shown that Nixon had taken money along the way, that he had in fact been paid off by Howard Hughes, by Adnan Khashogi, and ultimately by Tom Pappas a supporter of the Greek junta at the time. People forget that cover-ups do work.

So, week before last, I picked up my newspaper and saw that President Nixon's bosom buddy Bebe Rebozo had died. Re-bozo's obituary carried an account of how close he was to Nixon, how he was the one person who could talk to him about anything. In fact, in many ways he had been his fixer. This oth-erwise fine article by *New York Times* correspondent David Binder made no mention of Howard Hughes, no mention of Khashogi, no mention of Tom Pappas, no mention of the fact that Richard Nixon was, simply put, a crook, or why it was he became a crook or what the national security issues were. There was in fact no institutional memory. There were no facts left about Watergate. Nixon had washed them away over time.

It is this form of governmental cooperation with media and media's willingness to go along with it that distorts the jour-nalistic record. It occurs not only when officials are in office, but also after they've left office. No censor orders anyone to stop recording the facts. There is no clipping, no redaction, no threats or fatwas. For example, what obscured the Nixon case was the appearance of a series of lobbyists who stopped the Watergate hearings in midstream. Tommy Cochran, an old retainer of Roosevelt's, one of the Roosevelt aides that Blanche Cook cov-ered so well in her research, walked in to tell Sam Irvin, the chair-man of the committee, that the Democratic Party had also received money from the same individuals linked to Nixon. Cochran warned that their testimony would involve national security issues like the Glomar Explorer, the CIA's project to retrieve a Soviet submarine off of the floor of the ocean. There were matters involving the ownership of TWA, matters way beyond the competence of the Watergate Committee. And so the public never learned those facts. They got a partial account in a final report, but one that was easily suppressed, suppressed in a sense by the voluntary complicity of the media.

The issue was too complicated. One book, one series of newspaper articles were about all that ran in any detail on it. So my concern now is not that there's a conspiracy of intimidation but a conspiracy of inconvenience in reporting the facts. The American public has been victimized not so much by the embezzlement of our national patrimonies collectively than by the profit in certain types of journalism. There is less of a hidden master plan than of corporate pressure toward the lowest common denominator between the interests of capital and what the media feels is its minimal obligation to the public.

There are two contradictory forces at work here that are in many ways opposite sides of the same coin. There is the willingness of media and government to deny people access to information. Often it's the result of a simple failure to preserve or archive information. In the American bureaucratic system, where electronic data is the principal format, we have a constant problem with information being zapped away. It no longer exists a week, two weeks after the fact. The information is denied to us, not because of secrecy, but because there is no institutional memory. There is an unwillingness to sustain an institutional memory.

The people in the media are willing participants in this process. Major stories simply don't exist in certain newspapers. They just can't be seen, or they are not available in context. If covered, they are told with a sterility that defies the very vital nature of the information and dilutes the human impact. Again, there's no institutional memory within the media. Ronald

Reagan, a president who had very little institutional memory himself, was able to use that intellectual vacuum to reinvent reality on virtually a daily basis. And the press went along with it again and again and again.

There's an organization that I helped found in Washington, D.C. called the National Security Archive. If you work in the national security area, you will find it useful because it accumulates formerly classified information. It creates an institutional memory by taking information that's been declassified or released by government agencies and maintains it in the public domain.

In my view, nations that have free expression have a susceptibility to tyranny that is comparable to that of nations without such freedom, because of this phenomenon of media self-censorship, lack of institutional memory, and the willingness of the media to ignore the stories that are out there. We are deluded into seeking villainous plots buried behind the doors of oligarchs, behind the conspiracies of capital and government, when in fact we need only look at our own approach, whether it be alternate or establishment journalism, to what it is that's in front of us. The greatest threat walks among us. It's within ourselves, not in the cloisters of some secret corridors. If we allow secrecy, it works. And if we don't defeat it again and again on a daily basis, it begins to erode our ability to deal with it at all.

National security secrecy can be the most pervasively destructive underpinning of censorship in any society. In the United States, we often talk about the code words of classification: confidential, secret, top-secret. But in fact, it's not the stamping of information that causes the major problem. It's the creation of categories of individuals through what are called security clearances. The resultant compartmentalization of information isolates and taints loyal individuals within our government. A person who supports our Constitution and who advocates nothing more than an informed citizenry is unable to get information.

In the Pentagon alone, there are over 10,000 compartments within what are called "special access programs." Those are programs of sensitive compartmented information classified above top secret. Put differently, for the Secretary of Defense to get a briefing he would have to have about 9500 people come into his conference room because very few people hold multiple clearances. And every time one of them spoke, 9499 would have to leave the room. It's an absurd system.

Who needs censorship when you have this degree of control over information? And if you carefully inspect the methodology and practice of secrecy in the United States, you find out that public enemy number one is the public itself, along with the press, which is identified with the public. Second on the enemies list is the Congress of the United States. Third come the other Executive Branch agencies. If you're the CIA, you don't want the State Department to know what you're doing. If you're the Army, you can't have the Navy know what you're doing.

Fourth on the enemies list are our foreign allies. Not our nominal enemies. Our allies. We're more concerned with what the Brits learn about what we're up to than we are with what the Indians learn than we are with what the Chinese learn. It's not clear whether we even bother to declare our official enemies any more. Cuba, I guess, is our most fearsome enemy these days.

This kind of bureaucratic control allows manipulation through the selective release of information. The redaction of documents becomes trivial. It becomes a question of creating reality. There's no accountability, because again, it's easy to destroy the material itself. I've written a chapter in a book edited by Athan Theoharis called *The Culture of Secrecy* that examines this process. My article is called "The War over Secrecy."

We now have the media participating in this process by deciding whose institutional memory, as far as there is one, will enter the public domain. We have Henry Kissinger deciding how his personal and political history will be told, and he can't be contradicted because no one has access to his documents. Kissinger was careful to place them under a secret deed of trust in the Library of Congress, a supposedly public institution, but one that holds the documents in secret for 50 years. Al Haig did the same thing, not surprisingly, and after him Caspar Weinberger. Weinberger was actually indicted for the way in which he hid his papers, because he withheld information about criminal activities.

There are countless examples of such rigged history. The media chooses the tales of a Richard Holbrooke as the dominant account of events in Bosnia. We have media magnates in Russia choosing Alexander Kazakov, who is the author of the Russian Privatization Program, to write post-Cold War Russian history, and to write it for a very healthy advance, a choice that seems to me to be interesting as well as nefarious.

A recent example of news control occurred when U.S. jet planes shot down two helicopters over northern Iraq. People wondered why. They noted at the time that there was an invasion by the Turkish army into Iraqi-Kurdistan, one of the largest movements of troops that had ever occurred up to that point. News reports did not mention that such military action might have distracted the air control people that maintained a cap over that area. I mean, that's successful censorship. It required only minor manipulation of the final report, because, by and large, these were events that might as well not have happened.

In another example, a man showed up from Russia recently, an associate of Boris Yeltsin's, with eight billion dollars in assets that had been taken largely from the Russian conglomerate Gazprom. As we began to examine the story, we discovered that he was there to buy some 134 Uruguayan passports, which is legal to do in Uruguay, but not legal to do in the U.S. We began to ask the question, who owns Gazprom, who controls it, what are its real resources? We could not find the answers within the U.S. government. I'm not sure if that's censorship or if the answer is not there.

The relationship between the U.S. and the Saudis is another murky area. I won't bore you with details, but we found a 5.5 billion dollar program from 18 years ago that was to sell five $110 million planes. Now the only way five times $110 million equals $5.5 billion is if your abacus is missing a row, which it is in the Pentagon. That total has grown to almost $400 billion in Saudi purchases overall according to figures I saw in Britain last week.

We had the whole Hiroshima Nagasaki 50th anniversary wiped away by the Smithsonian. And when it was wiped away, there were very articulate protests. Gar Alperowitz and a number of other scholars protested very strongly, but they had no forum. The establishment media would brook them no forum. They had most of the documents, yet there was no place for their institutional memory to fit.

Then there are the human radiation experiments recently revealed by the Department of Energy. Things are so desperate in our country with respect to safety that the Secretary of Energy actually began releasing information on her own. She had no alternative but to do that to re-establish the department's credibility. That "openness program," I would submit, is something worth looking at.

The False Claims Act is legislation that allows whistle blowers to come forward and file claims on behalf of the U.S. government. It's interesting and unique, and it's created a number of routes around censorship. If anyone here in Greece is not aware of the details of the arms sales in progress for the advanced fighter program and missile programs, that information is available only partly in the U.S. and the gaps need to be filled. They need to be filled by whistle blowers, because we're not going to get them from our governments. But it's only our own fault if we don't get it out.

MEDIA REPORTING OF INTERNATIONAL EVENTS

BEN H. BAGDIKIAN

Historically, when it comes to reporting international affairs, the agenda of governments has become the agenda of the news. Obviously, a country's public policy toward other countries ought to be covered by its media. But simply reporting what the government announces is not enough. As we know, even democratic governments do not always disclose publicly what they are doing to whom. It is precisely the areas kept invisible, and therefore unaccountable, that so often go wrong and do wrong.

Even in democracies, the news media too often take it a step further. With few exceptions, they have reported at face value governmental recitations of facts and rationales of foreign policy. This is most obvious, of course, during times of war. With rare exceptions, when countries go to war, their media enlist. Few want their country to lose a deadly war, but being uncritical can have high costs. For example, Britain in the Crimea and France in Algeria paid heavily for uncorrected military errors and horrors.

It was true for much of our Vietnam War. The American phase of the Indochinese war began in 1954 and it was not until the mid-1960s that a handful of the correspondents in Saigon began reporting contrary battlefield realities they witnessed or that were told to them by combat commanders in the field. Our government took the position that if the United States withdrew short of victory, all of Asia would fall like dominoes until communists were at our shores. And each president announced that we were on the verge of victory. For 20 years, our government was mistaken. It lied or was deluded until, finally, after about two million dead, 58,000 of them American soldiers, we gave up. The dominoes did not fall.

Uncritical acceptance of governmental military rationales has continued in our invasions of Grenada and Panama and in the official versions of the Gulf War.

Unfortunately, governments usually suffer from their own disinformation or delusions. Our government said that failure in Vietnam meant a threat to the United States and, when most of the media took the same position, we were bound for a long and futile war.

John Kenneth Galbraith has made his own acid comment on the domestic version of this government-media circular process, once describing it as the only completely successful closed system yet devised for the recycling of garbage.

When the news media lack the capacity or will to create independent and informed knowledge, it increases the odds that wartime governmental errors, flawed strategies and incompetencies will go uncorrected. This is not to say that the press is superior to government in its knowledge or infallibility. But it can document objective evidence and draw upon informed citizens outside government who are able to provide independent information.

Unfortunately, the problem of a servile press is not limited to news about hot wars. It prevailed during our Cold War. In the forty years of the Cold War, the reporting of foreign news focused almost exclusively on the rivalry between the United States and the USSR. During that period, in both government and our major media, there was a frantic conditioned reflex to any hint of communism anywhere in the world. At the time, I heard foreign officials of smaller countries joking privately that for them, a real, live Communist was worth his weight in gold because as soon as the Communist was reported in the news, the United States would rush in with military and economic assistance.

Given the nuclear nightmare underlying the conflict between the U.S. and USSR, intensive coverage by the news media was justified. What is less understandable is that even when it had documented evidence to the contrary, most of the American press reported its news in conformity with the official line.

During the Cold War, the news establishment often failed to serve us well. In the years of Sen. Joseph McCarthy's rampages, only a half dozen metropolitan daily papers in the country adhered to their normal journalistic standards in covering the senator. I was fortunate to be working for one of those papers and discovered that reporters who followed McCarthy knew that he was a wild man who faked or distorted information and never exposed a spy not already identified. But many papers and broadcast stations ignored McCarthy's flaws, allowing the mantra of anti-communism to cover a multitude of political sins.

We paid dearly for that six-year period. We paid for it in the standards of respect and ethics in government. And we paid for it in our capacity for intelligent foreign policy. For example, the two most respected and knowledgeable American Foreign Service officers with firsthand knowledge of the upheavals in China were John Paton Davies and John Stewart Service. After attacks on them by McCarthy and other political Red hunters, both were cashiered by the craven Secretary of State, John Foster Dulles. Dulles knew the men were loyal, skilled and honest Foreign Service officers, but he was unwilling to take the political heat. The sin of Davies and Service was that they reported what was really happening in China, not what the powerful Nationalist China Lobby in the United States wished were happening.

As a result, for the better part of a generation, during a crucial period of world history, we were flying diplomatically blind with respect to a country of enormous importance.

It is significant that during the Cold War, the Western European democracies did not suffer our self-destructive domestic hysteria. Their government and press did not go through our feverish politics, and, indeed, some of them had significant indigenous Communist Parties. Perhaps the enemy at the gates is seen more realistically than a distant one whose invincibility can be fantasized.

Today the Cold War is over. With the collapse of the Soviet Union, the dynamics of international relations has changed. Suddenly, it is no longer a simple, two-nation rivalry. We find ourselves in a new international scene for which our news media are not well-equipped.

Many years ago, Walter Lippmann wrote that the news is like a searchlight flashing on a stage full of action. Where that searchlight rests becomes the news. Where you focus the light becomes the evening television news and Page One of the newspaper.

The world is full of innumerable events, and letting government aim the news searchlight is an easy solution for news companies. But sooner or later, it can have a high cost. The only responsible alternative for an independent news system is to support competent resources of its own. Major news organizations would have to maintain their own foreign bureaus, staffed by American nationals whose knowledge and length of continuous residence within their areas permit informed observation and competent judgment.

Unfortunately, just about the time that the simple news formulas of the Cold War disappeared, major American news organizations crippled their capacity for reporting international news. This is especially true of television networks, from which, for better or for worse, most Americans say they get their news. Our national newspapers do a somewhat better job, but most Americans read local, not national newspapers. The *New York Times* is read by fewer than two percent of the country's households.

As though arranged by an evil genius, just as the Cold War ended in the 1980s, all three radio and television networks were taken over by corporations that were strangers to news reporting. A real estate investor took over CBS, which had provided our best radio and network news. General Electric took over NBC, and Cap Cities Inc., a newspaper company with no foreign experience, took over ABC. These new owners were attracted by the networks' influence and handsome cash flow. And in that spirit, the first thing that each of these corporations did was to close most of their networks' foreign bureaus. Today, if you listen to foreign news on American networks, including CNN and Rupert Murdoch's new Fox network, you will overwhelmingly see and hear foreign news taken from two international wire services based outside the United States. Most of the journalists from those services are correspondents of the BBC or local reporters speaking British English. These are often competent and insightful journalists, but they may not be as sensitive to the news interests and needs of Americans as our own foreign bureaus once were.

I sometimes speculate that American dependence on foreign reporters for foreign news may mean that we will have a generation of children who will grow up thinking that if you discuss domestic American affairs, you use ordinary American English. But when you switch to discussing foreign affairs, you use British English, which is what they now hear on most American network foreign news.

It is not a serious problem that in these newscasts, "trucks" become "lorries" and "missiles" become "missyles." But it is a problem that the absence of long-term knowledge in foreign posts by American journalists means that our major news organizations lack a significant in-house information resource on important developments around the world. That is in dramatic contrast to the extensive foreign correspondence systems of England's BBC and the Japanese public network, NHK.

The shrinkage of foreign reporting resources in American news comes at a time when we are forced to face new complexities that follow the end of the Cold War. National boundaries are less reliable reflection of the dynamics inside those boundaries than before. Many of those national boundaries were drawn for Big Power purposes by the victors after World War I and World War II.

With the disappearance of the magnetic field of the old European colonial powers and the U.S.-USSR Cold War relationship, new forces within dozens of less developed countries are asserting themselves in ways that reflect their internal religions and ethnicities. The turmoil is intensified by poverty, disorder and unstable governments.

This accentuates another contemporary complication. During the Cold War, the United States and the Soviet Union flooded their client states with modern weaponry. Today, the United States overwhelmingly dominates the arms trade. People, who once fought with spears or single-shot Enfield rifles, now fight with heavy mortars and heat-seeking missiles. The world has escaped the dread of a full-scale nuclear war, but it has not escaped an uneasy global population with easy access to terrible weapons. A small group can make its point with a vehicle packed with explosives or a portable weapon that can shoot down an airliner in flight.

As our major media look out upon this confusing world, at least two external realities present themselves: 1) the end of geographic colonialism by a few major powers; 2) the advent of modern communications, ending the isolation of once-remote nations.

Communication satellites are now transmitting televised images for the first time to hundreds of millions of poor and illiterate people who were not reachable by radio or by print. Where serious American news organizations have left a void, American entertainment entrepreneurs like Rupert Murdoch have rushed in.

Most of the televised images now seen by people of the world are American in origin and focused on the enduring staples of American commercial television, sex and violence. American television makes about half of its profits from foreign exports, and one production executive has noted with approval that television focused around sex and violence is just fine because sex and violence need minimal translation and subtitles. To a large extent, the ideology of violence is replacing what used to be the ideological debate between the U.S. and USSR. Our major media, partly reflecting the indifference of our government, give insufficient emphasis to the obvious imperatives to move toward a peaceful world. One requirement is a huge increase in effective aid from rich countries to poor ones. The other is for a truly effective, permanent, international peacekeeping force designed for humanitarian purposes.

The developed nations and their modern technology are, in a way, victims of their own inventiveness. American television has brought not only violence, but personal aspiration as well. There are hundreds of millions of impoverished people in the world who see for the first time that in the rich countries most babies do not die in their first year and that few people starve or die from preventable diseases. These realizations raise aspirations, but in the absence of palpable change, they also inspire anger and frustration. Ironically, our exported television, suffused as it is with violence, implies that the best reaction to anger and frustration is with a gun.

America's media have been hampered as well by the new corporate ethic that encompasses so many of our news companies. Despite generous profits in both the daily newspaper and broadcast industries, they have cut news budgets and staffs to satisfy Wall Street's demand for ever larger quarterly earnings. News executives may exercise lavish stock options, but the public receives a diminished diet of foreign news. It is not because of corporate poverty. Standard & Poor's states that publicly traded daily newspapers enjoy annual average profits of 20%. Broadcaster outlets make similar or better profits.

Today, staffs of professional journalists are increasingly small islands within the ocean of large multinational firms like General Electric, which owns NBC, Westinghouse, which owns CBS, Disney, which owns ABC, and Fox Network, which is owned by Rupert Murdoch's News Corp.

With the end of the Cold War, the new focus of both government and the news media is promotion of international trade. That is legitimate enough. But one wonders if corporate opportunity for American firms should be the only guiding principle in the effort to inform the American public about the important events in the world? Trade is not synonymous with peace and democracy.

That became symbolized for me recently when my wife and I were standing in Tiananmen Square in Beijing. The huge, 122-acre walled plaza is the monumental display center for the icons of the Chinese regime. But looming over the other side of the Tiananmen Square wall is an American icon, the golden arches of a McDonald's hamburger stand.

Like the rest of Beijing, this best known international space in China symbolizes what is happening in China—Communist Party rule side-by-side with galloping capitalism.

It is clear that today, our dominant organizing principle in foreign relations is maximizing trade. Commercial trade is inevitable, necessary, and sometimes helpful in spreading enlightenment. But should that be our basic message for countries struggling with national identities and torn by internal differences of ethnicity, religion, and ancient loyalties? We press democracy and the free market as though they were the same entity to be adopted simultaneously. Social change is more complicated. In Russia, capitalism has produced Mercedes and beggars.

The news has done too little in showing the political and social realities that lie beneath the simple incidence of free markets and America's share in them.

We do have redeeming rays of light. The most poorly financed of our broadcast operations have shown that, despite low budgets, they can provide better foreign news. I refer to National Public Radio, the independent network called Alternative Radio, and our educational stations that broadcast the BBC World Service.

There are other sources of hope. With all our social and educational problems, we have a generation of young Americans more cosmopolitan and more personally acquainted with foreign experience than any previous generation. Every year, more of our young people travel around the world—and it is no longer just the Grand Tour of upper class sons and daughters.

Another ray of light is a generation of American journalists better equipped than any previous generation, many of them graduates in foreign area studies and languages. Few other countries have so large a potential group of prepared men and women. We often underestimate the strength of our education system by comparing our average students to foreign countries' elites. Our averages are often better than foreign averages. We need that new generation of American journalists in world news. They are ready. Tragically, our networks are not ready for them.

Thanks to modern communication, the world is becoming smaller. We glory in our new communications technology. But technical communications are neutral machines. They transmit intelligence and idiocy with equal indifference.

What is to be done? As citizens, we can push for general reform of television, notably to end the domination of violence in commercial television. The Surgeon General of the United States has proven that television violence increases real life violence and aggression, yet that is ignored by the broadcasters. Unlike the printed press, broadcasting has been a regulated industry in order to avoid freelance jamming and serve the public interest. We need once more to require all stations to provide some systematic news coverage. The Federal Communications Commission once required it and still has the power to do so. But today, a majority of FCC members are wedded to the free market without social obligations. By law, the airwaves belong to the public. The public needs to reclaim their property.

More and better foreign news would make clearer the urgency of our stake in cooperating with other countries and the United Nations in the search for basic remedies to dangerous global violence and combating poverty. We are still enthralled with our own political yahoos who oppose working with allies in cooperative efforts for a more peaceful, democratic world, and who object to United States participation in peacekeeping forces.

We need to enhance our national awareness that we are a people skilled not only in selling hamburgers to the world, but also in sharing our historic search for human rights. What works in a country like ours cannot be automatically transferred to a different kind of society. Nevertheless, the multi-ethnic, multicultural nature of the United States is a closer picture of the world population than exists in any other major industrial country. We have some constructive history to offer and a serious role to play in world relations.

Without better international news coverage in the United States, we will be unable to effectively address global problems. This is not an intellectual nicety, but a matter of survival. There are fatal consequences to continued environmental degradation and antihuman national doctrines. The human race, in its cleverness, has created so much destructive power that inaction is dangerous to its health.

We look for intelligent life in space, but we need to exploit more of it on our own planet. Carl Sagan, the astronomer, dismissed the science fiction of an alien force from outer space invading Earth. He said any space civilization would need a million years to create the concentrated power required for intergalactic travel. And during that time, if these aliens had not eliminated violence and aggression from their societies, they long ago would have used that power to destroy themselves.

It is not aliens from outer space we must deal with. We need to deal with our personal values and collective behavior here on earth. We need to know more about the realities of our own world, knowledge that depends in large part on our news. We need that news to help us remember that rich and poor, Americans and non-Americans, will survive only if we all become more compatible passengers on our own shrinking planet.

MEDIA MANIPULATION OF FOREIGN POLICY

RAMSEY CLARK

If the United States of America ever elected a president with the moral character, the personal experience of lifelong service to others, the noble thoughts and compassionate values of Haiti's President Aristide, then it would become a democracy. I don't expect that to happen in my lifetime. Struggle as we may and must, the greatest challenge in the struggle for democracy is the search for truth. The question of human survival and, if successful, of human nature, will depend largely on whether we can see the truth in time. If the people of the U.S. had full, open, equal access to the truth, they could find and elect their own Aristides.

The philosopher Voltaire expressed a disturbing notion, one that caused Napoleon to like him so much. Voltaire wrote that history is but fiction agreed upon, which means that all struggle and all commitment for a just society and even for the truth is as nothing, because finally truth comes down to an agreement among a few conspirators. We now face a much greater struggle for the truth, not Voltaire's "history," but the truth of the world as it is. The power of wealth and the power of force are being combined through a controlled media to make the condition and events of the world today a fiction that they write.

In this week's *The Nation* magazine there's a quote from a station manager for Fox News out of Florida that makes you think of the Robber Barons of America's late 19th century. Some members of the public were protesting the media's silence on the question of the use of chemical insecticides in food products. The station manager's answer was this: "We paid $3 billion for these stations, and we have a right to make the news. The news is what we say it is."

In some ways, the title of this paper, "Media Manipulation of Foreign Policy," approaches the problem from the wrong perspective. There is a near perfect harmony and common control of the policies of powerful governments and the media in these countries. Their power is enormous, and together they determine the news. They decide what the people know as news.

How is it that Muhammad Ali can go to Cuba taking medicine for Parkinson's disease, which he has, and 11 million Cubans know it immediately and celebrate his presence throughout the journey, yet practically no one in the United States of America is aware that he did it? How is it that the United States can conduct a continuing genocide against Iraq, deliberately and in the cruelest way possible, taking hundreds of thousands of lives through hunger and sickness, yet no one in the United States becomes concerned about it?

The seepage of news is sufficient so that the American people cannot deny their awareness of the toll on Iraqi civilians, but few are concerned about it. Millions of Americans watched Madeleine Albright on *60 Minutes*, interviewed by Leslie Stahl in 1995, asked why 500,000 Iraqi children under the age of 5 have died. Why that's more than Hiroshima. Albright was asked whether the human price was worth any benefits from the American blockade and bombing. Madeleine Albright was able to look straight at the camera and say, "That's a very difficult question, but yes, we think the price is worth it." How could anyone dare say that any policy is worth the lives of 500,000 beautiful children. Nonetheless, she can remain a public figure, remain in public life without infuriating the American public to the point where they would want to tear the establishment down. Iraqis have been dying at the rate of 12,000 a month ever since.

Consider the case of our own nuns. Any meddlesome nun or priest who tries to help the poor is in trouble. When American nuns and a religious worker went to El Salvador and were raped and murdered on the way to the airport, our Secretary of State Al Haig could say, "They must have run a roadblock." And our ambassador to the UN designate Jeane Kirkpatrick could say, "They weren't nuns. They were supporters of terrorism." And years later we find out that our government knew in advance that their murders had been ordered. Yet figures like Albright and Haig and Kirkpatrick remain popular and dominant in the mainstream of American thought, if you can call it thought.

We send two of the few valiant journalists that our system seems capable of breeding, Susan Meiselas, a photographer, and Ray Bonner, a reporter, to a village near El Mozote in El Salvador where they determined without question that hundreds and hundreds of villagers were slaughtered. Children lying on the floor were shot and stabbed. But such journalists try in vain to report these stories. The story is covered up. Only years after the fact does the media report and the government acknowledge, "Oh, that was El Mozote."

Ron Ridenhour died last week. He broke the story about the My Lai massacre. Hugh Thompson, who was the real hero at My Lai, who stopped the massacre after it was 80 percent finished, is unknown in America. We can write obituaries for Ron Ridenhour, saying good things we never said when he was alive, yet still not face up to what happened at My Lai.

We're creating an enormous, artificial, false culture, and it's very difficult for people born into that culture to ever penetrate and understand it. As the great poet Pindar told us, and it remains true, "Culture is lord of everything, of mortals and immortals king."

We might think for a minute about how it was that ancient Greece never knew incertitude, as Jorge Luis Borges wrote. I find this one of the most perceptive ideas about ancient Greece. They had their Stentor, whose voice could carry louder and farther than anyone, over the din of the battle on the plains of Troy. They had their Demosthenes, who would practice speaking with pebbles in his mouth to perfect his diction, who would parade in front of a mirror and write out his speeches to the great disdain of his contemporaries. Historians, including Greeks of the time, could agree that he was the greatest orator and greatest persuader of his time, for all of his failures of character. They could produce a Socrates, who didn't have to write a word. None from his hand have come to us intact, and yet he is one of the most influential thinkers in all of history. At that time, there were few obstacles obscuring the perception of the people from the facts. What they saw was palpable. What they heard was direct, its credibility measurable. What they carried with them was authentic. On the other hand, our children were born with a TV set in a room. They watch television more than they watch their teachers or their friends or even their parents. TV becomes a major part of their culture and their world. It's an incredibly soporific culture and its message is not easily weighed.

The Romans created the idea of bread and circuses. Give the people enough bread to keep them alive and enough circuses to distract them from their problems. Television and the broader media are by far the best circus that has ever been devised. Its message represents the modern fiction its directors intend the world to agree upon.

The means of communication are controlled by a handful of interests. Ninety percent of all television fare comes from six or seven companies. A General Electric or a Rupert Murdoch can marginalize a Socrates. A cup of hemlock might seem to do the same, but the fact of Socrates' existence and authenticity abides.

This is not an easy time to be a thinker. When the media marginalizes a Socrates of our time, if there be one, where will memory of his words abide? How will the message prevail? It's true that a spear could stop Stentor, but the power of his voice and all it could reach survived through Homer and others. People in ancient Greece knew the reality of their lives. Today the media can turn a great calamity such as that in Rwanda into an appearance that makes Europeans and Americans and many others believe that Africans are hopeless savages. That's the message. Not just Hutus or Tutsis. All Africans.

I am representing a Rwandan pastor from the Seventh Day Adventist Church, a Hutu, 70 years old, four times elected president of the church, the second largest Christian church in Rwanda, a man who never had a machete or weapon in his home, who always opposed violence. He lived the first half of his life in colonial violence and the second half in post-colonial violence and was always a peacemaker. He is charged with genocide. It is a total fabrication designed to consolidate government power. This power has already linked Uganda, Rwanda, Burundi and much of Zaire, now the Democratic Republic of the Congo, into an enormous empire, controlled by the old imperial surrogates, the Tutsis, who comprise less than two percent of the total population of those countries and less than ten percent of the population of Rwanda, a fragile structure that can't endure. The elimination of 250,000 Rwandan Hutus in eastern Zaire went virtually unnoticed.

Our ability to manipulate and admit without alarming the public is overwhelming. There was a review in the *New York Times* last week of the new book called *To Win a War* by Richard Holbrooke. It's written in the first person, telling how he did it. He didn't title his narrative *To Establish a Peace*. That wasn't what he was about. He chose *To Win a War*. And in his tale he reveals the horrors of ethnic cleansing. But pride overcomes discretion, and he writes boastfully according to a review, of how, even as Washington was condemning the Croatian purge of more than a quarter million Serbs from the Krajina, he was in Zagreb making sure that the Croatians did exactly that, identifying the cities to be purged, the deaths and the massive forced emigration.

Earlier U.S. diplomats marked villages on the maps of Cambodia for elimination. It took 25 years for a president of the United States to suggest an international war crimes tribunal for Pol Pot, but the president didn't mention the illegal bombing of Cambodia that preceded the tragedy. Most historians would agree that the bombing led to the descent of Cambodia into anarchy and terror. It didn't have to be. Why no war crimes trial there?

The power of the media to demonize is perhaps its most dangerous and vicious power. It can't create demons among the people who really know their place and culture. It can't demonize President Aristide among the Haitian people, because they've suffered a long time, and they know that he's shared their suffering. There's very little in their lives that they can trust, but they trust him. That doesn't mean that the United States of America didn't do everything it could to prevent his being elected, or didn't play a role in stealing 60 percent of his five-year term from him and exact a commitment that he would not run for reelection upon his return. We retrained their military and police forces to continue the same sort of terror against the people that we identify with the words FRAPH, Tonton Macoute, and all of those terrible forces that these beautiful people have suffered. These brave people, who are the darkest and the poorest, have never been forgiven for the boldness of Toussaint Louverture, because they dared to liberate themselves from slavery.

It's absolutely unreasonable to believe that the plutocratic, capitalistic media of this world, which controls the flow of nearly all of our information and the world awareness of the great majority of the people, will ever meaningfully address the key issues that humanity must address if it is to survive. When is the last time you've seen in the media any examination of the status of U.S. nuclear arms, or an analysis of how many Trident II submarines are presently commissioned? Or how many new and perhaps more dangerous nuclear submarines are being planned right now? Absolutely maniacal weapons.

What moral people could ever permit their construction? The Trident is capable of launching 24 missiles simultaneously while submerged, each with 17 independently targeted, maneuverable nuclear warheads. They can reach 7,000 nautical miles and hit within 100 feet of a predetermined target. That's a radius of 14,000 nautical miles, more than half way around mother earth's ample waist at the equator, enabling it to strike

408 centers of human population and incinerate them with a blast ten times more powerful than the one that destroyed Nagasaki. Why don't we face that problem? What madness permits such excesses?

And how do we ignore the fact that when one of the new nuclear destroyers was named after President Jimmy Carter, our human rights president, he said how proud he was to have this instrument of homicide named for him. God help us. And when asked what was the purpose of this new weapon, he answered, "To protect us from our enemies." If that's our perception of the earth, the earth better dig a deep foxhole on another planet, because there's no place to hide here.

When was the last time you saw the major media address the problem of the world's armament expenditures? Why is it that today, a decade after the end of the Cold War, the U.S. is spending $265 billion a year on arms, and the next largest expenditure is $49 billion by the Russian federation? The new evil empire, the People's Republic of China, spends $32 billion. Why are we exporting all these arms, including depleted uranium, to regimes all over the world? Anybody facing enemy armor wants DU ammunition. Why can't the media bring this to our attention? It's simply because the media is owned by the same interests that profit from exploitation of foreign people and weapons sales. The media will not run these stories, because the news is whatever it says it is. They're not about to get into these matters. Why do we constantly glorify violence, so that its employment by our forces or surrogates is ignored, accepted, even praised?

Above all, we need to raise the question addressed so sensitively by President Aristide this morning. The great question of the next century, perhaps of the next millennium, will not be the question of race, which W.E.B. DuBois identified as the dominant issue of the twentieth century in our country. Instead, it will be the more complicated question of poverty and the poor. There will be a billion more people born in less than ten years. The numbers are absolutely mind-boggling. Eighty percent will have beautiful dark skin and will live lives of hunger, sickness, fear and violence ending in an early death unless we act radically. The poorest, most corrupted country can feed its people, provide model health care, save its babies by strongly reducing mortality, educate all, help other nations, excel in arts, literature, music, scholarship. Look at Cuba.

The free male population of Athens was less than the residents at a major university in the United States or western Europe today. The citizens of Athens knew each other, so their truth and actuality was inescapable among themselves. Such a community cannot be compared to our universities, which are fragmented. One school doesn't know what the other school is doing. The speaker in one school is not known in the other schools.

Celebrity, fame is a form of incomprehension, perhaps the worst. A professor's fame isn't generated from what he says on campus, but which TV host puts him on his program, which publisher touts his book, a truly artificial standard. The best reporters are those who serve their masters the best. They're the ones that stay on, the ones that achieve fame in their field. But where are they? On the fifteenth of January 1991, when the world knew that something big, a great story, was about to occur, for better or for worse, in Baghdad, the major media was at the cashier's desk in the Al Rashid Hotel literally checking out. They were leaving. A young journalist in school, wanting to earn fame as a reporter like Ernie Pyle or perhaps an Ed Murrow reporting from London, would have done anything to remain there to cover the story. But at the Al Rashid fifteen famous journalists were checking out, leaving the story behind. One person remained, Peter Arnett, who was condemned as a traitor for a few camera shots that told the truth.

The media did not intend that the devastating effects of the U.S. bombing on Iraq be known. We proudly admitted to 110,000 aerial sorties, 88,500 tons of bombs, seven and a half Hiroshimas. We were proud of it. But what happened to the bombed people? No story there. Nobody to cover it. Sure, a hit on the al-Ameriyah bomb shelter was revealed, just to show that mistakes can happen. But what about the length and breadth of the land? Twenty million people subjected to a bombing unprecedented in history, absolutely defenseless, while not an armored vehicle of the allies, as we called ourselves, was hit by enemy fire. We lost fewer planes than in NATO's war games where they don't use live ammunition. There was no war, there was a slaughter.

When we took John Alpert, who had won seven Emmys for TV documentaries, into Iraq to report on the devastation, the media wouldn't show his tapes. He had six hours of tape that showed the devastation in Basra and elsewhere. They wouldn't show it. NBC, with whom Alpert had won most of his Emmys, wouldn't touch it. CBS wouldn't touch it. ABC wouldn't touch it. PBS wouldn't touch it. No one would air his tape. It was never shown until it was put out on little cassettes like home movies and taken out to churches and such places to show to a few hundred people. The facts were not to be known.

It's imperative that we recognize the nature of the beast that we're struggling with and find every way we can to overcome it. It's easy enough to say the truth will out, but the truth will not out in time to help unless the people demand it, unless we struggle with all our might. There are many alternatives to major media. We can hope for Web sites and all the potential of the Internet, but, realistically, it takes an unusual person to scan all these Web sites and it's a solitary activity. When they come across something there, they're interested, but they don't see it in the real world where they live and work, on the evening news, in their daily newspaper, in the weekly magazines. It's not there. It's only on this little Web site. Under these circumstances, how do you mobilize, how do you organize?

There may be enough news seepage to make it necessary for even the most powerful media to begin to report, because they can't afford to lose public credibility. When people begin to suspect that they are being denied information, they will be fed it in small and manipulated doses. But the fact remains that the media is in the business for money, and media owners make money by superior capacities for violence and exploitation.

You won't hear anything about the debt of poor countries from them, and those debts will grow. We'll steal corn from the mouths of hungry children in Mexico and pay them back, if it all, with things they never needed and didn't want. Similarly, we will impose privatization, forcing countries to sell the last social support systems that the poor people have. We'll demand free trade, preventing the development of any local economic power, even food production, that can resist the onslaught of concentrated wealth in what we call the West. We have to resist those things, and we have to work to overthrow them. It will require three qualities in the character of the people, the qualities that Anatole France described in his great book *The Revolt of the Angels* as the reason that Lucifer was banned from heaven: liberty, curiosity, and doubt.

In ourselves and in each person we can touch, let us try to instill a commitment to freedom of the mind from prejudice, from misinformation and disinformation and manipulation; then to a steely commitment to exercise that freedom, a curiosity driving us to want to know, to get our sack of potatoes off the couch to seek the truth. Finally, use skepticism and doubt to hone truth fine and to bring us to the facts in time. Liberty, curiosity, and doubt.

MEDIA EVASION

MICHAEL PARENTI

We often think of the news media as sensationalist and intrusive. In fact, the press's basic modus operandi is evasive rather than invasive. More important than the sensationalist hype is the artful avoidance.

Omission. The most common form of news evasion is outright omission. Information and analysis that reflects poorly upon the higher circles is least likely to see the light of day. Sometimes not just vital details but the entire story is suppressed. Thus, in 1965 the Indonesian military—trained, financed, and advised by the U.S. national security state—overthrew President Sukarno and eradicated the Indonesian Communist Party and its allies, killing half a million people (some estimates are as high as a million) in what was the greatest act of political mass murder since the Nazi Holocaust. The generals destroyed hundreds of clinics, libraries, schools, and community centers that had been opened by the communists. Here was a truly sensational—as opposed to sensationalist— story if ever there was one, but it took three months before it received passing mention in *Time* magazine and yet another month before it was reported in the *New York Times*, accompanied by an editorial that actually praised the Indonesian military for "rightly playing its part with utmost caution." [1]

Information about the murder and torture perpetrated by U.S.-sponsored surrogate forces in the Third World, the CIA's longtime involvement in drug trafficking, and most other crimes committed by the U.S. national security state are either omitted from the mainstream media or denied by media editorialists and commentators with a vehemence and unanimity that would be called "totalitarian" were it to occur in some other countries.

Labeling. A label predefines a subject by simply giving it a positive or negative tag without benefit of any explanatory details. Some positive labels are: "stability," "the president's firm leadership," and "a strong defense." Some negative ones are: "leftist guerillas," "Islamic terrorists," and "conspiracy theorists." The press itself is falsely labeled "the liberal media" by the hundreds of conservative columnists and commentators who crowd the communication universe while claiming to be shut out of it. In the June 1998 California campaign for Proposition 226, a measure designed to cripple the political activities of organized labor, union leaders were repeatedly labeled as "union bosses," while corporate leaders were never called "corporate bosses."

A strikingly deceptive label is "reform," whose meaning is inverted and misapplied to the dismantling of social reforms. So the media talked of "welfare reform" when referring to the elimination of family assistance programs. Over the last thirty years, "tax reform" has repeatedly served as a deceptive euphemism for laws that have reversed the progressive tax reforms of past generations by reducing upper-income taxes, including inheritance taxes, corporate taxes, and capital gains, shifting the payment burden still more regressively upon middle and low income strata.

In Eastern Europe and the former Soviet Union, "reform" has meant the expropriation of the public economy by private investors, complete with massive layoffs, the abolition of human services, and a drastic increase in unemployment and human suffering. So with "IMF reforms" throughout much of the Third World. Yet these "reforms" are portrayed in the press as bringing greater free-market prosperity to the targeted populations.

"Free market" itself is a pet label, evoking images of economic plentitude and democracy. In reality, free-market policies undermine the markets of local producers, provide state subsidies to multinational corporations, and create greater gaps between the wealthy few and the underprivileged many. Free markets are free for those who have lots of money.

A favorite negative label of late is "hard-liner." Anyone who resists the heartless "reforms" of the free-market plunderers is deemed a hard-liner. An article in the *New York Times* used "hard-line" eleven times to describe Bosnian Serb leaders who opposed attempts by NATO forces to close down the "hard-line Bosnian Serb broadcast network."[2] This repression of a network that was the only dissenting voice for ordinary Serbs in Bosnia was considered "a step toward bringing about responsible news coverage in Bosnia." The story did note "the apparent irony" of using foreign soldiers for "silencing broadcasts in order to encourage free speech." The troops, who shut down the stations were labeled "NATO peacekeepers."

It is no accident that "hard-liner" and various other labels are never subjected to precise definition. The efficacy of a label is that it not have a specific content that can be held up to any test of evidence; better it be self-referential, employing an undefined but distinctly evocative image.

Preemptive Assumption. Frequently the media accept as given the very policy position that needs to be debated. During the 1980s when the White House and the military-industrial complex proposed a sharp increase in military spending, the press discussed how much increase was needed. Absent was any opinion that called for substantial reductions in the arms budget. When policy elites call for cuts in Medicare or welfare or various other human services, media pundits discuss the amounts to be cut and the possible effects. The policy itself is preemptively accepted without critical debate.

Likewise with the public discussion on "Social Security reform," a euphemism for the privatization and eventual abolition of a program that is working well. In the United States, Social Security operates as a three-pronged human service. In addition to retirement pensions, it provides survivors' insurance (up until the age of 18, or 21 for students) to children in families that have lost their breadwinner, and it offers disability assistance to persons of pre-retirement age who have sustained serious injury or illness. From existing press coverage you would never know the good that Social Security does. Instead the media assume the very thing that needs to be debated: that the program is in danger of collapsing (in thirty years) and therefore needs drastic "reform."

Face-Value Transmission. One way to lie is to accept at face value what are known to be official lies, uncritically passing them on to the public without adequate confirmation. U.S. governmental and business leaders forever talk about "global leadership," "national security," "free markets," and "reforms," when what they mean is "All Power to the Multinationals." And the press uncritically echoes them, transmitting their loaded vocabularies and policy agendas to wider publics.

When challenged on this, reporters insist that they cannot inject their own personal ideology into their reports. Actually, no one is asking them to. My criticism is that they already do. Their conventional ideological perceptions usually coincide with those of their bosses and with officialdom, making them faithful purveyors of the prevailing political orthodoxy. This confluence of bias is experienced as the absence of bias, and is described as "objectivity."

Slighting of Content. One has to marvel at how the media can give so much emphasis to style and process, and so little to actual substance, so much focus on what policy will get through with no thought about who will benefit or be harmed by the policy, so much speculation about the future with hardly a glance at present politico-economic realities. A glaring example is the way elections are reported. The political campaign is reduced to a horse race: Who will run? Who will win the nomination? Who will win the election? News commentators sound more like theater critics as they hold forth on what candidate is projecting the most positive image, and whose ads are most effective. The actual issues are accorded scant attention, and the democratic dialogue that is supposed to accompany a contest for public office rarely takes place.

Accounts of major strikes—on those rare occasions the press attends to labor struggles—offer a similar slighting of content. We are told how many days the strike has lasted, the inconvenience and cost to the company and the public, and how negotiations threaten to break down. Missing is any reference to the *content* of the conflict, the actual issues: the cutback in wages and benefits, loss of seniority, or the unwillingness of management to negotiate a new contract.

False Balancing. In accordance with the canons of good journalism, the press is supposed to offer us both sides of an issue. In fact, both sides are seldom accorded equal prominence. One study found that on NPR, supposedly the most liberal of the mainstream media, right-wing spokespeople are often interviewed alone, while liberals—on the less frequent occasions they appear—are almost always offset by conservatives. Furthermore, both sides of a story are not necessarily *all* sides. Left-progressive and radical views are almost completely shut out.

False balancing is evident in a BBC report that spoke of "a history of violence between Indonesian forces and Timorese guerillas"—with not a hint that the guerillas were struggling for their lives against an Indonesian invasion force that had slaughtered some 200,000 Timorese.[3] Instead, a terrible act of aggression was made to sound like a grudge fight, with "killings on both sides." By imposing a neutralizing gloss over the genocidal invasion of East Timor, the BBC announcer was introducing a distortion.

The U.S.-supported wars in Guatemala and El Salvador were often treated with the same false balancing. Both those who burned villages and those who were having their villages burned were depicted as equally involved in a contentious bloodletting. In an attempt to neutralize oneself, one neutralizes the subject matter and thereby drastically distorts it.

Looking at the Bright Side. It is sometimes amazing how the media will paint a positive picture if it is in keeping with what the higher circles want us to believe. In a story about two former South Korean presidents who were being tried for crimes against their people, the *New York Times* reported: "While a relatively small number of South Koreans were tortured to death under Mr. Chun and Mr. Roh, the great majority of people gained immensely in economic terms during their rule."[4] Imagine applying such a grotesquely upbeat observation to the U.S. context: "While a relatively small number of women are raped and murdered in America, the great majority have gainfully entered the job market."

Another example. To assure us that the economy was fine during the late 1980s, NPR reported: "If you take food, fuel, and housing out of the equation, inflation has been really quite moderate."[5] If you remove a few other major items, it disappears altogether.

Follow-up Avoidance. When confronted with an unexpectedly heterodoxical response, media hosts quickly change the subject, or break for a commercial, or inject an identifying announcement: "We are talking with [whomever], who is associated with [whatever]." The purpose is to avoid going any further into a politically forbidden topic.

During the pope's recent visit to Cuba, a BBC anchorperson enthused: "Christmas in Cuba: For the first time in almost forty years Cubans were able to celebrate Christmas and go to church!" She then linked up with the BBC correspondent in Havana, who observed, "A crowd of two thousand have gathered in the cathedral for midnight mass. The whole thing is rather low key, very much like last year." Very much like last year? Here was something that craved clarification. Instead, the anchorperson quickly moving to another question: "Can we expect a growth of freedom with the pope's visit?"[6]

On a PBS talk show, host Charlie Rose asked a guest, whose name escaped me, whether Castro was bitter about the historic failure of communism. No, the man replied, Castro is proud of what he believes communism has done for Cuba: advances in health care and education, full employment, and the elimination of the worst aspects of poverty. Rose looked at him stony faced for an instant then swiftly turned to another guest: "What impact will the pope's visit have in Cuba?" Rose ignored the errant one for the rest of the program.[7]

Framing. The most effective propaganda relies on framing rather than on falsehood. By bending the truth rather than breaking it, using emphasis and other auxiliary embellishments, breaking it, using emphasis and other auxiliary embellishments, communicators can create a desired impression without departing too far from the appearance of objectivity. Framing is achieved in the way the news is packaged, the amount of exposure, the placement (front page or buried within, lead story or last), the tone of presentation (sympathetic or slighting), the headlines and photographs, and, in the case of broadcast media, the accompanying visual and auditory effects.

Newscasters use themselves as auxiliary embellishments. They cultivate a smooth delivery and try to convey an impression of detachment. They affect a knowing tone designed to foster credibility, voicing what I call "authoritative ignorance" as in remarks like: "How will this situation end? Only time will tell"; or "No one can say for sure." Sometimes trite truisms are palmed off as penetrating truths. So we are fed sentences like: "Unless the strike is settled soon, the two sides will be in for a long and bitter struggle." And: "Because of heightened voter interest, election-day turnout is expected to be heavy."

Learning Never to Ask Why. Many things are reported in the news but few are explained. Little is said about how the social order is organized and whose interests prevail. Instead we are left to see the world as do mainstream pundits, as a scatter of events and personalities propelled by happenstance, circumstance, confused intentions, and individual ambition—never by powerful class interests—yet producing effects that serve such interests with impressive regularity.

Passive voice and impersonal subject are essential rhetorical constructs for this mode of evasion. So we read or hear that "fighting broke out in the region," or "many people were killed in the disturbances," or "famine is on the increase." Recessions apparently just happen like some natural phenomenon ("our economy is in a slump"), having little to do with the profit accumulation process, the constant war of capital against labor, and the contradictions between productive power and earning power. As Marx noted: recessions occur because workers cannot make enough money to buy back the goods and

52

services they produce. Needless to say, such heresies are rarely entertained in the press.

If we are to believe the press, stuff just happens. Referring to Los Angeles traffic problems, one NPR announcer observed that earlier in the century "LA had a labyrinth of electric cars" that spanned the entire metropolis, but it "disappeared as LA developed a massive freeway system."[8] In fact, the electric car system wasn't a "labyrinth" but one of the world's largest, interurban electric rail systems, covering a 75-mile radius with three thousand quiet, pollution-free electric trains that carried 80 million people a year without major accidents. And it didn't just "disappear." General Motors and Standard Oil, using dummy corporations as fronts, purchased the system, scrapped its electric cars, tore down its transmission lines, and placed GM buses fueled by Standard Oil on LA's streets. Then came the corporate push for more cars and freeways, all at great cost to taxpayers in money and lives. The transformation of Los Angeles's transit system, and that of numerous other cities, involved active human agency in the form of powerful special interests. It was not something that just happened.

"Globalization" is another pet label that the press presents to us as a natural and inevitable development. In fact, globalization is a deliberate contrivance of multinational interests to undermine labor, consumer, and environmental regulations in various nations. If by "globalization" we mean the integration of the world's population in productive cooperation, then what we actually are experiencing is *de*globalization, an ever greater concentration of politico-economic power in the hands of an international investment class, accomplished under such arrangements as GATT, which divest the peoples of the world of any protective input.

Never Going All the Way. Taught to never ask why, we fail to associate social problems with the socio-economic forces that create them and we learn to truncate our own critical thinking. Imagine if we attempted something different. Let's say, we tried to explain that wealth and poverty exist together not in accidental juxtaposition, but because wealth *causes* poverty, an inevitable outcome of economic exploitation both at home and abroad. How could such an analysis gain any exposure in the capitalist media or in mainstream political life?

Suppose we start with a particular story about how child labor in Indonesia is contracted by multinational corporations at near-starvation wage levels. In 1996, after decades of effort by some activists, this information finally did appear in the centrist mainstream press. Suppose we then crossed a line and said that these exploitative relations are backed by the full might of the Indonesian military government, which for more than thirty years has been completely supported by the U.S. national security state, and that this support is not an aberration but is given to numerous other repressive governments.

Then suppose we crossed that most serious line of all and instead of just deploring this fact we also asked *why* successive U.S. administrations have involved themselves in such unsavory pursuits throughout the world. Suppose we concluded that the whole phenomenon was consistent with the U.S. dedication to making the world safe for the free market and the giant multinational corporations. Such an analysis almost certainly would not be printed anywhere except in a few select radical publications. We crossed too many lines. Because we tried to explain the particular situation (child labor) in terms of a larger set of social relations (corporate class power), our presentation would be rejected out of hand as "ideological" or "Marxist."

In sum, the news media's daily performance is not a failure but a skillfully evasive success. Their job is not to inform but *dis*inform, not to advance democratic discourse but mute it. The media give every appearance of being vigorously concerned about events of the day, saying so much, meaning so little, offering so many calories and so few nutrients. When we understand this, we move from a liberal complaint about the press's sloppy performance to a radical analysis of how the media serve the ruling circles with much craft and craftiness.

1. *New York Times*, April 4, 1966.
2. *New York Times*, October 10, 1997.
3. BBC World News, December 11, 1997.
4. *New York Times*, December 4, 1995.
5. "All Things Considered," National Public Radio, April 17, 1989.
6. BBC World News, December 26, 1997.
7. The Charlie Rose Show, PBS, January 22, 1998.
8. "Marketplace," National Public Radio, May 11 1998.

OWNERSHIP AND CONTROL OF THE MEDIA

PETER PHILLIPS

Twenty-two years ago there were approximately fifty media corporations that dominated the U.S. news services. Today that number is less than a dozen. The Federal Communications Commission used to limit television and radio station ownership. Now, since the passage of the Telecommunications Act in 1996 a single corporation can own radio, television, book publishing, newspapers, and Internet services, all in the same market area, and up to a 1/3 market share nationally. This means that the major media corporations that own most of our news systems today will be down to 3 or 4 corporations in the next decade.

Mainstream media is in a gold rush of acquisitions and mergers including: Time Warner's merger with CNN; ABC being taken over by Disney; and Westinghouse (CBS) buying up Infinity Radio Group. Over one third of all the radio stations in the United States have been sold within the last 18 months. This is happening in the newspaper industry as well. Gannett and Knight-Ridder have taken the lead in ownership of newspaper chains, together holding close to 200 metropolitan news publications.

I was impressed to learn yesterday that Athens has some 15 daily newspapers. In the United States, 98% of all cities have one newspaper, and these are rapidly being taken over by giant corporations.

The U.S. media has lost its diversity and its ability to present different points of view. Instead, there is a homogeneity of news stories and the major media tend to look alike.

The media in the U.S. has created, to use Neil Postman's words, the "best entertained, least informed society in the world." Americans are ignorant about international affairs and alienated from their own social issues. A growing portion of the people in the U.S. live in gated communities, and as Cornell West says, the "vanilla" suburbs have built institutional barriers to segregate themselves from the "chocolate" cities.

The media provide entertainment and fear. The American public watches celebrity news, infomercials, titillation, and sex as entertainment. Crime reports, stories of the underclass, immigrants, and welfare cheats create fear and loathing. Crime reporting has risen significantly in this decade, while at the same time actual crime has declined in the United States.

Media develop target markets and audiences, focusing on upper middle-class people with money and the ability to buy products. Little wonder that a recent Associated Press story released nationally was entitled: "How to Decorate Around Your Big Screen TV."

Last summer, researchers at Sonoma State University looked up the names of the 155 people who served on the boards of directors of the eleven media companies that dominated the U.S. market. This is a group small enough to fit into this room. They are 90% white males. Recently, Rupert Murdoch, despite his marital difficulties, has graciously agreed to allow his wife Anna Murdoch to retain her seat on News Corp's board of directors.

Who are these 155 media elites—directors of the largest combined media news systems in the world? They include men like: Frank Carlucci, who sits on the board of directors of Westinghouse (CBS), and was former deputy director of the CIA and later Secretary of Defense under President Bush; Andrew Sigler, on GE's (NBC) board, also sits on the board of directors of Chemical Bank, Bristol Meyers, Allied Signal, Champion International and Chase Manhattan Bank; Douglas Warner III, who is on GE's (NBC) board, is also on the board of directors of Bechtel Group, Anheuser-Busch and is the CEO of J.P. Morgan Company.

The 155 media elite are mostly individuals who inherited wealth, were educated in private preparatory schools and ivy-league universities, and whose main social interactions occur at the Knickerbocker Club in New York, Bohemian Grove in California or the Piedmont Driving Range in Atlanta. They represent private wealth, private education, private clubs and they control immense media resources. These media resources provide most people in the United States with their sole source of news and information.

The top 11 media corporations in the U.S. form a solid network of overlapping interests and affiliations. The 155 directors of these 11 media corporations sit on the board of directors of 144 of the Fortune 1000 corporations and interlock with each other through shared directorships in other firms some 36 times.

NBC, Fox News, and Time Warner each has a board member who sits as a director on tobacco producer Philip Morris's board. CBS (Westinghouse) shares directorships on Fortune 1000 boards with the *Washington Post*, Time-Warner, NBC (GE), Gannett, Viacom and the Times Mirror Corporation (*LA Times*).

Little wonder that the U.S. news is so biased against democratic liberation struggles all over the world and is so favorable to multi-national capital flow, International Monetary Fund politics, GATT, MAI, NAFTA, and all the other neo-liberal economic policies that favor the free flow of international capital and wealth acquisition. Democracy to the media elite means freedom to economically exploit, freedom to move money anywhere in the world, and freedom to present their own ideological messages.

The U.S. media ignores big questions like: Who loses in the process of economic growth and wealth accumulation? What about the one billion people in the world who are surplus labor and un-needed in the international market place? How are they to survive? What about the global issues of environmental sustainability and the using up of our unrenewable natural resources.

These are the questions of a socio-environmental apocalypse. Free market capitalism is creating an evil empire of corruption and waste that generates wretchedness for billions of people. All the indicators are that wealth and resources do not trickle down but rather become increasingly concentrated in the hands of the elites in the nation states of the First World and their senior and junior partners around the globe.

What hope have we? What direction can resistance take? I do not believe that we can expect reform from within the international global media system, especially in the United States. Media wealth is too concentrated, too solidified, and too integrated into the corporate government elite to make social change possible.

We can, however, look to ourselves for the direction we must go. In the past two years there have been two Media and Democracy Conventions in the United States. One was in San Francisco two and a half years ago and the other in New York last October. They each brought together 1,500 to 2,000 independent/alternative media writers, editors, film producers and broadcasters, who jointly recognized many of the same concerns with corporate media that we have covered over the past three days.

Media and Democracy is rapidly becoming a grass roots movement based on a shared vision of building alternative news and information systems independent from corporate influence. Hundreds of pirate radio stations, many now under attack by the FCC (and defended in part by the National Lawyers Guild and Luke Hiken, here today) have sprung up all over the U.S. offering a diversity of programs. Fairness and Accuracy in Reporting (FAIR), Institute of Alternative Journalism (IAJ), and numerous First Amendment groups, Internet newsletters and news magazines are active all over the United States.

Progressive media networks exist in LA, Chicago, Denver, San Francisco, Houston, New York, and Seattle. TV producers from Free Speech TV, People's Video, Globalvision, Deep Dish, and Paper Tiger TV are being joined by small progressive shoestring-budget cable show producers all over the country, people like school teacher John Morearty in Stockton California, who for five years has been doing a weekly hour-long progressive TV show aired in his local community.

Our Pacifica Radio network has been joined with Hightower Radio and United Broadcasting, and over 100 alternative newsweeklys are published in almost every major metropolitan area in the U.S. Two video producers, Beth Sanders and Randy Baker, made the film "Fear and Favor in the Newsroom" that describes the consequences of media monopoly. This film is being shown at activist meetings all over the country.

Alternative/independent media sources in the U.S. are still small, often territorially competitive and under-financed. Yet they offer a hope for the future.

Academics, progressives and leftists have been rightly criticized for being intellectually elitist and condescending. Michael Moore criticized the Media and Democracy Congress in New York for its failure to incorporate working class people into its agenda. This is a failure that we cannot ignore! The 60% of the population who are blue and white collar workers surviving paycheck to paycheck are alive and well. Yet they are confused by a media system that can't or won't explain why the purchasing power of their paychecks continues to decline as health care costs rise, housing becomes unaffordable, and taxes keep increasing.

Major media has led working people towards racial hatred, immigrant bashing, and attacks on welfare. People are fearful of the homeless because they fear homelessness themselves. They blame and attack the victims of corporate greed. They pay high tuition to send their children to universities, and these students often end up back home after graduation with huge student loan debts and few professional prospects for employment. Most working people are politically alienated and more than one-half no longer vote.

Yet, working people have strong core values that honor hard work, freedom, democratic process, equal opportunity, freedom of expression, due process, and systemic fairness. Several times over the past 100 years working people have joined with progressives, forming social movements that changed the United States.

The Progressive Movement 100 years ago challenged the Robber Barons and corporate wealth concentration and instituted income tax on the rich, an 8-hour work day, the rights of governmental recall, and citizen proposition. The Suffrage Movement gave women the right to vote. The Labor Movement in the 1930s forced a New Deal that allowed unionism, national social welfare, old age pensions, and national public health.

The Civil Rights Movement broke the back of racial segregation and the Peace Movement challenged the illegal war in Vietnam. The Environmental Movement, the American Indian Movement, and the Women's Movement have all introduced needed changes in society. Each of these movements depended on thousands of working people, who contributed, marched and in many cases died for their beliefs.

We must, and we can reawaken the values of the working people in order to mobilize against the socio-environmental apocalypse. A free flow of ideas will only happen outside of corporate media, outside of the government-corporate spin doctors.

An alternative/independent press can be a key element in a social movement that empowers working people in the U.S. to take control of their government/corporate power structures for their own betterment and that of the world. "Free the Media" can become a real rallying cry that will allow the emergence of what the new democratized AFL-CIO calls "Common Sense Economics," an economics that unmasks corporate wealth exploitation and offers an alternative that benefits working people worldwide.

Can we strengthen alternative/independent news systems in the United States? I believe we can by sharing news stories, Internet connections, joint promotional/marketing plans, and by addressing the important socio-economic, environmental, gender and racial issues in the U.S. and in the world.

I think that the American public needs to know that the U.S. is now the arms merchant to the world, selling 60% of all export weapons, using 650 government employees in embassies all over the world to promote weapons sales for private corporate profits.

I think the U.S. public deserves to know that many of their cosmetics and body lotions are carcinogenic, that U.S. companies manufacture torture devices and that a national I.D. card system is just around the big brother corner. The public needs to know that their private e-mail, telephone, and fax messages are monitored by U.S and allied intelligence services and that their *public* universities have become dependent on *private* corporate funding.

These are issues that must be addressed in order to solve the apocalyptic problems of wealth accumulation, environmental sustainability, and surplus labor forces.

For people in the U.S. this means building and supporting alternative news and information systems, and becoming local activists with global awareness. For those outside the U.S. it means sharing viewpoints, news stories, and information with the alternative press in the U.S. and helping reeducate working people to our shared global problems.

Project Censored annually compiles a listing of over 400 alternative press publications and media outlets in the United States. We are willing to share this resource electronically with journalists anywhere.

Remember, we have had Reagan, Thatcher, and Yeltsen, but as Jim Hightower likes to say, "Three right turns make a left." So it is time to move forward, remembering that Robin Hood may have been right after all.

PART TWO

FILTERING THE NEWS:

STORIES KEPT IN MEDIA DARKNESS

CHARACTER ASSASSINATION OF PRESIDENT ARISTIDE

BEN DUPUY

Haiti, it is well-known, is the only country in world history which carried out a successful slave revolution. It began in 1791, on the heels of the French Revolution. The man who led the slave armies through most of our 13-year liberation war was a former slave named Toussaint Louverture.

While much can be said about his military genius, Toussaint was above all a master in the art of what we might call "diplomatic guile." In other words, he sometimes pretended to go along with his powerful adversaries—variously the French, English, and Spanish—in order to accomplish his goal, the abolition of slavery (at least in its classical form).

One modern figure who has deeply studied and borrowed from Toussaint's tactics is Jean-Bertrand Aristide. Just as Toussaint attempted to advance his people's interests by sometimes fighting against the French, then sometimes working with them, Aristide has been locked in a similar dance with Haiti's principal adversary in this century: the United States.

The debate about the viability or correctness of using Toussaint's tactics in the 20th century can be left for another time. But one thing is certain: President Aristide has fallen in and out of favor with leading sectors of the U.S. ruling class and government on several occasions, offering a very revealing case study of how the mainstream corporate media has alternately demonized or glorified him as a leader, not on the basis of his support from or attachment to the masses, but according to his professed attitude toward U.S. business interests and U.S. government dictates.

Let us briefly review a little history.

First we must recall that Jean-Bertrand Aristide emerged in Haiti as a liberation theologian with an anti-imperialist message. *"Capitalism is a mortal sin"* was one of the refrains of the fiery sermons he would deliver at a church located in the La Saline slum of Port-au-Prince, Haiti's capital.

Although his prestige in Haiti was growing, the U.S. corporate press made little mention of him, even though the U.S. Embassy in Haiti was watching his rise very carefully.

Of course, the U.S. mainstream media could no longer ignore him when he announced he was running for president in October 1990, thereby unleashing the euphoric uprising known as the "Lavalas," or flood.

The initial portrayal of Aristide by the mainstream press in that pre-election period is typified by the comment of Howard French in the *New York Times* on Nov. 12, 1990, who said Aristide was "a mix of [Iran's Ayatollah] Khomeini and [Cuba's Fidel] Castro."

But of course, it was hard to frontally attack a man who came to power, not through a revolution, but through elections which the U.S. government had sponsored and paid for.

So all the mainstream press could do after Aristide's overwhelming victory on Dec. 16, 1990 was to try to intimidate him. The *New York Times* in a Dec. 18 editorial warned Aristide that he had "acquired a duty to respect the constitutional procedures that assured his victory" and "to be patient, and to preach patience," cautioning that he "can now become either the father of Haitian democracy, or just one more of its many betrayers."

Well, we know who ended up betraying Haitian democracy. The U.S. government through its CIA would work with Duvalierism to overthrow Aristide after less than 8 months in power with a bloody coup on September 30, 1991.

Rather than condemning the coup, the mainstream press began attacking Aristide. "Returning President Aristide to Haiti is going to be difficult for reasons to which he himself has greatly contributed," stated a *Washington Post* editorial on Oct. 6, 1991. The next day, the *Post* reported that Aristide had a "seeming disregard of legal structures" and cited "independent observers and diplomats" who charged that the he "repeatedly has used explicit and implicit threats of mob violence."

"Mob violence." If you look through the mainstream press clippings for the period immediately after the coup, you will see this refrain throughout. According to Katie Orenstein of the *NACLA Review of the Americas*, "during the two-week period after the coup, the *New York Times* spent over three times as many column inches discussing Aristide's alleged transgressions than it spent reporting on the ongoing military repression. Mass murders, executions and tortures that were later reported in human rights publications earned less than 4% of the space that the *Times* devoted to Haiti in those weeks."

Even during the coup that removed Aristide, the mainstream press never stopped casting suspicion on him. American negotiations with the putschists were promptly initiated, but Aristide was always portrayed as "intransigent" and "inflexible," even though he was making the concessions and the putschists were scuttling every deal. But Haitians in the diaspora maintained constant demonstrations in support of Aristide and against the coup. The Democrats in the United States took advantage of this movement to help build support for Bill Clinton's 1992 election.

This is where there emerged a difference between the two factions of the U.S. ruling class. President George Bush and the Republicans were perfectly happy to leave Aristide permanently in exile and work with their old allies, the Haitian military and Duvalierists. The Clinton administration decided to attempt to coopt Aristide and to force him to accept what is known in Haiti as "the American plan." The essence of this plan is to discard justice and reconcile with Duvalierist criminals, and also to "structurally adjust" the Haitian economy, that is, privatize profitable state enterprises, lower tariff walls, lay off state employees, mainly from schools and hospitals, and slash social subsidies and price-supports.

Of course, even if Aristide were to accept the deal, Washington felt he could not really be trusted, so U.S. troops would have to militarily occupy the country as an insurance policy.

Well, the Republicans didn't like this arrangement at all. Neither did the "invisible government" in the U.S., that is, the Pentagon and the CIA. Therefore, the CIA began pumping up a death-squad in Haiti known as the FRAPH, which they called a "counterweight" to the Lavalas.

The FRAPH and CIA coordinated their strategies. First, the FRAPH staged a demonstration with a few dozen thugs at the Port-au-Prince wharf on Oct. 11, 1993, so that the Pentagon had an excuse to withdraw its troop carrier the Harlan County, which was to off-load 200 U.S. and Canadian soldiers. Then, the following week, Brian Latell, the CIA's chief Latin American analyst, launched an offensive in the U.S. Congress and mainstream media to portray Aristide as "mentally unstable" and a "murderer and psychopath," while the coup's leader, General Raoul Cédras, and his cohorts came from "the most promising group of Haitian leaders to emerge since the Duvalier family." Henry Kissinger went on TV to call him "a psychopath." Right-wing politician Patrick Buchanan called him "a blood-thirsty little socialist."

Despite the "invisible government's" temporary victory in stopping Aristide's return in 1993, Haiti kept coming back to haunt the U.S. Repression continued and refugees kept flooding out of the country, eventually forcing the Clinton Administration to reconsider the return of Aristide to Haiti under U.S. supervision. This time the Clinton administration opted for a massive military invasion of 20,000 U.S. troops on Sept. 19, 1994.

When President Aristide agreed to this intervention, along with the structural adjustment program, there was a major shift in the portrayal of Aristide. He was warily praised as a "statesman" who had "matured" and become more "realistic." He was the prodigal son, perhaps.

"I think the best thing that has happened to Aristide and his administration-in-exile is that they have had a crash course in democracy and capitalism, and come to understand that too much revolution scares away investors. Small countries can't afford too much social experimentation," said former Ambassador Robert E. White, a Carter Center agent, in the *Boston Globe* shortly after the invasion.

Time magazine also spoke candidly about Clinton Administration reasoning. "For the next 17 months or so, the U.S. must pin its hopes on Aristide. His 1990 election victory gives him an aura of legitimacy no other Haitian figure can come close to matching [note: 67.5% of the vote usually earns legitimacy, not its aura]; the U.S. can hardly pretend to be restoring Haitian democracy if it backs anyone else. If he is a leftist and no admirer of the U.S.—well, in a perverse way, that makes American intervention easier to defend against possible cries of Yanqui imperialism. Instead of overthrowing a populist reformer to install a military dictatorship friendly to the U.S., Washington will be doing the exact opposite."

Two or three months after his return, since there was no revolution, the corporate media was thinking they had won him over. Consider a Dec. 1, 1994 *Washington Post* article which quotes an official to provide the proper spin: "'He is doing more than we ever dreamed he would. He is doing everything right,' gushed a senior U.S. official who had long privately expressed doubts about Aristide. 'It's like a dream.'"

But the dream didn't last for long. As 1995 progressed, friction between Aristide and the U.S. began to surface.

Soon the laments over the assassination of the putschist political figure, Mireille Durocher Bertin, became a full-fledged trial of the Aristide government, which was accused of the murder. U.S. government officials said that the killing was "masterminded" by Haitian Interior Minister Mondésir Beaubrun, who vehemently denied the charge.

Leading the new attacks on Aristide were coup supporters like reactionary columnist Robert Novak, who claimed in an April 3, 1995 column to have unearthed an "enemies list compiled by President Aristide's supporters." Novak went on to assert that "it is common knowledge in Haiti that a shadow government is headed by notorious former prime minister René Préval" who oversees a "commando unit greatly feared by the political opposition" as well as "the flow of weapons to the commando units" through the coastal town of St. Marc. His insinuation was that the supposed "commando unit" rubbed out Bertin.

One might dismiss Novak's allegations of a 30-person "hit list" and other sinister acts as the mere rantings of the conservative fringe. But the same day, the Associated Press reported that Bertin "was among more than 100 people on a hit list discovered by the U.S. government days before the slaying." Other reports speak of a 96-person list. The simultaneous discovery of supposed "hit lists" point to a typical U.S. government/mainstream media coordinated campaign.

On April 4, the *Washington Post* launched another missile. Writer Douglas Farah said he was not "suggesting Aristide knew of or sanctioned the killing," but noted that Aristide's "unwillingness to take steps against Beaubrun, despite heavy U.S. pressure and the advice of some of his closest advisers, has revived old questions about the president's willingness to tolerate abuses among those who have shown loyalty to him." The assumption here, of course, is that Beaubrun is guilty! No trial, no evidence, just the accusation of the U.S. government and its media.

Other conflicts began to develop as Aristide disbanded the Army, resisted U.S. plans to double the size of the police force, and dragged his feet on privatizing the state enterprises. In October 1995, Aristide's pro-neoliberal prime minister Smarck Michel quit in frustration. "Relations between Mr. Aristide's Government and the United Nations coalition that brought him back to power have been fraying since Prime Minister Smarck Michel stepped down," said the *New York Times*.

Then on Nov. 7, Aristide's cousin, Deputy Jean-Hubert Feuillé, was assassinated. When Aristide ordered Haitian authorities to arrest former Haitian dictator General Prosper Avril for possible involvement in the murder, the U.S. intervened to protect Avril. The U.S.'s meddling set the stage for a dramatic speech Aristide gave at the Port-au-Prince cathedral on Nov. 11.

Standing before U.S. and UN officials, Aristide assailed their policies in Haiti. "The game of hypocrisy is over," he said. He condemned the failure of the UN occupation forces to help disarm anti-democratic forces, particularly the rich and powerful in their big houses. "We say again that peace must reign here, and for this peace to reign, there must be no accomplices," Aristide said, referring to the U.S./UN troops. "The big guns of the international community are here to accompany the Haitian police to disarm all the criminals, all the terrorists, all the extremists," Aristide said. "If not, I'm going to tell them it's over. . . I'm saying now, whosoever tries to block the legal operation of disarmament, if they're Haitian, we'll arrest them, if they're not Haitian, we'll send them back to their parents," he said in the mostly Creole speech.

Well, you can imagine the reaction of the U.S. government and corporate press. The Nov. 19 *New York Times* reported on "Mr. Aristide's tirade" saying that "foreign officials who have been working closely with the Aristide Government in efforts to build democracy here after nearly three decades of dictatorship [dictatorships which the U.S. government supported economically and militarily] described themselves as shocked and even betrayed by the President's unexpected behavior."

The *Times*'s editorial on Nov. 26, entitled "Mr. Aristide's Deadly Rhetoric," said that he had "alarmingly reverted to the demagogic political style that scarred his Presidency before the 1991 military coup that forced him into exile. That earlier performance, which included incitements to mob violence, [there's that word again] planted reasonable doubts about his commitment to the rule of law and fanned suggestions he was not fit to run the country. . . . America's ally in Haiti is democracy, not any individual politician. If Mr. Aristide means to prove his critics right and destroy Haiti's chance for democracy, he should not have American help."

So there you have it. Democracy is threatened not because the U.S. and UN occupying forces have shielded Tonton Macoutes (as Duvalierist thugs are called) and putschist criminals from arrest and prosecution, allowing them to hide and use their vast arsenals of weapons to create the worst climate of violence and insecurity which the country has ever seen. It is not because the austerity policies of the World Bank and International Monetary Fund have ruined farmers, destroyed small businessmen, and impoverished a country that was already the poorest in the Western Hemisphere. It is because of "Mr. Aristide's tirade" and those unruly "Haitian mobs."

In these same articles and editorials, all the mainstream press clamored in unison that Aristide and his supporters might want him to recoup the three years he spent in exile. "He may go back on his pledge to the United States and try to extend his term past its scheduled end next February," warned the *New York Times*. The *New York Daily News* said that Aristide was "becoming tiresome. The man who had to be prodded to say thanks to the 20,000 Yanks who restored him to power now is talking about ignoring his pledge—and the Haitian constitution—to step down early next year." Now who gives the U.S. government and its hireling press the right to interpret the Haitian constitution? Where in the constitution does it say that the clock is ticking on a president's term when he is removed from power by a bloody coup? The Constitution says nothing about what to do in case of a coup, and if a determination is to be made, it should be by the Haitian people, not Washington and its subservient media.

To make a long story short, the OPL or Lavalas Political Organization, the party which was formed to support the national democratic Lavalas agenda, made a deal with the U.S., betrayed Aristide, and ran René Préval for President. Aristide finally acquiesced and turned over power to Préval on Feb. 7, 1996, with the parting shot of establishing diplomatic relations with Cuba.

In the two years since that time, Aristide established the Aristide Foundation for Democracy, which has launched a credit union, a food cooperative, and a children's radio station among other things. Many mass meetings take place at the Foundation's large auditorium.

He also founded a new party, the Fanmi Lavalas, which largely won legislative and municipal elections held on April 6, 1997. The OPL has refused to accept the election results and has launched what Aristide has called "a coup d'état which is revised, corrected and improved." The result is that the country has been without a prime minister since last June and without even a caretaker government since last October. The OPL has blocked in the Parliament every prime minister proposed by President Préval.

But if you read the mainstream press, who do they say is responsible for Haiti's deadlock? You guessed it: Jean-Bertrand Aristide.

For example, "Aristide: An Obstacle to Haiti's Progress" was the title of a Jun. 29, 1997 news/analysis piece by the *Miami Herald's* Haiti correspondent Don Bohning. "The onetime-priest-turned-politician. . . is simultaneously the country's most popular figure and one of the biggest obstacles to its progress. And there are those who see him as a threat to democracy itself."

Why is Aristide now seen as such an "obstacle" when he is out of office: because he has become an outspoken critic of neoliberalism. In a bipartisan U.S. Congressional report from June 1997, which the *Herald* and other mainstream media heavily publicized, Aristide is taken to task. "The lack of a strong leader—particularly given Aristide's renewed prominent role in economic and political questions—poses a serious threat to U.S. interests in privatization and economic reform in Haiti," the report says.

And, for the U.S. government and mainstream media, there is no greater sin than being a nationalist. . . well, except being a blood-thirsty little socialist.

Meanwhile, President Préval, who has embraced the neoliberal austerity package, has become the new darling. Take this June 11, 1996 *Herald* report: "I think President Préval has done a fantastic job. He has really taken the bull by the horns and said 'either we are going to sit around and do nothing, or we will move forward on economic reforms,'" an official of a multilateral aid organization said. "You really get a feeling that things are moving. It's not the usual lethargy." Or here is Don Bohning's Feb. 13, 1997 glowing portrait of Préval in the *Miami Herald*: "Relaxed and informal, he responded to questions candidly with an occasional flash of humor." Other characterizations: "Low-key and unpretentious" or "Préval's modesty and low-key personality."

In recent months, as the crisis has dragged on, the press has begun to criticize Préval for not acting strongly enough in support of the "American plan" and against Aristide. Thus, when one follows the American guidelines, one is rewarded. Depart from them, and you will feel the whip.

So this is why they now attack Aristide regularly for blocking everything in Haiti because he no longer plays along. Take for example a Mar. 20, 1998 *Miami Herald* article by Bohning entitled "Political impasse puts elections at risk in Haiti." He claims that Aristide's Fanmi Lavalas has "refused to go along" with elections in Haiti.

This isn't only bad spin, it's just plain false. The Fanmi Lavalas has been calling for elections to continue. And how can it block elections? Aristide's party has no members in the executive branch or in the parliament. The mainstream press doesn't castigate and vilify the OPL, even though this party has blocked three different attempts to ratify a new Haitian prime minister. But if OPL were aligned with Aristide, you would see it in the headlines and on your TV every day.

As you all know, the sheer volume of disinformation is so vast that it is difficult to show or repudiate anything more than a small fraction of it. There are so many other lies and distortions to denounce. But I will finish with the latest and most insidious mainstream media campaign.

To show the insidious nature, I just want to give a little anecdote. When we were coordinating President Aristide's participation in this conference—airfares, hotels, and the like—we encountered some financial obstacles. One of the conference organizers, who will remain nameless, asked "Why are we going through all of this? Doesn't Aristide have money?" Here is a very conscious, engaged, and progressive person helping to organize a conference to combat the big media's lies, who has unconsciously absorbed the media's lies. This shows you the power we are up against.

So this is their new campaign: to portray Aristide as a "millionaire," who is corrupt and manipulative and living in a palace. Take the lead of this April 5, 1997 Reuters piece: "Ensconced in a luxury villa behind pink walls, Haiti's former president Jean-Bertrand Aristide still wears the mantle of a champion of the poor as he snipes at the government of his successor and one-time ally."

A May 14, 1998 article in the *LA Times* is another good example of the smear job being attempted. The article relies chiefly on two Aristide critics. Let's hear one of them: "After he came back in 1994, Aristide got the taste of power," said Gerald Dalvius, an opposition politician who has announced his presidential aspirations for 2000. "Now he only believes in power. Maybe he looked for the money to get the power or maybe to make more money."

Let's hear the other: "In every case, I believe power changes people, but in the case of Aristide more than any other, power aggravated the true personality," said Gerard-Pierre Charles, leader of the OPL. Pierre-Charles also compared Aristide to Duvalier, accused him of being "fascist," of smuggling arms into Haiti, and then "blamed Aristide for the political impasse that has paralyzed Haiti."

In short, Aristide is a devil in the eyes of the U.S. government and the mainstream press because he criticizes their plans for Haiti. He is the "obstacle," the great manipulator, the "threat to democracy." Well, the real manipulator, the real threat to democracy is the corporate media and more generally the capitalist system of which it is a pillar. In "Corporate Media and the Threat to Democracy" professor Robert McChesney tells us that "fewer than 10 colossal vertically integrated media conglomerates now dominate U.S. media," companies like Time Warner, Disney, News Corporation, Viacom and TCI.

I think most of the participants in this conference are already pretty clear about the undemocratic, distorting, and falsifying nature of the corporate mainstream media. But the question is what is to be done, how to fight back.

To our way of thinking, there is no way to "reform" the mainstream media, to make it more reliable or truthful. It is not just a bad approach or policy. The mainstream media, just like the state, functions to preserve and defend the interests of monopoly capitalism, and can only function that way.

We might win some media battles, build some media alternatives, denounce the lies, and raise consciousness about the corporate media in various ways. We print *Haïti Progrès* each week as some kind of antidote to and analysis of all the lies they spread each week.

However, the only real solution is to take control of the means of communication from the increasingly tiny ruling class which also owns all the means of production. A truly democratic media will only result from the revolutionary change of capitalist society. Let us use every media resource possible in our fight to reach that end.

ROARING MOUSE: PEOPLE'S MEDIA TAKE THE HIGH GROUND

LAURA FLANDERS

Recently I traded in my position as a long time media critic with the media watch group FAIR for that of the Critics Target at Pacifica Network News. I direct a daily national news broadcast heard on about 65 stations around the country. Pacifica is a community-supported noncommercial radio network that tries to bring alternative news. How can we become the mouse that roars and a people's media that takes the high ground? That is, the high ground of justice and equality and of being right.

The components of how we move into an assertive high ground, roaring mouse kind of position are three fold. The first is criticism of the status quo, content analysis and careful articulation of what the problems are. The second is confrontation with power, confronting and taking on those who have the power that we want to share. Cultivation comes third. I will put my biggest emphasis on the cultivation of our own courageous creativity. What is it exactly about us that makes us alternative, makes us special? These are the three points that I'm going to cover.

When it comes to criticism, the best type of media criticism is not simply the exchange of assertions, my opinion versus yours as to whether a story or a news outlet is biased or unbalanced or ideologically spun. The best criticism is data-based. It is research-based. One finds information to back up one's arguments. Not all media are the same. Not all mainstream media are the same. We need to remember that this is a heterogeneous field that we are talking about. When we fall into the rhetoric of "the media this and the media that," we are ignoring the places where there are real vulnerabilities that we can target and real strengths that will enable us to grow.

FAIR, the media watch group, has been in the forefront of pioneering this type of media research content analysis. Just to give you one example, beginning in 1990 the people at FAIR sat and watched *Nightline*, the nightly news program on the ABC network, over a period of 40 months. At that time it was the most serious evening news discussion show on the air nationally. We sat and watched all 40 months in order to document, among other things, a list of those people most often invited to speak on the show. Who were the guests that were most often asked for their expertise and for their interpretation of the world? We came up with some not very surprising statistics about their demographic details. The data showed eighty-nine percent were male and 92% were white.

The really important part of the story was that we took our information and confronted the powers that be with it. We found out that the top four guests in 1990 were: Henry Kissinger, Al Haig, Elliott Abrams and Jerry Falwell. Which means: a war criminal, a Watergate co-conspirator, a man who had admitted lying to Congress, (which we thought made him a really good expert for interpreting the news), and Jerry Falwell, an evangelist for white Christian supremacy. The confrontation part of the story is that we did not just take the research and leave it there. We went to ABC. We went to Ted Koppel and said, "What do you make of this? What kind of news are you bringing the people? What kind of news makers do you consider fit to talk on your program?"

Ted Koppel, the *Nightline* anchor, said a very interesting thing. He said, "We are a news program and we talk to those who make the news." We took that information and went back to the mainstream media to document the names that *Nightline* thinks make the news. We found that *Nightline*'s "newsmakers" were overwhelmingly connected to Washington, D.C. Is power only in the hands of those in Washington who have served inside the beltway or hope to do so? That stimulated an interesting debate. It made some headlines and it spoke volumes about what mainstream media is about.

In 1998, another group called "Rocky Mountain Media Watch," led by Paul Clight and a tiny handful of volunteers in Boulder, Colorado, put out a call for local colleges to do a day-by-day assessment of their local television news. They used outlets like the radio program *Counter Spin*, the weekly radio program of FAIR, to solicit volunteers and people who would participate in the study about their local television news channels. They found out that 47% of all the air time was dedicated to what they called mayhem, that is, trivia, cat in a tree stories, inter-anchor chit chat and jokes about the weather. The far larger section of the news programming was about crime and violence. There was very little dedicated to the serious consideration of local politics.

They then compiled this data on the local news and challenged the licenses of four commercial television stations in their area. They submitted a petition at the formal re-licensing session for these stations. Every eight years the licenses granted to the stations by the Federal Communications Commission (FCC) are up for renewal. The FCC made the mistake of asking the public for their ideas, assuming they wouldn't get any. Usually they do not. But on this occasion in Boulder, Colorado, they did get input.

The folks from Rocky Mountain Media Watch sent in petitions asking that the licenses be repealed on the grounds that the news being presented was toxic and was not covering local politics adequately. They called for nothing that would contravene the free speech rights of the station, but requested that warnings of violent content in the news be broadcast, just like the surgeon general's warnings on cigarette packages. They called for media literacy courses to be aired during the stations' air time. They called for sensitivity training for the news staff about the impact of violence on the people watching the news. And they called for sensible coverage of local politics. Of course, they did not get any of these things, but they asserted the right to speak the truth, to affirm the fact that the FCC is the peoples' arbiter as the administrator of publicly owned licenses.

What Rocky Mountain Media Watch actually did was a repeat of what had been done almost thirty years ago by black civil rights workers in Jackson, Mississippi. These black activists had challenged the license of their local TV station because it was failing to cover what was going on in the civil rights movement and, in particular, what was going on in Jackson, Mississippi. The stations would not quote Martin Luther King, nor would they quote the more outrageous statements of the white administrators in a majority black town. They simply refused to cover the conflict that was taking place, including the violence and the actions of the police.

In response, this black civil rights groups got together and challenged the license of that station. They not only won their case, but actually acquired the license of the station. Because of this victory they were able to turn that station into the most successful news outlet on the air in that town for a long period. That was really where the whole notion of public interest was born and defined, establishing the principle that stations should cover the local news in order to serve the public interest and their community.

From criticism to confrontation, we then come to creativity. The commercial media are serving their own interests very well. They are not about to admit their failures and give us the editorial pages of the *Wall Street Journal*. They are serving their interests, and we must define ours. What are our resources? Who are we, other than an alternative to them? There is a lot of talk about "we" and "they," but "we" have yet to be defined. It seems to me that "we" are the folks who care about democracy. Not the every-fourth-year-at-the-polls part, but the people involved in the process of democracy.

We care about an Athenian model of politics, people talking with each other and public exchange. And here, with all due respect to Athenians, I think it's important to remember that the republic, at least as it's described by Plato, only represented land-owning men. No women and no slaves were allowed into those wonderful all-encompassing discussions about what the mutual interest was and who we are or should be. A democratic society requires a media that treats women and children as subjects, not objects. Democracy requires that we take ourselves seriously, and that means all of ourselves. If we are the people, then the majority of us on this planet are people of color.

It takes time to challenge so-called conventional wisdom, challenge a line that we are already familiar with. There was a very disturbing study done recently at UCLA about crime reporting. They played a tape to people, black and white, of a crime story in which no perpetrator was depicted. Then they asked the participants in the study, black and white, to describe the perpetrator. What was the race of the perpetrator? And, black and white, the participants identified the perpetrator as black, though they had actually seen no one. The story line was already running in their heads. They did not need to see any facts to confirm what they assumed to be the truth. It takes time to, as Nawal said, unveil our own minds.

At Pacifica Network News, when we cover the news we rely, at least in part, on the news wire services to get our news stories. We have the same AP and Reuters news wires coming in as do the other papers. The woman who writes headlines is trying to keep up with what is happening hour after hour. She does not have 24 hour programming from deep dish television or public access cable to bring her the information necessary to make headline decisions each day. So she listens to CNN and MSNBC and the local channels.

As a result, she and I are in constant disagreement about what is the breaking news that day. She feels we have to say something about Monica Lewinsky if we want to be taken seriously as a news show. And I say, if we want to be taken seriously, we should say something about that black family farm that was just foreclosed by their bank, despite a pending law suit charging discrimination by that very bank. Well, that is not in the headlines on CNN and MSNBC. Yet my headline writer thinks she's not doing her job if we cover the black farmer instead of Monica Lewinsky.

So I think that Nawal's comment about unveiling our own minds is very crucial. It takes courage to do what we are trying to do. We are engaged in a project that not only attempts to reclaim history, but also tries to retell our current reality. Retell the facts of our daily lives, which, at every moment, are being distorted. Archbishop Juan Gerardi in Guatemala, just a month ago was killed for releasing what he called his historical memory recovery project. This was an assessment of the human rights abuses that had taken place and who had committed them during the years of civil war in Guatemala. He was killed two days after releasing this project. He was killed for producing a project that was about recovering memory. This is more dangerous than our project, which is about recovering contemporary reality. This also takes a certain amount of courage, and it takes time to instill that kind of courage in the journalist standing alone and under attack.

In Washington, D.C. we see journalists competing to attend presidential news conferences. The first eight rows of the press conference seats are reserved for members of the mainstream media, so if you are from the alternative media you stand at the back. You can't be heard unless you shout, and if you shout you sound like a crazy person. If you shout while challenging a question you sound crazy because you are using a tone that isn't normal. Why isn't it normal? Because you're not sitting in the normal seats. You don't have normal access. They don't call on you, so you have to wave your hand like a maniac.

We need to instill courage in our colleagues, and to instill that courage we need to tell those stories that will serve as inspiration. For example, I think we need to be very realistic about the failure to have total revolutionary change in Indonesia. I was inspired listening and talking to the Indonesian students in the parliament building, hearing them say how they were not going to go home. Hearing their words of commitment to their vision of change. If we dismiss that vision because it was not realized with the appointment of B.J. Habibie in Indonesia, then we are missing a story that could feed our spirits, inspire us and move us forward.

When it comes to telling the stories that inspire us, I think we have to go to some nontraditional places. We need to tell the stories, for example, of the roll back in civil rights. We hear a lot about the fact that affirmative action in the U.S. is being repealed. In places like the University of California there has been an attack on affirmative action that re-authorizes segregation in education. Now this is a very important story, but we also need to look around the country and see that in nine out of ten places where anti-affirmative action proposals have been introduced, they have been defeated at the local level. To get that real story about the roll back as well as the resistance to reauthorizing segregation, we need to bring the protagonists in that story into the room, not for their sake but for ours. It's not just a question of showing tolerance, it's a question of getting the information that we all need as a people about what is happening on our planet, with all its inspiration, with all its fire, with all its fun.

Liberty, curiosity, doubt: The qualities that Ramsey Clark said that we needed to embrace and practice. I think he's right. We need to hold each of those close to our hearts. But we also need the courage to listen, to remain open, and to conduct that public exchange with the surprisingly untamed many who certainly have more to tell us than the privileged and predictable few. What they have to say and what we have to say can be unsettling to some. The orthodoxy that is challenged when we have a genuine debate or exchange with "we the people" can sometimes be our own.

I'll close with a reiteration of the fact that there is no wisdom too conventional to be wrong. For as long as I can remember, it has been the conventional wisdom that females outnumber males on earth, but before we went to press I checked, opening the United Nations 1995 report on the world's trends and statistics on women. It begins: "There are fewer women in the world than men." I heard a statistical thunder clap. Isn't that news? I asked one of the UN researchers if that was really true. "Well, yes actually," she replied excited, "but you are the first to call about that."

A week later the same researcher got back to me with answers to my other questions, and this time she sounded chagrined. "Women are a majority in the U.S.," she said, "but women haven't had the numerical upper hand world-wide since 1965." My shocker story was 31 years old and had yet to break. The only detailed discussion I could find of the documented decline of the world's women was a 1990 *New York Review of Books* article that estimated that although women now actually outlive men, the denial of food and health care to females had engineered a man-made shift in the planet's demography. The article was titled, "One Hundred Million Missing Women."

One hundred million of us were missing? And for more than three decades it hadn't made the news? That is serious sidelining. Stumbling across the silence I felt I had downed a dose of the same contempt that determines who gets born and who survives. Simone de Beauvoir said that an understanding of the genuine conditions of our lives is what gives rise to the strength to change things. But for my entire life I had been 100% wrong about the basic composition of the company I was in. The cost of sidelining women in this story was what it always is, the facts, but also the possibilities for astute action. Neglect claims peoples' lives.

THE ACHILLES HEEL OF MEDIA POWER: LOSS OF CREDIBILITY

SARA FLOUNDERS

This conference in Greece on the Media's Dark Age seems to be the right place to talk about the Achilles' heel of the corporate media. If we discuss only the media's power, we run the risk of demoralizing ourselves and losing perspective about what we can still accomplish.

It's true that today the media is more powerful, more concentrated, more controlled than ever before. But in a system where crisis is inevitable there is a dialectic to this powerful tool of corporate control. It is also more vulnerable.

We need to discuss this Achilles' heel of the major media. And how, even within the United States, small opposition forces and a small alternative media were able to turn the tables on the seemingly omnipotent mainstream forces of government, television and press.

I spend a great deal of my time and energy trying to focus attention on the very issues that the major media have chosen to ignore. I work organizing opposition to U.S. militarism and war. These are hardly minor issues. But a daily reality check shows that the public has no access to information and hears no real debate about life-and-death issues involving millions of lives.

The International Action Center publishes books and fact sheets, produces videos, maintains a web site, and utilizes the Internet, often sending or receiving thousands of email messages a day. We organize actions, protests, rallies and forums. All these are potential media events. But they are usually censored. Our focus is to challenge the role of U.S. bases, which are now in 100 countries. We seek to expose U.S. nuclear testing and development—now at an all time high. We oppose the expansion of NATO, the U.S. role in the break-up of Yugoslavia and the use of radioactive depleted uranium weapons. We are part of the international opposition to the growing use of sanctions, a brutal anti-personnel weapon of mass destruction. We challenge the policies of globalization that are creating poverty on an unprecedented scale.

Try to think back to how you felt when, as a new young activist, you first realized that something was terribly wrong with the society you live in. What was the first step in consciousness, beyond opposing war or racism or in taking part in a strike or a student action? So often the first breakthrough to a more radical view of society can be described by the phrase, "The media lies," "It is a cover-up" or "I've been duped." There is genuine outrage that the media lies. Outrage that there is so much information, but none of it tells about what is real.

Our role as alternative media activists is to explain, that, yes, the media lies, of course the media lies. When they lie, they are just doing their job. The corporate media isn't free. It isn't accessible to community voices. It isn't neutral. It is an expression of this class society.

Information empowers people. Those who control the media do so to keep us isolated and alienated. "The ruling ideas of each age are the ideas of its ruling class." This is a great observation from Karl Marx—someone the ruling class in the West tries to overlook these days.

Change Breaks Through

Every ruling class imposes on society as a whole the lies, deceits and biases that justify their existence. This has always been true. But historically this control of ideas and information has not been able to stop great change from breaking through.

It is hardly surprising that those who have great corporate fortunes to protect own more than just industries and banks. In order to protect those grand investments there is also a drive to control and own communication, information and culture.

Today the concentration of wealth has grown far beyond what it was in any prior stage in history. Monopolization and globalization, the concentration of ownership and control has taken place not only in banking, in auto, in airlines, in computers. The same process of mega-mergers is underway in information, communication, in entertainment and in mass culture. Wealth and control is in the hands of fewer and fewer.

Twenty-eight billionaires own more than the population of half of the world's countries. In the U.S. today four corporations control most of the daily newspapers, TV and radio stations, cable franchises and almost everything else that is perceived as information and news. These same corporations also shape our culture, values and our entertainment. They control the major magazine and book publishers, music industry and movie studies.

There are no longer hundreds of independent newspapers and locally owned radio stations. According to Ben Bagdikian, today 20 corporations around the world own almost all the major media. By the year 2001 there will be only six corporations that own all information, entertainment, and mass culture. There is no room for new competitors.

Like any concentrated mass exerting a pull of gravity, this concentrated control draws into itself all independent efforts. But what makes all of this more dangerous, more ominous? It is not only the tighter concentration of media into fewer and fewer hands. It also depends on whose hands.

Growing Militarism & the Media

In the U.S. today militarism fuels the economy. This is the center of an empire. There are U.S. military bases in 100 countries. The Pentagon absorbs a majority of the federal budget. The U.S. economy and its largest corporations are utterly dependent on military contracts. The total spent on the military budget is larger than what the rest of the world put together spends on its military. How can this enormous and ever growing expenditure be sold to the population in the U.S.?

General Electric and Westinghouse, the two largest military weapons manufacturers, own much of the U.S. media. GE owns the whole NBC network. Westinghouse owns CBS. It is no accident that these giant weapons contractors use the news media as the public relations arm for their primary product—war and the weapons of war.

Loss of Socialist Media

There has been another development in this decade. It is not only capitalist consolidation on a new unprecedented scale that has pushed out any alternative information. The last ten years have also seen the loss of alternative information and debate from a whole number of socialist countries. The Soviet Union had an infrastructure that on every social issue provided a different point of view. Even for those who didn't agree, there was a conscious, alternative source and distribution of information.

There were thousands of journals, magazines, movies and daily radio broadcasts produced in the Soviet Union and Eastern Europe in every academic and social field. There were hundreds of small publications of liberation struggles, unions and mass organizations throughout Africa, South America and Asia which were financed or printed in Eastern Europe or the Soviet Union. In the 1990s most of these publications and news services have disappeared.

There is a third ominous development that has curtailed news and information globally. The IMF and the World Bank policy now require as part of their approval for continued loans and credit that debtor nations privatize every nationalized or subsidized industry. This same pressure to end all subsidies and to pursue a policy of aggressive privatization is part of the GATT, the World Trade Organization and part of the consolidation in Europe. What this means is that along with being forced to privatize railroads and steel mills and airlines, what is up for sale in countries throughout Asia and Africa includes national press bureaus, TV and radio stations and subsidized film industries.

This is surely the first time that news, information and entertainment have been under such concentrated control on a global scale. At many times in history, however, and in many diverse societies, a few priests and local despots have totally controlled ideas and information. Anyone who spoke out risked charges of heresy or treason. But just because everyone genuflects doesn't mean that they believe—or that explosive opposition will not erupt from below.

Absolute Control Is Vulnerable

The more absolutely controlled and homogenized news and information become the more it lacks credibility—and the more vulnerable it is to the truth. A generation ago in the U.S. the average American accepted or believed what government officials said and what they heard on the news.

Now the distrust of the media goes even deeper than the alienation from government. Today the average person knows that the politicians lie. They lie about their personal lives and sexual affairs, of course. They lie about taxes and finances and they lie about the reasons for going to war. This distrust is reflected first in apathy and alienation. The U.S. today has the lowest voter turnout of any "industrialized democracy." There is not yet a crisis of sufficient proportion to cause millions of people to actively seek an alternative to the media's version of the truth.

However, the media as a mechanism of mass control, allegiance and loyalty seems to be losing its grip even as it becomes more absolutely concentrated.

One little deviation, one little crack and the ideological stranglehold begins to slip. There is consensus only as long as there is no debate.

Consider the response on issues of U.S. military action. Historically, war is one issue where every strata and class in society is aroused, apprehensive and has an opinion. The rulers in any society know they must find a way to whip up popular support. Wild claims of self-defense or demonizing an opponent are hardly new tactics in the annals of war. Great wars of conquest and plunder have always been masked by noble appeals.

Consider the wild swings of U.S. public opinion in the continuing war against Iraq. Just days before the January 1991 bombing began—this was after five months of war build up and propaganda—over 50% of the population was still against the war.

During the 40 days when more than 110,000 aerial sorties were flown against Iraq, under a 24-hour-a-day media barrage calling on the public to "support our troops," approval ratings of President Bush and the war reached 80%. This was the highest approval rating of any president since these polls began. The U.S. casualties seemed low, the expenses were hidden and the war was of short duration. But the support was shallow and short lived. Six months later this approval rating for President Bush had plummeted to 30%. A year later as an incumbent, Bush lost the election.

It takes greater hype and in heavier doses to achieve even temporary support. In the civil war in Bosnia even after five years of almost daily news reports of atrocity stories, more than 50% of the population opposed sending U.S./NATO troops to enforce the Dayton Accords.

Cracks in the Veneer

Or consider the fiasco the Clinton Administration faced in Columbus, Ohio in February 1998. There had been seven years of unrelenting propaganda in the major western media to justify seven years of continuing sanctions against Iraq and U.S. military occupation of the Persian/Arabian Gulf region—costing $50 billion a year. Charges that Iraq manufactured nuclear weapons, VX gas and germ weapons were a constant din. Clinton had announced to the world he fully intended to bomb Iraq for supposed non-compliance with inspection.

The aircraft carriers, the cruise missiles, the jet bombers had been moved into place. Madeleine Albright declared that the U.S. needed no one's approval, not the UN, not U.S. allies, not even the feudal oil regimes in the Gulf dependent on U.S. backing.

In the U.S. at the grass-roots level there were a number of organizations which for years had opposed the sanctions. These groups called the ongoing sanctions a war against Iraq, since this policy was responsible for the death of more than one-and-a-half million Iraqis from malnutrition and disease.

At the International Action Center we had built a website, produced books and videos, and gathered several thousand email addresses of people opposed to sanctions. There were small demonstrations. But it was slow going, with modest results. Still, there was an activist network in place.

To give the image of overwhelming support for a new strike on Iraq the Clinton administration organized a staged media event at Ohio State University, considered typical middle America. Secretary of State Madeleine Albright, Defense Secretary William Cohen and National Security Adviser Sandy Berger were set to present the administration's case. CNN would carry the event live to the whole world.

As some students protested, others asked probing questions that put the administration on the defensive and shattered the veneer of consensus. Millions had felt apprehension about a new bombing, and when they heard the protesters at Ohio State express it for the first time on national television, it aroused them to action. It woke them up like the little boy in the folk tale who proclaimed the obvious, "the Emperor has no clothes." A few minutes of opposition breaking through on TV was able to unravel seven years of war propaganda.

Within three days more than 25,000 people had logged onto our website. This number kept growing. Thousands and thousands. How did they find us? Suddenly people had a reason to look, to search out alternative information.

Along with several other organizations, we called for nationally coordinated demonstrations. Before this, our full mobilization could only raise local picket lines in 25 to 30 cities. But this time within a week there were demonstrations in more than 300 cities, towns, and universities. Thousands, then tens of thousands were in the street. Around the world, the mood was electrified. The administration's policy was in disarray.

The mood had so changed that it was the U.S. that was isolated. Once people are in motion the whole policy is called into question. We were in touch by e-mail with thousands of new student activists. We were able to provide instantaneously slogans, fact sheets and talking points.

Take Advantage of the Moment

For seven years the sanctions policy had never been criticized, questioned or even debated in the U.S. media. This was the collective punishment of an entire people, an unrelenting war that had taken a far greater toll in human lives than saturation bombing. Within weeks we were able to get out over a thousand copies of our video *Genocide by Sanctions.* Hundreds of Cable Access programs, universities and grassroots meetings were using it. There was opposition not only to a new bombing, but for the first time in years we had a response on the issue of the sanctions.

After the administration was forced to accept the agreement which UN General Secretary Kofi Annan had forged with Iraq, things didn't return to the way they were before. They never do.

The media censorship of debate on the sanctions policy had been broken. We initiated the Iraq Sanctions Challenge. This was an open defiance of a criminal U.S. law, an international act of civil disobedience and the response was incredible. Despite Washington's threats of 12 years in prison and one million dollars in fines, we were able to organize 100 people to travel to Iraq. The delegation included major religious groups, peace organizations trade unionists, doctors and students. In less than six weeks, tens of thousands of people sent donations, helped gather medicine and serve as a support network. $4 million dollars worth of medicine weighing more than 4 tons was publicly gathered.

This one experience is worth consideration by media activists. Those who succeed in putting forth an alternative view in times of crisis are those who have succeeded in creating their own voice. This requires a two-part strategy. It requires creating our own media forms that are credible and attractive. While this is always difficult, it is easier in today's electronic world. Small groups of talented people with almost no budget can produce educational videos or build websites.

And it requires fighting for access in the major media, struggling to break through. There are always real divisions, antagonisms, disputes among the powerful ruling forces that open up in any crisis. For a short window of time the media can seem less monolithic. This can only be taken advantage of by those media activists who are linked to the struggle, who have material prepared and who have no illusions that this is a free and open ended discussion.

The 100 activists who traveled to Baghdad saw the misery in the Iraqi hospitals. But instead of being overwhelmed by this horror, they took action to stop it. We discussed this strategy of networking and building our own voice using videos, websites, while organizing from every direction, pushing our local media and developing connections with local reporters. And most important, we discussed how to turn the cynicism growing out of the knowledge that the media lies into activism.

We won't accept the lies. We have a right to the truth and we have a right to make history. We had with us in Baghdad students who had embarrassed Madeleine Albright at Ohio State and students from Minneapolis who drove Assistant Secretary of State Richardson off the stage.

There was a time during the Vietnam war when U.S. officials couldn't go to any campus or to most major cities without facing confrontations and disruptions. Thousands of activists need to think about how to plan confrontations, disruptions, and challenges. Be audacious. We need to change the terms of debate.

Of course this administration and the major corporate media are not likely to make again the same mistake that they made at the orchestrated meeting in Columbus, Ohio. But they will make other big miscalculations. Because their seeming control leads them to overestimate the depth of their influence. Those most deceived by the media are the very people immersed in it.

We are told this is a time of apathy. It is true that there is great alienation Yet we find people starving for information and hungry to hear of opposition. A last example of the potential of alternative media is the grassroots movement mobilized to save the life of Mumia Abu Jamal, an African-American political prisoner on death row in Pennsylvania. When an execution date was suddenly announced in 1995, it seemed unstoppable. Activists put a video explaining this case on satellite and sent hundreds of copies to public-access cable stations. Tens of thousands of people responded. They made a special website. Their material became an organizing tool. In six weeks time the escalating demonstrations, rallies and protests won at least a postponement pending court appeals.

Journalists, videographers and media activists who are linked to movements for social change can have an enormous impact in the crises that are built into the fabric of this society.

Today the seeming omnipotence of the corporate media gives the veneer or the illusion that a historic process has been arrested. That it can be controlled and channeled. There is a drive to be free—a continuing struggle of the nationally oppressed and colonized people to be independent and sovereign. Even absolute control of the media cannot alter the historic relation of forces. Past efforts at all-encompassing state religions, inquisitions and dictatorships have shown this again and again. The structure of lies can crumble overnight The more monolithic the control, the more fragile. The new ideas that represent reality break through and take hold.

An explosive movement for change will grow because this is an economic system based on ruthless competition and unending war. Capitalism has no solutions to the horrendous social problems of hunger and unemployment of millions. Activist alternative media can be a powerful force if they see themselves as part of the historic struggle.

Socialist Breakup in Eastern Europe Devastates Workers

UN reports grim facts NY Times ignores

Brian Becker

It looked like an expensive paid advertisement. One of those $15,000 per quarter page announcements located prominently on the top of page 8 of the *New York Times* of Aug. 2, 1999: "Yugoslav Opposition Plans Big Rally in Capital Aug. 19." It wasn't an advertisement, well it wasn't a paid advertisement. It was a "news story," written by Steven Erlanger for a newspaper that has openly called for the overthrow of the elected government of Yugoslavia.

Not only was the "Aug. 19 opposition rally" to President Milosevic advertised by the leading capitalist-owned newspapers in the United States. We learn from Erlanger that the rally was organized and inspired from the United States, principally by the Clinton Administration no doubt using the Central Intelligence Agency.

"Opposition figures had been saying there would be no rally here until at least September, when students return and it is easier to turn out big numbers. But Washington has been pressing the fractious opposition to unite and not to lose momentum," Erlanger reports, apparently unembarrassed by "his governments'" gross and illegal efforts to overthrow a sovereign government.

Devastation of the working class

While the *New York Times* reported daily in July and August 1999[1] of every manifestation of opposition to Milosevic in Yugoslavia, the newspaper did no serious coverage of a major UN report detailing the devastating impact on working people in the countries that used to make up the Soviet Union and in the other Eastern European countries in the period following the overthrow of their socialist governments.

By all objective standards this is an important story that would be immediately relevant to the 11 million people in Yugoslavia.

The United Nations Development Program's *1999 Annual Report on Human Development*[2] reveals a shocking growth of poverty and gross inequality in these countries.

This report provides hard evidence that living conditions are plummeting for working people as capitalism is established. Except during wartime, it is hard to find a comparable social catastrophe in this century.

The report's findings should give pause to all those who are being glibly swept up in the U.S.-inspired campaign to carry out a counter-revolutionary overthrow of the elected government of Slobodan Milosevic in Yugoslavia.

Much more is at stake than the fate of one leader, or even of the Serbian Socialist Party and the Party of the United Left.

The consequences of capitalist counter-revolution are unambiguous. In Russia between 1989 and 1996, the report says, wages fell 48 percent.[3] Income derived from rent, meaning landlords' profits, jumped to 23 percent.[4]

During the days of the Soviet Union, rent was restricted to no more than 5 percent of a worker's wage. The money went into social funds administered by the state. There was no such thing as landlords.

The report goes on: "There are [other] serious human deprivations. Between 1989 and 1996 male life expectancy [in Russia] declined by more than four years, to 60."[5]

Throughout Eastern Europe and the Soviet Union "the transition from centrally planned to market economies was accompanied by large changes in the distribution of national wealth and income. Data on income inequality indicate that these changes were the fastest ever recorded."[6]

What counter-revolution means for women

The streets in the Soviet Union were considered very safe. The crime rate was very low.

The report documents how homicides, illegal drug trafficking, prostitution and organized crime have come to dominate the new capitalist Russia and the other Eastern European countries.[7]

Women are being killed in Russia in record numbers. A report published in 1997 revealed that the murder rate of women had risen sevenfold between 1990 and 1997.

Sexual slavery has returned with a vengeance. "An estimated 500,000 women are trafficked each year from Eastern Europe and the CIS [former republics of the Soviet Union] to Western Europe. An estimated 15,000 Russians and East Europeans work in Germany's red light districts. In the Netherlands 57 percent of the trafficked women are under 21," according to the new UN report.[8]

Absence of Soviet Union worsens conditions worldwide

The UN report documents that growing inequality, class polarization and poverty are rampant around the globe. Before the counter-revolutionary overthrow of the socialist governments from 1989 to 1991, the countries associated with the USSR and the socialist bloc in Eastern Europe were largely protected from the ravages of world capitalism. State-owned or publicly-owned property, central planning and a state monopoly on foreign trade prevented Western corporations from plundering their land, resources and labor.

So-called globalization, or the unhindered movement of private capital, took on momentum after the collapse of the socialist governments. This was also devastating for the so-called Third World countries. No longer enjoying a trade alternative to the world capitalist economy, many developing countries have been forced to accept the dictates of the International Monetary Fund's Structural Adjustment Programs.

This meant privatizing industry, usually to be bought up by foreign corporations. It also meant slashing social programs for the people and reducing wages.

New wealth does not even alleviate poverty

"The world's 200 richest people more than doubled their net worth in the four years [up] to 1998, to more than $1 trillion," the report states.[9]

"The assets of the top three billionaires are more than the combined Gross National Product (GNP) of all the least developed countries and their 600 million people." [10]

This is not a momentary trend of world capitalism. The flow of wealth from the people of the world to a handful of imperialist countries is rapidly increasing as a result of globalization.

"The income gap between the fifth of the world's people living in the richest countries and the fifth in the poorest was 74 to one in 1997," the report states.[11]

It was 30 to one in 1960.[12]

Of course, the statistics about the "richest countries" don't really tell the whole story. In these countries a small handful of the population controls and benefits from the lion's share of the wealth. In the United States, for instance, just 1 percent of the population owns 40 percent of the wealth; the top 10 percent controls 80 percent of the wealth.

Capitalism has rapidly developed industrial and technological capability. It creates new wealth. One might think such a capability would alleviate or end poverty and hunger.

But because this staggering wealth belongs to the capitalists rather than society, the opposite is true.

"About 840 million people are malnourished. . . nearly 1.3 billion live on less than a dollar a day, and close to 1 billion cannot meet their basic consumption requirements," the report states.[13] "Nearly 160 million children are malnourished and more than 250 million children are working as child laborers." [14]

A social catastrophe

During its existence the Soviet Union's economy grew consistently. In spite of Western trade embargoes and sanctions and the devastation and the loss of 20 million people in World War II, the USSR grew to be the second- or third-biggest economy in the world.

With the exception of 1941 to 1944—the years of the Nazi invasion—the Soviet Union never experienced a period of economic recession, or negative growth, between 1921 and 1985. Recessions and depressions, which are fundamental to capitalist society, were avoided altogether.

Since 1989, just before the counter-revolution, production in Russia has fallen 43 percent. [15] According to World Bank estimates, if the current trend continues, Russia will slip to 13th in total production by 2010—behind Brazil, Taiwan, Indonesia and Italy.

Unemployment, unheard of until 1990, now includes at least one out of every 10 workers. The real average income of working-class families has dropped to about one-quarter of what it was in 1990. [16]

The International Labor Organization, a United Nations agency, describes what it calls the "appalling growth" of the number of people living in poverty in the USSR and the former socialist camp. The ILO reports that 100 million people in Russia live below the official poverty line.

These shocking statistics are replicated in other former socialist countries in Eastern Europe. In Bulgaria, 73 percent of the people now live in poverty. The rate is 50 percent in Poland. [17]

Meaning for Yugoslavia

In Yugoslavia eight years of war and economic sanctions imposed by the United States and the major European countries have already brought significant damage to the workers' living standards. [18]

Considerable damage was also inflicted in 1990 when Yugoslav Prime Minister Ante Markovic launched a program of privatizing or shutting down state-owned industry, cutting back on social programs and freezing wages. The United States backed Markovic in his effort to fully restore capitalism.[19]

Between January and October 1990, Markovic's "market reform" led to a sharp decline in workers' living standards. Within nine months it dropped by 18 percent, while industrial production fell by 10.4 percent and the prices for consumer goods doubled.[20]

But U.S. plans for a cold counter-revolution in Yugoslavia were suddenly stymied when the "reforms" were halted in October 1990. Even more unhappily for the United States, Markovic was ousted.[21]

The current Yugoslav government led by Slobodan Milosevic was widely criticized in the U.S. media in 1996 for reversing the path toward privatization in the economy. As the *Washington Post* wrote in its Aug. 4, 1996, edition: "Milosevic failed to understand the political message of the fall of the Berlin Wall. . . . [W]hile the other Communist politicians [in Eastern Europe] accepted the Western model . . . Milosevic went the other way."

How is it that Milosevic could change course and reverse the trend to full-scale capitalist restoration? It is because the Yugoslav state apparatus, which was created in the cauldron of a profound socialist revolution during World War II, is not under the domination of a Yugoslav capitalist class.

Milosevic, and Tito before him, made many harmful compromises with imperialism. They promoted economic decentralization as against centralized planning. This spurred the growth of an acquisitive bourgeois class among the various nationalities and republics in the old Yugoslavia. But the class character of the state apparatus has not been fundamentally altered. It has not fallen under the domination of the Yugoslav bourgeoisie.

The Clinton administration's efforts to destabilize and overthrow the Milosevic government are not intended simply to remove one leader and replace him with another. More is at stake.

The imperialist governments want to change the class structure in Yugoslavia to guarantee the full-scale restoration of capitalism. The dire consequences of such a counter-revolution are evidenced by the now evident catastrophe that has befallen the working class in Russia and throughout the region.

Milosevic is the elected leader of Yugoslavia. He still retains a solid base of support among many workers who may not agree with all his policies but fear a takeover of the country by out-and-out capitalist forces of reaction.

The United States has often demanded "elections" in other countries so that CIA-supported candidates could stand a chance. But this is not the case in Yugoslavia today.

"Let's forget about elections. I'm in favor of putschist methods. He's got to go without elections," said Vesna Pesic, a leader of the anti-Milosevic opposition.[22]

Pesic has close ties to U.S. imperialism. She was granted the National Endowment for Democracy biannual prize in 1993, according to their webpage. NED is funded by the U.S. Congress. Along with Zoran Djindjic and Zuk Draskovic, other top "opposition leaders" in Yugoslavia, she was received by Secretary of State Madeleine Albright in her office in April of 1997. (German Press Agency, April 6, 1997). She was even a fellow of the United States Institute for Peace in 1996-97, according to their webpage. The USIP is another congressionally funded institution, headed by Chester Crocker, undersecretary of state for Africa during Reagan's presidency.

The *New York Times* reflects the current U.S. government position that, in this case, it is better to use methods combining CIA covert operations and civil war to oust an elected government.

This might come as a shock to those who take seriously the *Times* editorial positions, written in such pious prose, about the need for a "transition to democracy." Its long-standing advocacy of anti-democratic CIA subversion tactics against governments that resist U.S. imperialism is more familiar to those who have followed the paper over the decades. The *Times*, like the other U.S. mass media, has learned better to disguise its real, that is, its pro-imperialist position over the years.

When the CIA overthrew the elected government of Dr. Mohammed Mossadegh in Iran 46 years ago for the crime of having nationalized western oil companies in his country, the *New York Times* revealed its true orientation. Thousands were killed in the 1953 CIA coup, very similar to the one they are trying to organize now in Yugoslavia. The reaction of the *Times* to the CIA-induced bloodbath: "Underdeveloped countries with rich resources now have an object lesson in the heavy cost that must be paid when one of their number goes berserk with fanatical nationalism." [23]

---

1. The July 9 *New York Times* carried a large photo of an anti-Milosevic demonstration in the city of Prokuplje, Serbia. A picture of an even smaller demonstration from the city of Valjevo filled up an entire half-page of the July 12 *New York Times*.

2. *United Nations Human Development Report 1999*, published by Oxford University Press.

3. Ibid., p.85.

4. Ibid., p.85.

5. Ibid., p.88.

6. Ibid., p.39.

7. Ibid., p.89.

8. Ibid., p.89.

9. Ibid., p.3.

10. Ibid., p.3.

11. Ibid., p.3.

12. Ibid., p.3.

13. Ibid., p.22.

14. Ibid., p.22.

15. Wall Street Journal, January 28, 1998.

16. Vladimir Bilenkin, "Russian Workers Under the Yeltsin Regime: Notes on a Class Defeat," *Monthly Review*, November 1996.

17. Ibid.

18. Richard Becker, "The Role of Sanctions in the Destruction of Yugoslavia," *NATO in the Balkans*, p. 107., published by the International Action Center

19. Ibid., p. 111.

20. Facts on File, December 31, 1990

21. Richard Becker, op. cit., p.111.

22. *New York Times*, July 19, 1999.

23. *New York Times*, August 6, 1954 cited by William Blum in *Killing Hope: U.S. Military and CIA Interventions Since World War II*, published by Common Courage Press.

FOR LIGHT IN THE DARKNESS

DANNY SCHECHTER

When I left the United States to attend this conference in Greece on the media's dark age, I thought I would be trading that darkness for the sunlight of Athens, the cradle of democracy.

But, no, the darkness followed me onto the plane. Sitting behind me was a young woman who works for a well-known public relations firm in Washington. She had come to frolic on the islands, I to trade analytical insights with fellow media critics and practitioners.

I told her about my book, *The More You Watch, The Less You Know* and its assault on the trivialization, that is, dumbing down the news.

She laughed. "My job," she told me, "is to keep it that way."

And so the gauntlet was thrown down once again, this time at thirty thousand feet. I doubt if my flight mate knew that PR flacks in America now outnumber journalists by a factor of two. But then again, that news wouldn't trouble her because, as she told me, she believes that her firm and the TV networks they service are only "giving the people what they want."

That is the mantra of the media industry, a belief that has taken on the weight of a religious conviction, a reflection of the faith that the marketplace and its guardians invoke at the slightest suggestion that there may be a public interest that should take precedence over the private interest.

We are living at the end of the first Media Century, an era in which the press, radio and television, and now computers, literally revolutionized our lives. In developed countries at least, but also in every capital of the world, few can imagine life without access to telephones, radio, television, beepers and cell phones, and for a growing number of the cyber savvy, the Internet and computer-based interactivity. The effect of these new media is total on social relations, on political culture and discourse, but also on entertainment and economics. Many of their implications are troubling for the intellectual, socio-cultural and economic life of our country and others, most profoundly for the future of democracy. The determinative role of modern commercial media is rarely examined by the media themselves, which have no interest in having attention focused on their own role.

Usually, media issues are downplayed in the business or feature pages of the newspaper. Yet they belong on page one, because this is the war story of our times.

The media war is an undeclared war, one that is chronicled in gossip columns but rarely examined in depth. Yes, the war's battles are often reported in a manner of speaking. If you want to find out which suit is now in charge or who has bought what, you can. But more often than not, this saga is covered only as a chronicle of business decisions, with the cultural and political implications rarely spelled out or followed up.

"This is a war on several fronts," acknowledges England's *Guardian*, "in which timidity won't be the winner. The world's telephone, wireless, and cable companies are battling it out to become the dominant conveyors of information, while media giants such as Disney, Viacom, Microsoft, and Rupert Murdoch's empire are restructuring to become the dominant suppliers of entertainment and software." In our country, ten years ago media critic Ben Bagdikian wrote his classic, *The Media Monopoly*, exposing the fifty companies that then dominated the media marketplace. Today, in his updated edition, he speaks of five to seven by the end of this century. Those companies are global entities with tentacles on every continent.

To compete effectively, these companies have opted to become colossal conglomerates through mergers and acquisitions, aided and abetted by government policies. These companies have become cartels, interconnected through a web of deals and strategic alliances, operating globally with little regulation or social responsibility.

Truth is as much a casualty in this media war as in any other. Intentional or not, one effect of what is called the information age is the continuing under-informing of the larger public, while an elite sector is inundated with more news and information than it can possibly absorb. In America, this has led to five business channels but no labor channels—Bloomberg for the elite classes, Jerry Springer and local news for the masses.

Don't laugh—all too often what starts as a trend in the United States spreads globally, especially as American companies take over TV channels or gain access to viewers through satellites and other delivery systems. In an era of globalization, consumerism is marketed far more successfully than citizenship. Television is now sellovision in world terms—-an instrument of a one trillion dollar marketing economy. Is it any wonder that the marketing view of the world marches in lock step with the images of glitzy lifestyles. All of this, of course, also propels the spread of conservative ideologies that are disseminated with all of the manipulative techniques of advertising and media control. In this world, image overpowers information and perception has come to be more than reality.

And it is not just the media corporations that have merged; there has been a merging of business and journalistic values as well, such that the different companies have become practically indistinguishable from one another. As the companies grow, often by taking on vast loads of debt, the inevitable downsizing and scaling back of news divisions has contributed to this sameness.

This media war is being fought not with guns but with marketing strategies and corporate logos that value entertainment more than information, diversion more than democracy. No wonder that Larry Gelbart, the screenwriter who created M*A*S*H, reached for a military metaphor as the title of his 1997 TV drama skewering media moguls, calling it *Weapons of Mass Distraction*. Those weapons, he told Howard Rosenberg of the *LA Times*, "take our eye off the ball. We are more concerned with who is sleeping with whom, and who is having a baby. The real problems in America and in the world go unnoticed while the prurient side of us is appealed to."

Media executives speak in the language of war, of bombarding audiences, targeting markets, capturing grosses, killing the competition, and winning, by which they mean making more money than the other guy. Some news organizations even refer to their employees as the troops. This high-tech war deploys technologies whose goal, in part, is to expand, domestically and globally, an entertainment-information economy now valued, in the United States alone, at $150 billion a year. Already, well over 50 percent of the revenues for America's cultural industries are raised overseas. As the companies duel, countries and communities often find themselves in the crossfire.

Consider this reality flowing from the merger between show biz and news biz. According to a recent survey, feature stories covering celebrities, scandal and human interest have increased from 15% to 43% of the total coverage provided by the three nightly network TV newscasts, major newspapers, front pages and weekly news magazines from 1977 to 1997. *Variety* reports that the network news magazines like ABC's *20-20*—the show I used to work for—and NBC's *Dateline* say that "celebrity stuff got them better ratings than the more newsy stuff they were airing." Remember this phrase—"More newsy stuff"—because it is indicative of how journalism itself is regarded in a time in which some scholars already pronounce the coming of the post-journalism era. This is the stuff of commodities, not consciousness.

Fast forward into the present—literally, the last few weeks before this conference convened. What's happening in the media war?

■ In New York, the Canadian liquor mogul Edgar Bronfman Jr. of Seagram, owners of Universal Studios, the Home Shopping Network, and the USA Networks, shelled out $10.6 billion dollars to buy the music giant Polygram from the

Dutch-based Phillips conglomerate. This acquisition means that there are now only seven record companies with significant international distribution. The new company will control the largest market share.

■ In the UK, Steven Spielberg's Dream Works and Disney's Miramax swallowed up more British film companies, including Channel Four Films, a leading independent. The British regulatory agency meanwhile blasted Channel Four itself—which was set up to offer an alternative to the BBC and commercial broadcasters—for not being innovative enough. . . .And, alas, the people who publish the *Daily Mirror* say they may have to shut down their cable channel—LIVE TV. Live TV is home to the news bunny and the bikini clad weather girl.

■ In the world of TV, in the United States, after one of the biggest hypes in the history of the media, 70 million Americans tuned in to watch the final episode of Seinfeld, a program widely considered the "show about nothing." A perfect metaphor for the media landscape, wouldn't you say? On the day the program aired, I was invited to discuss it on Rupert Murdoch's Fox News Channel on a segment called *In-depth.* There were three guests and a host all scrambling for air time in the five minutes allotted for this "in-depth" debate. Meanwhile, Murdoch's Fox Studio has become a major supplier of prime time network programming while his Fox network beat ABC in the key 18-49 demos. What that means is that they have become more of a force with the viewers most prized by advertisers.

Meanwhile, William Simon, the conservative Reagan Administration Treasury Secretary, has become the president of Paxon Communications, which now owns more TV stations than any other company. CBS, now under the control of the man who made shock jock Howard Stern a household word, revealed that its fall schedule will be stacked only with programs the company owns.

■ The *Wall Street Journal* announced that the advertising industry is about to start its own merger wave with more concentration expected in that crucial media sector.

■ On the journalism front, in England, critics discovered that a Carleton TV documentary on Colombian drug dealing that had been aired in part on *60 Minutes* in the U.S.A. had been faked. . .Totally made up with interviewees paid to tell tall tales. A journalist, Nate Thayer, turned down the prestigious Peabody prize for his scoop on the trial of Pol Pot in the jungle of Cambodia. He sold his pictures and story to ABC's Ted Koppel of *Nightline* fame, and claims that Koppel stole his material, did not give him credit or pay him, disseminated it world-wide so he couldn't sell it, and reedited it without his permission. "I have just become incredibly disillusioned in the last year," he told the *New Yorker*. "My main objection is that the industry has taken control of journalists, and part of our job is to fight for the integrity of our profession." Koppel said he was pained by the charges, while ABC said the journalist didn't seem to understand how TV companies worked. "It might be that he had no idea that this is what happens when you deal with a large news organization," said ABC. Meanwhile, CBS's Dan Rather went on CNN's Larry King Show—not his own network—and admitted journalists today have gone from being watchdogs to lapdogs.

In media coverage of world affairs, the mainstream has become a mudstream. Suharto of Indonesia fell without any serious analysis of the role of the IMF. After Secretary of State Madeleine Albright appealed to Suharto to step down to "preserve his legacy," few news organizations pointed out that that "legacy" included responsibility for the murder of 500,000 Indonesians and 200,000 East Timorese, a slaughter that has yet to be reported on widely.

And so it goes—the beat of a media system that sees news as "stuff" and prefers infotainment to information: The question is—what can we do about it?

And that question leads to others.

How can we help launch a campaign for real news, for media and democracy? How can we fight for more coverage of issues that matter—abuses in Algeria, oppression in Cyprus, torture in Turkey, human rights violations against women worldwide? How can we promote more racial and ethnic diversity, more visibility for women's issues and a broader spectrum of debate. How do we get the media to promote peace and tolerance instead of war and racial stereotyping? How do we challenge state propaganda posing as news and commercial interests using the news? How can we get the public to become as indignant towards the media companies as they are at the tobacco companies—at least in the U.S.A.? How do we foster and sustain our own media companies and alternative channels to compete against the junk media? How does this issue get on the agenda when the media themselves are unwilling, for obvious reasons, to give it the coverage it deserves? How do we learn to talk to ordinary people about media reform without seeming to be strident conspiracy nuts who are against popular culture and fun?

I can go on with my questions. My book offers some concrete proposals and suggestions based on my thirty years as a journalist in print, radio, at CNN and ABC News and today at Globalvision, an independent company known for its human rights television programming.

Our collective challenge is to find a way to link movements and NGOs, journalists and editors, unions and activists across borders and boundaries to build a movement to make the media a tool of democracy—not a threat to it.

PART THREE

MEDIA

AND

WAR IN THE BALKANS

NATO: THE STORY THE MEDIA WON'T TELL

MICHEL COLLON

During the Cold War, the media gave us an apocalyptic image of the "Soviet peril," systematically inflating the Soviet military threat (as recent studies have shown) in order to justify enormous military spending in the United States. Similar exaggeration was employed in the coverage of Iraq before and after the Gulf War. Now we see the logical extension of such press hyperbole: The entire Third World represents a threat to the West.

By 1990, the North Atlantic Treaty Organization (NATO) found itself without a mission, its awesome military might unemployed. This should have come as no surprise to the public, since they had always been told that NATO was a strictly defensive alliance, limited to protecting Western Europe from "the Soviet threat" represented by the Warsaw Pact. Of course, we were not told that NATO had been created five years *before* the Warsaw Pact, the latter alliance having been formed in response to the dramatic admission of Germany into NATO. Today, five years after the dissolution of the Warsaw Pact, NATO is more active than ever.

In the post-Cold War world, NATO has emerged from its defined "area." In September 1993, three analysts close to the U.S. Department of Defense wrote, "NATO must go out of the area or it will go out of business." [1] Subsequent events in the Balkans proved opportune for NATO. Was this mere chance?

Western officials and media representatives have justified NATO intervention in Bosnia as the only way to "save the various ethnic groups living there." Was this really NATO's objective, and was intervention prompted by a genuine emer-

116

gency? Or had NATO been preparing for this military action, and numerous others in Eastern Europe and elsewhere, for some time? Are Washington, Bonn and Paris as unified on the issue of NATO intervention as their press releases indicate? These are important questions to analyze since, according to the Secretary General of NATO, Javier Solana, the intervention in Bosnia served as "a model for future operations. The Bosnian experience has had a profound influence on the role of security in Europe and in particular on the role of NATO." [2]

For the first time in its forty-seven-year history, NATO has been able to deploy ground forces outside of its "area" and even use those military forces in an aggressive way. This is why Solana regarded the Bosnian intervention as the consummation of a project that had been in preparation for years.

As dramatic as NATO's use of offensive military action has been, its involvement in the civil governance of the region has been even more unusual. As Solana himself said in March 1996, "Even if the role of IFOR [NATO troops sent to Bosnia] is focused on military tasks, we can guarantee close coordination with various civilian organizations." [3] This position was confirmed three months later by a statement issued during a meeting of the Conseil de l'Atlantique in Berlin recognizing that IFOR brings enhanced support to the deployment of some civilian aspects of the Dayton Accords.

Would NATO's oversight of "civilian aspects" of the Accords consist of peacekeeping or colonization? The German Minister of Foreign Affairs soon laid claim to the coordination and execution of military and civilian matters, but one must keep in mind that the "reconstruction funds" for the area would come from German bankers. No one can believe that they were acting philanthropically. In reality, Bosnia was to become a NATO protectorate, a neo-colony.

Carl Bildt, the European mediator who administered Bosnia under the Dayton Peace Accords, was given control over the existing civil government there. He collaborated directly with NATO command and had complete control over "reconstruction funding." The central bank of Bosnia is controlled by the

IMF, whereas BERD (The European Bank for the Reconstruction of Eastern Europe) has taken control of enterprises such as the post office, water, energy, and public transportation. Fifteen hundred foreign policemen are under the command of an Irish official. Thus, all of the conditions are in place for the control and systematic exploitation by foreign multinationals. We have a "protectorate," just like the one the great powers created in the Balkans at the beginning of the century.

All this leads one to pose the question: Is NATO intervening to keep the peace or to protect capitalism?

In Rome in November 1991, European heads of State and their governments assembled solemnly. The order of the day: what is going to become of NATO now that its enemy has disappeared? Who is the enemy of this Alliance or has it actually disappeared? After two days of deliberations, prepared far in advance, the Declaration of Rome was issued defining three main axes for future NATO military interventions. NATO would not only survive in the post-Cold War, but would be more active than ever.

NATO would no longer play a defensive role, but would assert itself eastward. The Rome Declaration said "Risks to Allied security are less likely to result from calculated aggression against the territory of the Allies, but rather from the adverse consequences of instabilities that may arise from the serious economic, social and political difficulties, including ethnic rivalries and territorial disputes, which are faced by many countries in central and eastern Europe." [4]

In fact, after having liquidated its old enemy, the USSR, NATO redefined itself with three new tasks. According to this strategy, the situation associated with several strategic regions would be more complex from now on, as would the risks involved. The regions would be 1) Eastern Europe and Russia; 2) southern Europe; 3) the Third World in general.

The Declaration of Rome evoked the "necessity" of intervening in Eastern Europe as soon as the socialist regimes had collapsed. But the instability of Eastern Europe stems precisely from the restoration of capitalism and the unbearable inequalities which it produces. In order to decipher NATO's official jargon it is important to understand that "stability" is a code that signifies "uncontested capitalism." "Instability," on the contrary, signifies a situation where Western multi-nationals are not allowed to act with impunity.

The opening paragraph in the Declaration celebrates the fact that the Warsaw Pact, NATO's former adversaries, "have, in varying degrees, embraced and begun to implement policies aimed at achieving pluralistic democracy, the rule of law, respect for human rights and a market economy."[5]

Thus, the essential task is to protect capitalism from possible popular revolts. Yes, NATO really is the armed gunman of multinational corporations.

Also during 1991, Secretary General Manfred Worner explained NATO's "mission" with respect to the countries of Eastern Europe: "Their security is of singular importance to us. The consequences of each attempt to annihilate the positive advances achieved over the last three years in democracy and freedom cannot be made clearer in the future than they are now."[6]

"Democracy?" "Liberty?" It is difficult to believe that these are really the goals of NATO, which has supported and still supports a number of fascist powers, Greek colonels of yesteryear, and today's Turkish generals. What is it about, then? It is to prevent any delay in the re-establishment of capitalism. This is a task that retains all of its currency today. In May 1996, the *NATO Review* wrote, "The European community and NATO are involved in firmly anchoring the countries of Eastern Europe. . .in order to consolidate the gains of the Cold War."[7] The reference to Cold War victory confirms that it is a question of assuring the victory of capitalism over socialism, now and forever.

The Declaration of Rome defined a second strategic area for NATO control: "The countries that lie in the southern Mediterranean and the Middle East; stability and peace in this peripheral area of Europe are important for the security of the Alliance, as the Gulf War has shown."

Today, NATO analysts describe "the Mediterranean basin, from Gibraltar to the Black Sea, [as] an area of crises with as many potential conflicts as open ones. The United States and its European Allies can indeed see themselves adding instability in North Africa to the conflict in the ex-Yugoslavia and the Balkans. Algeria—or Egypt—could be the next candidate for a crisis necessitating a coordinated Western response."[8]

The French periodical *Defense Nationale* also insists on this rationale for intervention: "A number of European countries—France among them—consider the Mediterranean to be the principal area of instability in the years to come. The collapse of the Soviet Union and its satellites, the Gulf War, the pressure of Islamist movements in Egypt and the situation in Algeria, the energy dependence of the European nations are all elements which justify this evaluation."[9]

The Declaration of Rome indicates a third axis of eventual military intervention: "The security interests of the Alliance could be tested by the proliferation of weapons of mass destruction." The Alliance went even farther three years later in Istanbul: "NATO ought to rely on using the necessary military means in order to counter the proliferation and usage of weapons of mass destruction."

Shocking! The master of NATO, namely the United States, is the only country that ever used the atomic bomb, and that for the sole purpose of intimidating the Soviet Union, as was demonstrated in the book *d'Hiroshima à Sarajevo*.[10] Even today, the United States claims the right of "first use" of atomic weapons and has arrogated the right to ceaselessly develop and perfect its own weapons of mass destruction. And to crown it off, they pretend to decide who in the world may possess such arms. Because the Alliance perceives "threats" of weapons proliferation throughout virtually the entire world, this gives NATO the right to intervene anywhere. Let us recall, according to its strategy analysts, that the organization must "go out of its area or go out of business." In fact, it more and more openly claims an unlimited area of action.

The small Belgian community, Kleine Brogel, has been sheltering bombs warehoused there by NATO for years. In 1997, NATO announced their replacement by an "improved" weapon, the B61-11 nuclear bomb. It's a tactical weapon, which has air explosive force twenty-five times greater than the bomb which destroyed Hiroshima. The B61-11 bomb was designed to be used in the Third World in an "offensive and preventive" manner, that is to say, before an enemy attack. In fact, this high-tech weapon permits the great powers of the North to attack wherever they wish to impose their law.

Where can NATO intervene militarily? In the beginning, NATO affirmed that it would intervene only to defend the territories of its member states. But since 1990, the United States and Germany have openly proclaimed that these limits were unduly restrictive. Also, in 1992, NATO Secretary General Manfred Worner declared that any discussion about "in the area or outside of the area" was pointless. NATO has the right to intervene, he claimed, if the security of the Alliance or one of its members is threatened. That's a foggy notion. The same year the organization proclaimed itself to be "the armed gunman" of the United Nations as well as the OSCE (Organization for Security and Cooperation in Europe).

Bosnia was going to permit them to leap to a new stage of development. The new Secretary General, the Belgian socialist Willy Claes, first presented NATO as a tool to help the UN secure peace. But Claes's true goal—and that of his patrons in Washington and Bonn—was to use the crisis in Bosnia to reverse the roles of the two organizations: it was no longer NATO which was under the control of the UN, but the reverse. This served to demonstrate that the UN was "powerless" and that only NATO could be effective. Then, after drawing up the final balance sheet for war, Claes claimed the freedom to initiate independent action based on the unhappy NATO experience with the UN mandate in ex-Yugoslavia. Claes claimed that there were circumstances under which NATO ought to decide upon entering into an action on its own authority, even in the absence of a UN mandate.

What does all this mean? That the UN serves as a cover for actions of the great powers whenever possible. And if the UN cannot serve as cover, NATO will ignore it.

Since 1991, NATO has been announcing its desire to establish arrangements with the countries of Eastern Europe under which they would work in concert for the solution of concrete problems of politics and security. Five years later, the secretary-general of NATO joyfully anticipated seeing "our partners in Eastern Europe placed under the command of NATO." [11] They moved from working in concert with these countries to placing them under its guardianship.

But why is it important to enlarge NATO? What are NATO chiefs preparing? Manfred Worner has been confirming since 1994 that an intervention is possible in Eastern Europe "if those countries have to face a direct menace to their territorial integrity, their political independence, or their security." [12] This concept of "security" is sufficiently vague to allow broad interpretation.

In reality, the new NATO strategy does not concern the defense of the countries of Eastern Europe, but an effort to weaken Russia and prepare for an eventual attack against it. Washington and Bonn want the ex-USSR to remain divided and weakened. And it is to guarantee this dismemberment that NATO has launched the "Partnership," which may permit expansion as far as the Ukraine. But NATO is very careful about keeping Russia outside of this enlarged Alliance.

Signed in Brussels in January of 1994, the "Partnership for Peace" prepared the expansion of NATO into the countries of Eastern Europe. These countries committed themselves to realize "plans, training, and joint exercises to increase their ability to undertake humanitarian as well as peacekeeping missions." [13]

"Humanitarian" intervention once again, even though not one endangered population had been identified! The NATO generals have decided to swear their oath of allegiance upon this word. When they launch a new war for petroleum, there is no doubt that Kouchner will be the first sent on television news programs to elaborate on this theme.

In reality, the "humanitarian" preoccupations are more often than not the kind that consist of doing good for people against their own wills. Under pressure from the west, the Hungarian parliament initially refused to hold a referendum on joining NATO, and then it avoided the question. As far as the word "partnership" is concerned, it is equally hypocritical. The participation of a Czech or Hungarian unit, for example, at the side of the great western powers, cannnot in any way be an equal partnership, but serves merely as an alibi, an alibi which will serve to present a military intervention by the United States and/or Germany in a less than colonialist light.

In fact, the "partnership" is concerned with placing the Eastern European military under the control of the West. "The Partnership will stimulate a transparent national defense plan and budgetary process as well." Of course, the "transparency" goes in only one direction. Do not imagine that the United States will confide its little secrets to its new friends in Eastern Europe. In reality, they are simply looking at one OPA regarding the defense forces of these countries. Any vestige of sovereignty or independence has been liquidated.

This enlargement of the Western Alliance toward the East portends new threats to peace, including nuclear threats. Since 1991, General Galvin, supreme commander of Allied forces in Europe, has insisted: "The nuclear capabilities of NATO will continue to enjoy a vital role in safeguarding stability and security."[14] Since the enlargement will permit western forces to be present in the territories of its new members, it is quite probable that these countries will be obliged to accept nuclear weapons on their territories. On the day when a war is launched against Russia, strategic risk of this kind will have serious consequences.

In the days immediately following the Gulf War, NATO Chief of Staff, General Galvin, showed his colors: "Our forces must be sufficiently multi-purpose. We must be ready to deploy our forces from region to region, a quality that requires a mobility identical to that which we observed in the Gulf conflict." [15]

NATO wants to be prepared for quick and decisive intervention in strategic areas that are extremely diverse and spread over the globe. For chief NATO military strategists, the ability to wage new Gulf Wars almost anywhere requires a complete reorganization of military structures and troop composition.

The characteristics of the new intervention forces are:
1) Speed; 2) Mobility; 3) Effortless Adaptability.

The global police force wants to be able to dictate its law in any number of different situations. The NATO forces of the future will, however, exhibit another important characteristic: they will be increasingly multinational. There are two reasons for this:

1) the world economic crisis has forced NATO countries to slash their military budgets, forcing Washington and Bonn to redistribute costs to their allies by establishing integrated forces.

2) Integrating troops from other countries is also a convenient means to subordinate smaller armies to U.S. and German command.

The president of the NATO Military Committee, Vigleik Eide, emphasizes this latter aspect. "In the long term, multinationality could also encourage a greater specialization of forces between nations." [16]

"Specialization" here means that small and medium sized nations will be increasingly subject to the strategic demands of the U.S. and Germany, eventually losing their independent defense capabilities.

The new intervention forces will combine not only land, sea, and air operations, but also troops originating from numerous NATO member countries as well. This evidently poses practical integration problems. It is precisely for this reason that real war situations are "useful." If NATO wants to find and work out the kinks in the new system, a real military intervention is worth a hundred exercises.

In August 1992, NATO Military Committee President Vigleik Eide was ecstatic: "The rapid deployment of a maritime operation to oversee the United Nations embargo against Serbia and Montenegro provided NATO with invaluable experience. Most notably, when involving efficient operational coordination with European Union Forces involved in the same task." Even more positive bulletins were issued after the 1995 bombardments against the Bosnian Serbs.

The European armies will therefore be integrated further. But who will dominate this ensemble? NATO strategic documents abound with the word "interoperability." This means that if they engage multinational forces, it is necessary to harmonize the armies, which comprise it, and therefore unify them in a number of different fields of activity: military doctrine, joint combat plans, and standardization of weaponry and equipment.

As we have already discussed, standardizing weaponry exacerbates the struggle between leading arms producers. On the other hand, as NATO undertakings foresee, to improve "the intelligence, long range detection, surveillance, telecommunications, command structure and control," is to find itself on a field where the United States has acquired a superiority which its rivals would like to challenge.

In fact, the "Alliance" is much less united than it seems. It is striated by growing rivalries between the great western powers. And above all, the rivalry between the two greats: Washington and Bonn.

Bonn is not counting on remaining number two forever. Its Minister of Defense, Volker Ruhe, has suggested that the NATO treaty ought to be replaced by a new treaty between the European Union and the United States. Ruhe claimed that, on a global scale, Europe and the United States must be considered as equals and Europe must therefore be able to intervene strategically as a global power alongside the United States.

The Germans have led grand maneuvers in conjunction with France under the guise of preparing a future European army. These exercises were presented as composing a NATO program, "The Partnership for Peace," but most Europeans saw them for what they were. The era of NATO intervention as a unified military bloc was approaching its end.

Indeed, Bonn has been overcome by a frenzy of "joint maneuvers": it inaugurated a joint German-Danish-Polish army; it is directing the formation of a joint navy of three Baltic states; it has undertaken in Hamburg and Munich the long-term formation of an Uzbek army which receives German "advisors"; it has incorporated two Albanian platoons with its active troops in Bosnia; and it is delighted to see the formation of a Slovene army based on the principles and regulations of the German military.

All of these measures are viewed with anxiety by Moscow, which sees potential military danger in NATO's enlargement.

But Washington has not remained indifferent in the face of this German will for independence. President Clinton has no intention of abandoning the international supremacy of the United States, and will not allow its stature as sole superpower to be questioned again regardless of the form it might take. It is preoccupied with avoiding the breakup of the camp that they have assembled against Eastern Europe and avoiding any challenge to their leadership while maintaining the disequilibrium of forces that was in place at the end of the Cold War.

Remain Number One; maintain the Western camp under their direction; protect their advance. To keep control of their allies, the U.S.A. must ultimately play on its strong points: nuclear supremacy, great advances in the field of logistics, transportation, espionage, and communications. Most of all, they must keep the upper hand in NATO's military command structure.

These factors, Washington has concluded, should serve as impediments to the development of a new German empire in Eastern Europe. Bonn, however, has been contesting U.S. domination of NATO more frequently. An intense rivalry exists behind the officially warm relations. Who will command the next military interventions, Washington or the Bonn-Paris duo? Who will fix objectives? One thing is clear. The Bundeswehr remains the backbone of NATO in Europe, being the only European army able to mobilize on a large scale.

Germany is counting on using NATO to further its own ends and enlarge its domination of Eastern Europe and the former Soviet republics. It has already succeeded in launching NATO against its hereditary enemy, Serbia. In the future, Germany wants to confront Russia, its only traditional rival in the East. As usual, Germany is playing on two gameboards: the North Atlantic Treaty Organization, and the European Union. It is skillfully alternating emphasis on and combining the two in order to maximize its gains.

Rivalry among the great powers is not limited to the conflict between Bonn and Washington. France has presented its own obstacles as well, not only with the United States but also with Germany.

The British publication *Searchlight* analyzed this subtle chess game between the great capitals: "The French government wants to contain Germany for the short-term through the Eurocorps and the army of the Union of Western Europe. The United States and Great Britain have another idea: to keep Germany subordinated through the persistent presence of NATO in Europe, and granting Bonn greater involvement in NATO affairs. Bonn, meanwhile, plays intelligently against the two opposites while pretending to be in favor of both." [17]

Will the relationship between Bonn and Paris be that of equal partners, or master and servant?

In the spring of 1996, Jacques Chirac announced major reforms for the French military: Conscription would be eliminated and the army transformed into a professional corps. Bonn got nervous. German leaders were surprised by the scope of the reform projects for the French military, and they were unhappy about being poorly informed about it.

Bonn wants to direct everything in Europe, including restructuring the French military. But why does this transformation into a professional army generate such anger with the Germans? The response can be found only by turning to a defense industry magazine. The real goals of armies are not discussed in media destined for the general public. Accordingly, we find the real answer in the military publication, *Defense Nationale*: "Reform of our armed services has generated intense reactions on the other side of the Rhone. The German Minister of Defense, Volker Ruhe, sees quite clearly that NATO, European defense, and the Franco-German partnership divided between France and Great Britain specializing in missions of intervention, while Germany continues to assume territorial defense. This fear is underscored by the loud proclamations of France's global ambitions by Jacques Chirac." [18]

The problem is suddenly clear. The president of the Defense Commission of the German Parliament has called for a professional army geared for foreign operations. Bonn, in fact, suspects Paris of committing itself to imperialist intervention abroad while German troops must be content with staying on guard in Germany. The German suspicions are well founded: France has given evidence of its "global ambitions" in Rwanda and the Congo.

Even if France declares "adaptations," it continues to play a pivotal military role in order to compensate for its economic weakness against an economically all-powerful Germany.

Even after Washington's victory in Bosnia, the struggle for control of NATO continues to rage between the U.S. and Europe. In June 1996, at the Berlin Summit, the U.S. had to back down in the face of pressure from the European Union, spearheaded by the Bonn-Paris duo. A decision was reached giving Europe the right to conduct military operations independently of Washington.

Six months earlier, France had been reinstated in NATO, but demanded a visible European identity, politically as well as militarily, at the core of the Alliance. On the eve of the Berlin Summit, French Foreign Affairs Minister Herve de Charette demanded that the European identity have a lasting, visible, and operational character, including its own planning, training, and command structure. He insisted that strategic control of operations and political decisions must be built on the Union of Western Europe.

De Charette was supported by his German colleague, Minister of Foreign Affairs Klaus Kinkel. "We need to reinforce the European capacity for direct involvement. To do this, the military structure of the Alliance must be available for missions under European command."[19] France and Germany are demanding that NATO's command structure, communications, and logistic capabilities be placed in European hands for autonomous military operations.

North American military commanders strongly opposed this mandate. Even the commander-in-chief of NATO, Gen. George Joulwan, threatened to resign, claiming that the European armed forces were attempting to split up NATO.

The United States demanded control of each phase of military operations. The rift was smoothed over by provisionally accepting that NATO gives political approval to any autonomous European intervention. The struggle continued mercilessly, however, with the European countries demanding that the Berlin decision become operational.

Kinkel stated diplomatically that it was in neither the European nor the American interest to call Americans to arms every time something goes wrong somewhere. Translation of this polite, but hypocritical language: Our American colleagues should no longer interfere in Europe.

The Americans were not anxious to accept such a passive role. After the Berlin Conference, a U.S. diplomat reaffirmed that the United States intervenes whenever a menace arises anywhere in the world. Translation of this polite language: Our German colleagues should not dispute the fact that the U.S. leads the world.

Disturbing threats. But isn't this rivalry between great powers also a positive factor for peace? Could it not re-establish equilibrium between the world's forces and neutralize all-powerful U.S. imperialism? To the contrary, we think that this rivalry between great powers increases the risks of war. Why?

The great powers have always divided the world on the basis of their military, economic, and political power. It must be noted, however, that the development of empires does not proceed in equilibrium, but unevenly. When the ratio of forces shifts, the ascendant imperial power demands a re-partitioning of its sphere of influence.

What has the history of the last centuries shown us? One after the other, various powers have dominated the world before ceding it to a rival: Spain, the Netherlands, England, France. Each time the transfer of power was accomplished by major wars. The period between two reigns is characterized by great instability and the risk of conflict. The two world wars, which marked the 20th century, have no other cause. During WWI, an imperialist Germany, the ascendant power, demanded a new partition of the world, which France and England refused to allow. During WWII, German and Japanese imperialism again wished to overturn the existing order.

What about today? The U.S. still dominates the world, but is in decline, holding on only because of its political and military clout. Germany is economically stronger (a condition to submitting to Europe) and is working to regain its political and military might. Japan is showing the same tendencies. We have already lived through this growing rivalry for domination twice in this century. If we want to keep the 21st century from becoming an even worse disaster, we must quit reassuring ourselves with illusions such as "They won't go that far!" After the unimaginable butchery of 1914-1918, the world cried "Never again!" Was that enough? No. Defending peace implies that progressive minded people wake up and see the capitalist system for what it is: a system that needs wars.

The deep causes of conflict between imperial powers have not disappeared. Their struggles start with political and economic confrontations that always end up decided by military means. During the past 40 years, the great powers have been more or less unified in ensuring their domination of the peoples of the Third World. They are also cooperating to control the evolution of the nations of Eastern Europe. But none of them wants to take risks without any profit for themselves. The deepening economic crisis is only aggravating the situation; they are fighting not only to exploit the weakest nations but also to take control of industrially developed areas, the second tier of European countries. The fact that these countries are "allies" remains irrelevant.

Imperialism is not a defect proper to the character of any country, political party, or leader. It is the fundamental tendency of capitalism itself. The laws of economics demand control of more and more countries. If one power doesn't seize new territory, a rival will. Dominate or be dominated, such is the law of capitalism. Sooner or later, this giant Monopoly game ends when war breaks out. NATO has under its command the most powerful military force on earth, an armada capable of overturning and destroying any region of the world. And this armada is not in good hands.

---

1. Ronald D. Asmus, Richard L. Kugler and F. Stephen Larrabee, *Foreign Affairs*, vol. 72, no. 4, p. 31.
2. *Revue de l'OTAN*, March 1996, p. 4.
3. Ibid, p. 3.
4. *NATO Basic Documents*, 7th-8th November, 1991, Rome "The Alliance's New Strategic Concept," www.nato.int/docu/comm, p.3-4.
5. Ibid., p.2.
6. *Revue de l'OTAN*, December 1991, p. 4.
7. Ibid., May 1996, p. 25.
8. Ibid.
9. *Defense Nationale*, February, 1996, p. 93.
10. Pierre Pierart and Wies Jespers, *d' Hiroshima à Sarajevo*, EPO, Bruxelles, 1994.
11. *Revue de l'OTAN*, March, 1996, p. 3.
12. Ibid., February, 1994, p. 3-6.
13. Ibid.
14. *Revue de l'OTAN*, December 1991, pp. 14-18.
15. Ibid.
16. *Revue de l'OTAN*, August 1992, p. 23.
17. "Reunited Germany," *Searchlight*, 1994, p. 31.
18. *Defense Nationale*, Juillet 1996, p.41.
19. Courrier *de l'OTAN*, Mai 1996, p. 10.

THE PULITZER PRIZE AND CROATIAN PROPAGANDA

THOMAS DEICHMANN

Like few other Western journalists, Roy Gutman has built his reputation through his reporting of the war in former Yugoslavia. From 1990 until summer 1994 he was chief of the *Newsday* Europe office in Bonn and won great credibility for his coverage of the Balkan tragedy. After his report on the alleged "Death Camp" in Omarska, which appeared in *Newsday* on August 2, 1992, Gutman rapidly became well known all over the world. He was awarded the prestigious Pulitzer Prize for journalism in 1993 for his rape and death camp stories and other reports about atrocities in Bosnia.

Today, it is clear that Croatian political interests were involved in at least one of his big stories from Bosnia. In the article "One by One" he told the story of Jadranka Cigelj—a paid Croatian propagandist—who acquired international fame partly as a consequence of Gutman's representation of her as a credible source for tales of war crimes.

Lowering Standards

Many of Gutman's articles on the early period of the Bosnian civil war are reassembled in his book *A Witness to Genocide*, which has been published in many countries. Though it is an impressive publication based on extensive research, the credibility of some of its reports is open to question, and Gutman has been criticized by other journalists for persistent bias[1]. There can be no doubt that he has sometimes failed to observe very elementary standards of journalistic rigor and balance. Clearly, his influential death camp article on Omarska ·in

August 1992 lowered the standards in ways, which were unfortunately widely adopted by many of his press colleagues [2].

Much of his early work on Bosnia was based solely on hearsay, stimulating a whole series of speculative reports about Serbian atrocities that established a pattern for blaming only one side in the conflict. Such stories profoundly influenced public opinion in Western countries.

Croatian Propagandist as Gutman's Witness

It is striking that throughout his work, Gutman frequently relied on the official pronouncements of one of the parties in the conflict and its political representatives, despite the obvious danger that the warring parties in any conflict will seek to promote their own cause. In one important case, Gutman used a paid Croatian propagandist in order to lend greater authenticity to one of his famous stories about Omarska. The article, dated February 21, 1993 and titled "One by One" ["Eine nach der anderen"], concerns mass rapes in Bosnia, one of the most sensitive issues of the war. It deals specifically with women held in Omarska prison camp in Bosnia. Gutman tells the story of Jadranka Cigelj, a then 45-year old Croatian lawyer from Prijedor who says she spent several months in Omarska and was raped by camp commander Zeljko Mejakic and other Serb men.

In a telephone interview in August 1994, Roy Gutman affirmed that he still regarded Cigelj, his rape witness, as a reliable source. In his article from the year before he acknowledged that she was a "political activist" and "vice chairperson" of Tudjman's ruling party, the Croatian Democratic Society (HDZ), and that she worked for the Croatian Information Center (CIC) in Zagreb. Nonetheless, Gutman maintained that he never saw cause to doubt her credibility.

Until his return to the U.S. from Germany in 1994, Gutman maintained contact with Cigelj on a regular basis. Amelija Janovic, wife of the then president of the Croatian World Congress in Germany and a leading member of the Croatian Cultural Association Rhein-Main, acted as Jadranka Cigelj's contact person in Germany. In a telephone interview she claimed that Cigelj and Gutman had remained in close contact since their first meeting in early 1993 and that she herself had arranged several meetings between them. The fact that Gutman met with Cigelj when he launched the Croatian edition of *A Witness to Genocide* in the Zagreb Culture and Information Center in June 1994 also suggests that they have maintained a close relationship. The CIC has also stated that Cigelj helped Gutman with his research trips in Bosnia and that it continued to pass "valuable information" to him.

Upon closer inspection, Cigelj's political activities raise many questions, which shed a different light on her person and on the quality of Gutman's reporting. It is easy to uncover information suggesting that Jadranka Cigelj is a paid propagandist of radical Croatian nationalist circles linked with the government in Zagreb. Due to her background and her dubious connections, objective journalism would provide Cigelj with no more, or less, credibility than the Serb Omarska camp commander Zeljko Mejakic, who—as Gutman acknowledges in the article—repeatedly denied having committed the alleged rape of Cigelj and other women.

Credibility Worldwide

Because Gutman chose to present Cigelj's words as truth, her tale won credibility worldwide. Indeed, by late 1993, Cigelj assumed an important role in the investigations for indictments against alleged Bosnian Serb war criminals. The Croatian Information Center has confirmed that Cigelj assisted a German TV team in research which resulted not just in a TV feature, but in the arrest of alleged war criminal Dusan Tadic in Munich in February 1994 on the basis of a warrant from the German Federal Prosecutor. Cigelj also testified against Tadic to the German Federal Police (BKA) and contacted the International Criminal Tribunal for the Former Yugoslavia (ICTY) in The Hague in order to become a witness against him there as well. Tadic became the first individual indicted by the Tribunal.

The Croatian Information Center

The Croatian Information Center (CIC), for which Cigelj operated, was a war propaganda institution, which replaced the former Croatian Ministry of Information. The CIC was set up with exile Croatian funds. The main role of the Center was to provide Western journalists, governments, academics and intellectuals with pro-Croat information. Its publications are on display in Croatian bookshops, despite the fact that war and economic crisis have severely constrained most other publishing activity. One of the Center's influential publications, "Genocide—Ethnic Cleansing in North-Western Bosnia," edited by CIC-director Ante Beljo, appeared in English, German and French. Apart from eyewitness reports of Serb atrocities in the civil war, it also contains reports of Croatian suffering during World War II. The Center's objective evidently was not just to portray present-day Serbs as cruel beasts, but to rewrite Croatian history, which was intimately associated with German fascism and the Holocaust.

The CIC was located in the former History Department of Zagreb University in Opacity 10, in the immediate vicinity of the Croatian government building "Saber" and other state institutions. Opacity 8, which had previously housed the former Croatian Ministry of Information under Branko Salaj, became the seat of the press office of the Croatian Ministry of Foreign Affairs. Few Western journalists were aware of the fact that during the war in Croatia and Bosnia, all the "Foreign Press Centers" in Croatia—the main ones being located in Zagreb and Split—were also run by the supposedly non-governmental CIC, the successor of the Ministry of Information. This whole propaganda machine was a highly professional operation and it has played an important role since the beginning of the war. A large staff was available to deal with the inquiries of visiting Western journalists and to assist them by providing interview contacts. Almost all the staff spoke fluent English, since many came from Canada and the U.S., where exile information centers bearing the same name were in operation. In addition to the press accreditation of UNPROFOR, the CIC issued its own press cards bearing the name and photo of visiting journalists.

Publicity Machine and Armed Forces

Before Croatian independence, CIC-director Ante Beljo had already formed exile HDZ sections in Canada and the U.S.A. He returned to Croatia after independence, was general secretary of the HDZ under president Franjo Tudjman in 1990-91, later joined the Ministry of Information under Branko Salaj and then formed the CIC, whose staff included Jadranka Cigelj as a senior person. Beljo was also chairman of the Croatian Homeland Foundation, which looked after exiles returning to Croatia.

The former Croatian Minister of Defense Gojko Susak—also a former Canadian exile—was Croatian Immigration Minister in 1990-91 and already had close contact with Beljo in Canada. It is no secret in Croatia and elsewhere that exile funds were used to finance Tudjman's election campaigns and that they formed a major source of the wealth of the new Croatian elite and helped fund its propaganda apparatus and the armed forces. The Croatian writer Zvonco Ivankovic Vonta is convinced that Ante Beljo was also involved in illegal arms deals. There are further links between the CIC and the presidential office and immigrant groups, some of whom openly co-operate with pro-fascist Ustasha supporters.

Society for Human Rights & Croatian Ustashas

Roy Gutman's key witness for mass rapes in Bosnia, Jadranka Cigelj, played an important role in the Croatian propaganda network. From early 1992 she was working for the CIC, and in December 10, 1993 she became the vice-chair of the Croatian section of the International Society for Human Rights (ISHR), whose headquarters is situated in Frankfurt am Main, Germany. The ISHR predecessor organization had well-documented historic links with the Nazi authorities in World War II and later with the American secret service, the CIA, and its German partner BND. In the 1980s the ISHR had developed close contact with exiled Croatian nationalists such as Dobroslav Paraga, who returned from the U.S. to Croatia after independence and became chairman of the Croatian Party of Rights (HSP).

Together with a further associate of the ISHR, Ante Paradjik, Paraga organized the paramilitary activities of the notorious neo-fascist HOS-troops, who perpetrated anti-Serb violence during the war in Croatia in 1991 and were later integrated into the Croatian army. The HSP claims adherence to the tradition of Ustasha-leader and Hitler-collaborator Ante Pavelic. The ISHR Zagreb office and personnel double as the CIC. In Opacity 10, one of Jadranka Cigelj's colleagues, Albert Bing, variously operated as chairman of the ISHR or as a member of Ante Beljo's CIC. [3]

Perplexing Contradictions

Moving in these circles, Jadranka Cigelj became well known to Western journalists like Roy Gutman, who frequently stayed in Zagreb. Cigelj not only figures in Gutman's war coverage, but in numerous publications of the ISHR—under the names Jadranka C., Jadranka Cigelj, Jadranka Cigev, Jadranka Cigay or simply Mrs. Jadranka. She is sometimes described as a 44-year old Croatian from Prijedor, sometimes as a Croatian in her early 40s from Vukovar. When asked about how Gutman came into contact with Cigelj, he stated that he first met her by chance in Zagreb in January 1993 and subsequently verified that she was a credible witness. But this verification process was not taken seriously.

Since the Serb authorities had refused to permit him to visit Omarska, he had asked the press officer of the Bosnian Serb army in Banja Luka to procure a response from the Omarska prison camp commander, Zeljko Mejakic, to the accusation that he had raped Mrs. Jadranka. The arrogance of Mejakic's denial confirmed Gutman's impression that Jadranka could be trusted. Gutman resolutely affirmed that he procured sufficient information about the identity of his witness, but in his letter to Banja Luka he referred to Jadranka "Siget," which could suggest that he did not even know her real name. In his article written only 10 days later, Gutman wrote of Jadranka "Cigelj." Gutman explained that as a mere oversight.

The ISHR-brochure "God's Forgotten Children" includes an eyewitness account of a Jadranka C.[4] Without doubt the witness in question is Jadranka Cigelj, since her statements about the length of her imprisonment in Omarska and other details are identical with those in Gutman's story. But there are also some contradictions. For example, in Gutman's report she says that she was "released" on August 3, 1992, when the prison camp in Omarska was closed down. In the brochure of the ISHR we learn that she still had to spend four days in the "concentration camp Trnopolje" after leaving Omarska.

Different Serb Criminals

What is rather more puzzling is that Cigelj accuses different Serbs of having raped her in her two accounts. In the ISHR story she only charged the reserve officer Nedeljko Grabovac with this crime: "Grabovac not only insulted me on account of my nationality, but also threatened me.

Suddenly the lights went out, he took my hand and pushed me in the hall. Then he forced me into the bathroom. . . Then he raped me." She also reported that "the same happened" in the following nights, but mentioned no other names.

At the end of this eyewitness account she underlines the impression that she was raped by only one person in Omarska: She states that the camp commander—Zeljko Mejakic, whose name she never mentions in the ISHR-brochure—had asked her five days after these incidents whether she had received any maltreatment. She expressed her outrage at this question, since he had been present in the first night when Grabovac had grabbed her hand and then raped her. She supplemented her account of the commander's role, stating: "He acted as if he had not been present during that night. But he was the one who had brought this man in. I later found out that the man [the rapist; note of the ISHR-editor] was a member of the Serb territorial defense forces."

In this account Zeljko Mejakic appears merely as the camp commander—not as a rapist. He is not even mentioned by name. In Gutman's article, however, Jadranka Cigelj claims that she was raped by commander Zeljko Mejakic, the guards Mladen Radic and Kos Milojica, in addition to Nedeljko Grabovac. Roy Gutman said the explanation for this may be that Cigelj only overcame her trauma in stages, until she was finally able to articulate all the details of her horrific experience. This seems unlikely, since the ISHR brochure was published in February 1993, the same month as Gutman's article.

Two months later a long interview with Cigelj was published in the German *Frankfurter Allgemeine Zeitung* (April 5, 1993). As in the ISHR brochure she claims that the camp commander did not rape her. However, in this interview it became again clear that she was not seeking to relate the facts but rather operated as a propagandist. She claimed that in the Omarska camp alone 11,800 people had already been killed before she arrived there on June 14, 1992. This figure is a pure fiction, as every serious investigator will confirm.

Cigelj and the Croatian Ministry of Information

An earlier ISHR publication sheds some light on Jadranka Cigelj's links with the former Croatian Ministry of Information[5]. It reports that a human rights activist of the ISHR in Frankfurt had been introduced to "Mrs. Jadranka" by Marika Riser, a member of the ministry staff. A photograph in this brochure shows Jadranka Cigelj in a fur coat and hat, smoking a cigarette and looking well. In the brochure "God's Forgotten Children" Marika Riser is listed as Maritza Risek alongside Jadranka Cigey (not Cigelj) as contacts in Opacity 10 in the information section "Contact addresses in Zagreb." The same page also features the "Center for the Investigation of War Crimes" in Zenica, another propaganda organization that cooperated with the German pro-Muslim activist and leader of the Society for Threatened Peoples (Gesellschaft fuer bedrohte Voelker) Tilman Zuelch[6]. In other ISHR publications Jadranka

Cigelj is listed in various capacities, such as chairperson of the "Women's Group Omarska"[7].

Famous War Victim

As a result of the professional PR work organized in Zagreb, Gutman's witness Cigelj is better known abroad than in Croatia. Rarely has a single war victim become so famous[8]. This appears to be a consequence of her being systematically introduced to Western journalists by the CIC staff and Gutman's use of her as a source. In addition, Cigelj was sent abroad and invited to participate in international meetings. For example, she appeared at the annual conference of the ISHR in Koenigstein near Frankfurt in March 1993 as Jadranka Cigev[9].

Cigelj had already visited Germany on several occasions before then. For example, she spoke at the public hearing of the German parliament about "systematic rape in Bosnia-Herzegovina" in December 1992. The hearing was held in response to the revelations about alleged mass rape in Bosnia in the "Mona Lisa" TV program. Amelija Janovic of the Croatian Cultural Association Rhein-Main acted as Cigelj's translator. In 1994, Janovic's husband was the president of the Croatian World Congress and a friend of Hans Peter Rullmann. Rullmann himself has close contacts to the ISHR and was the editor of the Ost-Dienst (East-Service), a radical right wing publication based in Hamburg. Like the ISHR, Rullmann lobbied for Dobroslav Paraga and published pro-Croatian propaganda.

Cigelj has appeared on international TV various times—in Germany, France, Great Britain and the U.S. Due to her influential connections, she also won official recognition in the U.S. and France. She was honored by the Minnesota Advocates for Human Rights (MAHR) in Minneapolis "For outstanding contributions to international women's rights" in June 1993, alongside Dr. Shana Swiss of the organization Physicians for Human Rights (PHR). On June 3, 1993 the U.S. paper *Star Tribune* featured an article on the ceremony along with a photograph of Swiss and Cigelj, in which Cigelj was referred to not as a Croatian, but as a "Bosnian Muslim victim."

Witness for the Tribunal

The French non-governmental barristers' association Institut des Droits de l'Homme du Barreau de Bordeaux further awarded Cigelj the "Ludovic Trarieux Prize" with FF 30.000. The Institute met with French intellectuals associated with Bernard Henry Levy, a forceful proponent of Western military action against the Serbs. Amelija Janovic of the Croatian Cultural Association Rhein-Main explained to the author that these and other organizations planned to act as prosecutors in the International Criminal Tribunal for the Former Yugoslavia in The Hague in an early stage. Jadranka Cigelj, of course, was billed as a major witness at the Tribunal. She was to put forward in the witness box her charges against Dusan Tadic and other indicted Bosnian Serbs. According to Amelija Janovic, representatives of the French barristers' association accompanied by Austrian colleagues visited Zagreb in August 1994 to discuss the proceedings with Cigelj.

However, their initiative did not succeed. Although Jadranka Cigelj offered to become a key witness for the prosecution during the Tadic case, she was rejected by the Tribunal because she was seen as an unreliable source. So far, neither in the Tadic case nor in any other case has she been called as a witness for the prosecution.

Anti-Serb Propaganda

The legitimacy she had being a credible source for a Pulitzer Prize winner helped her to continue her anti-Serb work. In 1996 together with Nusreta Sivac she won further credibility when both women were featured in the documentary *Calling the Ghosts: A story about Rape, War and Women.* Human Rights Watch launched the film in June 1996 at their International Film Festival. Following that event Amnesty International sponsored a 25-city U.S. promotional tour. The message of this film as others of Cigelj's political activities follow the same line: With moralistic and biased accusations she blames the Serbs as new Nazis and the other parties in the civil war in former Yugoslavia as pure victims.

No surprise that in *Calling the Ghosts* Roy Gutman is the man referred to by Cigelj as an American top journalist. Cigelj expressed her revisionist and radical political views in spring 1996 at a conference in the Italian city Merano with the disputed International Society for Human Rights. "Compared to the methods of torture used by the Serbs," she said, "the Gestapo was only an apprenticeship of a far lower level than this university of torture. In those days people were at least a number. We were nothing at all."[10].

More recent political activities, in which she was involved, occurred in Boston. On January, 31, 1999, *The Boston Globe* published an article entitled "Debate swirls around ex-Serb prison guard" about Jezdimir Topic, a former guard of Trnopolje transit and refugee camp in Northern Bosnia, who settled with his family as a refugee in Everett, a small city outside of Boston. The local Immigration and Naturalization Service (INS) started to investigate his refugee status, concerned that he was accomplice to "ethnic cleansing." INS officials said Topic could have his status revoked and be expelled from the country. The background for the INS investigation was an inquiry of the *Globe*, which was based on accusations against Topic by three women, amongst them Jadranka Cigelj[11]. The journalists of *The Boston Globe* immediately spoke of a "fake refugee issue"[12].

Stuttering Pulitzer Prize Winner

Whatever her background and intentions, the uninitiated reader will perceive Jadranka Cigelj in Gutman's *A Witness to Genocide* as an ordinary victim of terrible crimes. Maybe Cigelj was really raped by the Omarska commander and his guards and she can offer some explanation for all the murky links and relationships detailed here. But there can only be grave doubt as to her credibility as an unbiased source.

When I asked Roy Gutman in August 1994, on what occasion he had last seen Jadranka Cigelj he failed to mention the

presentation of his book together with Cigelj in Zagreb which
had taken place only a few weeks before our conversation. He
began stuttering and pretended having forgotten this event,
which made him the most important and celebrated Western
journalist in Croatia. He also stated that, apart from a very brief
and insignificant contact in summer 1994, he had never heard
of the International Society for Human Rights and that he did
not know that Jadranka Cigelj has been the vice-chair of its
Croatian section in Zagreb since December 1993.

However, when Gutman wrote his article about Jadranka
Cigelj in February 1993, he was fully aware of her connections
with the governing Croatian party HDZ and the Croatian Information Center which organized war propaganda. It is perplexing that Gutman has never expressed any doubt about the
credibility of this institution and its personnel.

Notes and References

Roy Gutman, *A Witness to Genocide*, Macmillan Publishing
Company, New York and Maxwell Macmillan Canada Inc.,
Ontario, 1993

1. See for example Joan Phillips: "Who's making news in
Bosnia," in: *Living Marxism*, May 1993, London
(www.informinc.co.uk). Phillips wrote about the British merce-
nary Robert Loftus who went to Bosnia in 1992 to fight for the
Muslim forces. Loftus supplied the British and American media
with anti-Serb propaganda, amongst them Roy Gutman.
2. Another striking example for circulating a misleading
picture of the escalating civil war in Bosnia was the broadcast of
Independent Television News (ITN) from Trnopolje camp on
August 6, 1992. Four days after Gutman's "Death Camp" article had appeared in Newsday ITN broadcast the famous image
of an emaciated Bosnian Muslim seemingly caged behind
barbed wire. The image was interpreted as proof for the existence of Nazi-style concentration camps. For a detailed study of

this image and why it was misleading see Thomas Deichmann: "The Picture that Fooled the World," in: *LM magazine*, January 1997, London (www.informinc.co.uk/ITN-vs-LM); see also: T.D.: "Misinformation: TV Coverage of a Bosnian Camp," in: *CovertAction Quarterly*, Fall 1998.

3. For a detailed study of the ISHR see Thomas Deichmann: "IGFM—Menschenrechte im Visier," in: NOVO, No12, September/October 1994, Frankfurt (Germany); an English translation was published in *The Balkan war*, Sefa Martin Yurukel (ed.), Aarhus University, Denmark 1995. A copy of the article can be obtained from the author.

4. Internationale Gesellschaft fuer Menschenrechte e.V.: Bosnien-Herzegowina: Gottes vergessene Kinder. Das Drama der vergewaltigen Frauen und deren Kinder—Dokumentation, Feb.1993, Frankfurt/Main

5. Menschenrechte, 1/1993.

6. The "Center for the Investigation of War Crimes" in Zenica in Bosnia-Herzegovina operated during the war as a state sponsored propaganda institution. When war broke out in Herzegovina between Croat and Muslim forces in spring 1993 the Center cut all its connections with ISHR branch in Zagreb.

7. Fuer die Menschenrechte, 4/1993 & 6/1993.

8. This is symptomatic for the personalized and victim centered PR operations and the media coverage during the war in the Balkans. Another example for that is the story of the first "war crimes trial" in Sarajevo against Borislav Herak. For a detailed study see Thomas Deichmann: "I think I will be their main witness in The Hague. The first trial of war criminals in Sarajevo and the double standards of the media and big politics—The trial against Borislav Herak, Sretko Damjanovic and Nada Tomic. A case study," in: NOVO, No31, November/December 1997, Frankfurt (Germany). The text was also published in the Dutch weekly *De Groene Amsterdammer* in November 1997. A copy of the article can be obtained from the author.

9. *Fuer die Menschenrechte*, 3/1993; Menschenrechte, 2-3/1993.

10. Rheinischer Merkur, 12/4/96.

11. The other two women were Nusreta Sivac who had featured with Cigelj in "Calling the Ghosts" and Tesma Elezovic who during the war had been involved in similar propaganda activities as Cigelj for the Bosnian-Muslim side. During the war Elezovic appeared in the European press repeatedly and co-operated with Tilman Zuelch's disputed Society for Threatened People, based in Goettingen, Germany.

12. Another article in the *Boston Globe* entitled "INS official urges questioning of Serb ex-guard" appeared on February 2, 1999. The *Globe* staff promised to "look at all possible angles for further exploration" of the case. The author, however, did not receive a satisfactory reply, when he offered his own information about Cigelj and her background to the *Globe* journalists.

SEEING YUGOSLAVIA THROUGH A DARK GLASS:

The Ideological Uniformity of the Media

DIANA JOHNSTONE

Years of experience in and out of both mainstream and alternative media have made me aware of the power of the dominant ideology to impose certain interpretations on international news. During the Cold War, most world news for American consumption had to be framed as part of the Soviet-U.S. contest. Since then, a new ideological bias frames the news. The way the violent fragmentation of Yugoslavia has been reported is the most stunning example.

I must admit that it took me some time to figure this out, even though I had a long-standing interest and some knowledge of Yugoslavia. I spent time there as a student in 1953, living in a Belgrade dormitory and learning the language. In 1984, I warned of the danger of Yugoslavia's disintegration in a piece for *In These Times*.[1] Even so, as the country was torn apart in the early nineties, I was unable to keep up with all that was happening. In those years, I was working as press officer for the Greens in the European Parliament, and had no time to investigate the situation myself. I realised that there were serious flaws in the way media and politicians were reacting, and I managed to write an article warning against judging a complex situation by analogy with totally different times and places.[2] It was only later, when I was able to devote considerable time to my own research, that I gradually figured things out for myself and realised the extent of the deception—which is in large part self-deception.

Even journalists or media outlets that are characterised as "alternative" are not necessarily free from a society's dominant interpretation and the dominant ideology. In fact, in the case of the Yugoslav tragedy, "alternative" or "left" activists and writers have frequently taken the lead in likening the Serbs, the people who most wanted to continue to live in multi-cultural Yugoslavia, to Nazi racists, and in calling for military intervention on behalf of ethnically defined secessionist movements[3]—all supposedly in the name of "multi-cultural Bosnia," a country which, unlike Yugoslavia, would have to be built from scratch by outsiders.

The terrible paradox is that very many people of left and liberal persuasion have contributed to demonizing an entire people, the Serbs, thereby justifying both ethnic separatism and the new role of NATO as occupying power in the Balkans on behalf of a theoretical "international community."

Political Motives

The political motives that launched the anti-Serb propaganda campaign are obvious enough. Nationalist leaders in the Yugoslav republics of Slovenia and Croatia used the claim of Serbian oppression as the pretext for setting up their own little statelets which, thanks to strong German support, could "jump the queue" and get into the rich men's European club ahead of the rest of Yugoslavia.

Demonization of the Serbs began in July 1991 with a virulent anti-Serb campaign in the German media, led by the major conservative newspaper the *Frankfurter Allgemeine Zeitung* (FAZ). In almost daily columns, FAZ editor Johann Georg Reismüller justified the freshly, and illegally, declared "independence" of Slovenia and Croatia by describing "the Yugo-Serbs" as essentially Oriental "militarist Bolsheviks" who have "no place in the European Community." Nineteen months after German reunification, and for the first time since Hitler's defeat in 1945, German media resounded with condemnation of an entire ethnic group reminiscent of the pre-war propaganda against the Jews.[4]

This German propaganda binge was the signal that times had changed seriously. Only a few years earlier, a seemingly broad German peace movement had stressed the need to put an end to "enemy stereotypes" (*Feindbilder*). Yet the sudden ferocious emergence of the enemy stereotype of "the Serbs" did not shock liberal or left Germans, who were soon repeating it themselves. Had the German peace movement completed its historic mission once its contribution to altering the image of Germany had led Gorbachev to endorse reunification? It would seem so. In the Bundestag, German Green leader Joschka Fischer pressed for disavowal of "pacifism" in order to "combat Auschwitz," meaning the Serbs, accused of abusing Bosnian Muslims. In a heady mood of self-righteous indignation, German politicians across the board joined in using Germany's past guilt as a reason, not for restraint, as had been the logic up until reunification, but on the contrary, for "bearing their share of the military burden." In the name of human rights, the Federal Republic of Germany abolished its ban on military operations outside the NATO defensive area. Germany could once again be a "normal" military power—thanks to the "Serb threat."

The near unanimity was all the more surprising in that the "enemy stereotype" of the Serb had been dredged up from the most belligerent German nationalism of the past. "Serbien muss sterbien" (a play on the word *sterben*, to die), meaning "Serbia must die" was a famous popular war cry of World War I.[5] Serbs had been singled out for slaughter along with Jews during the Nazi occupation of Yugoslavia in 1941. One would have thought that the younger generation of Germans, seemingly so sensitive to the victims of Germany's aggressive past, would have at least urged caution.

On the contrary, what occurred in Germany was a strange sort of mass transfer of Nazi identity, and guilt, to the Serbs. In the case of the Germans, this can be seen as a comforting psychological projection, which served to give Germans a fresh and welcome sense of innocence in the face of the new "criminal" people, the Serbs. But the hate campaign against Serbs, started in Germany, did not stop there. Elsewhere, the willingness to single out one of the Yugoslav peoples as the villain calls for other explanations.

Media Momentum

From the start, foreign reporters were better treated in Zagreb and in Ljubljana, whose secessionist leaders understood the prime importance of international support, than in Belgrade. The Albanian secessionists in Kosovo and the Croatian nationalist secessionists hired professional public relations experts to guide public opinion in their direction;[6] the Serbs did not. The Yugoslav story was complicated; anti-Serb stories had the advantage of being simple and available, and they provided an easy-to-use moral compass by designating the bad guys.

As the war in Bosnia-Herzegovina got underway in mid-1992, American journalists who repeated unconfirmed stories of Serbian atrocities could count on getting published, with a chance of a Pulitzer prize,[7] while there was no market for stories by journalists who discovered that a reported Serbian "rape camp" did not exist (German TV reporter Martin Lettmayer)[8] or who included information about Muslim or Croat crimes against Serbs (Belgian journalist Georges Berghezan for one). It became increasingly impossible to challenge the dominant interpretation in major media. Editors, of course, like to keep the story simple: one villain, and as much blood as possible. Moreover, after the German government forced the early recognition of Slovenian and Croatian independence, other Western powers lined up opportunistically with the anti-Serb position. The United States soon moved aggressively into the game by picking its own client state—Muslim Bosnia—out of the ruins.

Still, the one-sided view of Yugoslavia's collapse cannot be attributed solely to political designs or to sensationalist manipulation of the news by major media. It also owes a great deal to the *ideological uniformity* prevailing among educated liberals who are the consensual moral conscience in Northwestern Euro-American society since the end of the Cold War.

Down with the State

After the defeat of communism and collapse of the Soviet Union, the United States emerged as the world's sole super power, bringing with it a dominant ideology, expressed in moralistic terms, and a plan to reshape the world. United States foreign policy for over a century had been dictated by a single concern: to open world markets to American capital and American enterprise, by any means possible. Today this project is triumphant as "economic globalization." Throughout the world, government policies are judged, approved or condemned decisively not by their populations, but by "the markets," meaning the financial markets. Foreign investors, not domestic voters, decide policy. The International Monetary Fund and other such agencies are there to help governments adjust their policies to market dictates.

This economic globalization is being accompanied by an ideological assault on the nation-state as *a political community exercising sovereignty over a defined territory*. In fact, only the nation-state, so defined, can, in the name of protecting its citizens' welfare and environment, offer any resistance to the advancing dictates of "the markets." The goal of this ideological assault is to destroy the hitherto unsurpassed legitimacy of the nation-state as real or potential democracy.

Much of the left unwittingly helps to advance this project by eagerly promoting its moralistic cover: a theoretical global democracy that should replace attempts to strengthen democracy at the supposedly obsolete nation-state level.

Within the United States, the link between anti-nation-state ideology and economic globalization may be hard to grasp because of the double standard employed by U.S. leaders, who regularly invoke the supremacy of U.S. "national interest" over the very international institutions they promote in order to advance economic globalization. But such double standards are the function of the military power of the U.S., not available to small countries unless they are obedient client states. Thus, there is no real contradiction between asserting the primacy of

U.S. interests and blasting the nation-state barriers that might allow some organized defense of the interests of other peoples. Nonetheless, impressed by the apparent contradiction, some American liberals are comforted in their belief that nationalism is the number one enemy of mankind, and, therefore, opposing nationalism is progressive.

Indeed, an important asset of the anti-nation-state ideology is its powerful appeal to the left, whose internationalism has been disoriented by the collapse of any discernible socialist alternative to capitalism and by the disarray of liberation struggles in the South of the planet.

In the absence of any clear analysis of the contemporary world, the nation-state is readily identified as the cause of war, oppression and violations of human rights. In short, the only existing context for institutionalized democracy is demonized as the mere expression of a negative, exclusive ideology: "nationalism."

This is a structuralist rather than an historical construct, producing mechanical judgments. Whatever is smaller than the nation-state, or whatever transcends the nation-state, must be better. On the smaller scale, "identities" of all kinds, or "regions," generally undefined, are automatically considered more promising by much of the current generation. On the larger scale, the hope for democracy is being transferred to the European Union, or to international NGOs, or to theoretical institutions such as the proposed International Criminal Court.

The simplistic interpretation of the Yugoslav crisis as Serbian "aggression" against peaceful multi-cultural Europe is virtually unshakeable because it is not only credible, according to this ideology, but seems to confirm it.

It was this ideology that made it possible for the Croatian, Slovenian and Albanian secessionists and their supporters in Germany and the United States in particular to portray the Yugoslav conflict as the struggle of "oppressed little nations" to free themselves from aggressive Serbian nationalism. In fact, those "little nations" were by no means oppressed in Yugoslavia. The accusation could not stand up in any serious court of international law.[9] However, appeals to the dominant anti-state ideology led to frivolous acceptance in the West of the very grave act of accepting the *unnegotiated* break-up of an existing nation, Yugoslavia, by interpreting ethnic secession as a proper form of "self-determination," which it is not.[10] There is no parallel in recent diplomatic annals for such an irresponsible act, and as a precedent it can only promise endless bloody conflict around the world.

The New World Order

In fact, the break-up of Yugoslavia has served to discredit and further weaken the United Nations, while providing a new role for an expanding NATO. Germany had occupied Yugoslavia in 1941, setting up a Nazi-like nationalist regime in Croatia, enrolling Muslims in an SS division, and executing one hundred Serb hostages for each German killed by resistance guerillas. If someone had announced in 1989 that since the Berlin Wall had come down, Germany could now unite and send military forces back into Yugoslavia, people on the left would surely have raised objections. However, that is exactly what has happened, and people on the left have provided the ideological cover and excuse.

Perhaps dazed by the end of the Cold War, much of what remains of the left in the early nineties forgot the need for constant scrutiny of the geostrategic Realpolitik underlying great power policies and seemed to believe that the world politics would now be determined by purely moral considerations.

This has much to do with the privatization of "the left" in the past twenty years or so. The United States has led the way in this trend. Mass movements aimed at overall political action have declined, while single-issue movements have managed to continue. The single-issue movements in turn engender nongovernmental organizations (NGOs) which, because of the requirements of fundraising, need to adapt their causes to the mood of the times, in other words, to the dominant ideology and to the media. Massive fundraising is easiest for *victims*, using appeals to sentiment rather than to reason. Greenpeace has found that it can raise money more easily for baby seals than for combating the development of nuclear weapons. This fact of life steers NGO activity in certain directions, away from political analysis toward sentiment. On another level, the NGOs offer idealistic internationalists a rare opportunity to intervene all around the world in matters of human rights and human welfare.

And herein lies a new danger. Just as the "civilizing mission" of bringing Christianity to the heathen provided a justifying pretext for the imperialist conquest of Asia and Africa in the past, today the protection of "human rights" may be the cloak for a new type of imperialist military intervention worldwide. Certainly, human rights are an essential concern of the left. In a world now dedicated to brutal economic rivalry, where the rich get richer and the poor get poorer, human rights abuses can only increase. From this vast array of man's inhumanity to man, particular abuses may be selectively spotlighted by the media in places where corporate capitalism wishes to replace local rulers with more compliant defenders of global financial interests. In such situations, the humanitarian NGOs may play the role of the missionaries of the past—sincere, devoted people who need to be "protected," this time by NATO military forces. The Somali expedition provided a rough rehearsal (truly scandalous if examined closely) for this scenario. Closer to home base, Bosnia and Kosovo provide a vast experimental terrain for co-operation between NGOs and NATO.

Foreign news has always been much easier to distort than domestic news. Television coverage simply makes the distortion more convincing. TV crews, sent into strange places about which they know next to nothing, send back images of violence that give millions of viewers the impression that "everybody knows what is happening." Such an impression is worse than plain ignorance.

Today, world-wide media such as CNN openly put pressure on governments to respond to the "public opinion" which the media themselves create. Christine Amanpour tells the U.S. and European Union what they should be doing in Bosnia; to what extent this is co-ordinated with U.S. agencies is hard to tell. What is known is that the national secessionist movements in Yugoslavia, first the Albanians and Croatians and later the Muslims, hired an American public relations firm, Ruder Finn, to advance their causes by demonizing the Serbs [See Note 6]. Ruder Finn deliberately targeted certain publics, notably the American Jewish community, with a campaign likening Serbs to Nazis. Feminists were also clearly targeted by the Croatian nationalist campaign directed out of Zagreb to brand Serbs as rapists.[11] In short, people of naturally left, liberal, humanitarian persuasion are choice targets for the propaganda of all sorts of causes which are neither left, nor liberal, nor humanitarian. In the same way, sincere Christians in Europe and America were targeted for pro-imperialist propaganda a century ago.

Consumer beware. There is urgent need to take care to preserve genuine and legitimate efforts on behalf of human rights from instrumentalization. This is a delicate challenge. It is very difficult for people to admit having made a mistake. It is even more difficult to admit to ourselves that our own good intentions have been exploited. It is next to impossible for people who have actively taken up a cause to realize that they got it wrong.

NGOs and NATO, Hand In Hand

In former Yugoslavia, and especially in Bosnia-Herzegovina, Western NGOs have found a justifying role for themselves alongside NATO. They gain funding and prestige from the situation. Local employees of Western NGOs gain political and financial advantages over other local people. As a result, "democracy" is not the people's choice but whatever meets with the approval of outside donors. This breeds arrogance among the outside benefactors and cynicism among local people, who have the choice between opposing the outsiders or seeking to manipulate them. It is an unhealthy situation, and some of the most self-critical are aware of its dangers.[12]

Perhaps the most effectively arrogant NGO with regard to former Yugoslavia is the Vienna-based office of Human Rights

Watch/Helsinki. On September 18, 1997, that organization issued a long statement announcing in advance that the Serbian elections to be held three days later "will be neither free nor fair." This astonishing intervention was followed by a long list of measures that Serbia and Yugoslavia must carry out "or else" and that the international community must impose to discipline Serbia and Yugoslavia. These demands indicated an extremely broad interpretation of obligatory standards of "human rights" as applied to Serbia, although not, obviously to everybody else, since they included new media laws drafted "in full consultation with the independent media in Yugoslavia" as well as permission for all "unlicensed but currently operating radio and television stations to broadcast without interference."[13]

Human Rights Watch/Helsinki concluded its diatribe by calling on the Organization for Security and Cooperation in Europe (OSCE) to "deny Yugoslavia readmission to the OSCE until there are concrete improvements in the country's human rights record, including respect for freedom of the press, independence of the judiciary and minority rights, as well as cooperation with the International Criminal Tribunal for the former Yugoslavia."

Now, to mention only one of these demands, it is hard to see what measures would satisfy the demand to "respect freedom of the press," since press freedom already exists to an extent well beyond that in many other countries not being served with such an ultimatum. There exist in Serbia quite a range of media devoted to attacking the government. As of June 1998, there were 2,319 print publications and 101 radio and television stations in Yugoslavia, over twice the number that existed in 1992. Belgrade alone has 14 daily newspapers. Six state-controlled national dailies have a joint circulation of 180,000, compared to around 350,000 for seven leading opposition dailies.[14]

Moreover, the judiciary in Serbia is certainly no less independent than in Croatia or Muslim Bosnia, and almost certainly much more so. As for "minority rights," it would be hard to find a country anywhere in the world where they are better protected in both theory and practice than in Yugoslavia.[15]

For those who remember history, the Human Rights Watch/Helsinki ultimatum instantly brings to mind the ultimatum issued by Vienna to Belgrade after the Sarajevo assassination in 1914 as a pretext for the Austrian invasion which touched off World War I. The Serbian government gave in to almost all the demands, but was invaded anyway.[16]

The hostility of this new Vienna power, the International Helsinki Federation for Human Rights, toward Serbia, is evident in all its statements, and in those of its executive director, Aaron Rhodes. In a recent column for the *International Herald Tribune*, he wrote that Albanians in Kosovo "have lived for years under conditions similar to those suffered by Jews in Nazi-controlled parts of Europe just before World War II. They have been ghettoised. They are not free, but politically disenfranchised and deprived of basic civil liberties." The comparison could hardly be more incendiary, but the specific facts to back it up are absent. They are necessarily absent, since the accusation is totally false.[17]

This blanket condemnation of a government which, like it or not, was elected, in a country whose existence is threatened by German-backed secessionist movements, contrasts sharply with the traditional approach of the senior international human rights organization, Amnesty International.

What can be considered the traditional Amnesty International approach consists broadly in trying to encourage governments to enact and abide by humanitarian legal standards. It does this by calling attention to particular cases of injustice. It asks precise questions that can be answered precisely. It tries to be fair. It is no doubt significant that Amnesty International is a grassroots organization, which operates under the mandate of its contributing members, and whose rules preclude domination by any large donor.

Aaron Rhodes displays none of the scrupulous concern for facts which is the hallmark of Amnesty International. He deals in sweeping generalities.

For Yugoslavia, the Human Rights Watch/Helsinki approach differs fundamentally from that of Amnesty International in that it clearly aims not at calling attention to specific abuses that might be corrected, but at totally condemning the targeted State. By the excessive nature of its accusations, it does not ally with reformist forces in the targeted country so much as it undermines them. Its lack of balance, its rejection of any effort at remaining neutral on issues between conflicting parties contributes to a disintegrative polarization rather than to reconciliation and mutual understanding. It therefore contributes, deliberately or inadvertently, to a deepening cycle of violence that eventually may justify, or require, outside intervention.

This is an approach which, like its partner, economic globalization, breaks down the defenses and authority of weaker states. It does not help to enforce democratic institutions at the national level. The only democracy it recognizes is that of the "international community," which is summoned to act according to the recommendations of Human Rights Watch. This "international community," the so-called IC, is in reality no democracy. Its decisions are formally taken at NATO meetings. The IC is not even a "community"; the initials could more accurately stand for "imperialist condominium," a joint exercise of domination by the former imperialist powers, torn apart and weakened by two World Wars, now brought together under U.S. domination with NATO as their military arm. Certainly there are frictions between the members of this condominium, but so long as their rivalries can be played out within the IC, the price will be paid by smaller and weaker countries.

Media attention to conflicts in Yugoslavia is sporadic, dictated by Great Power interests, lobbies, and the institutional ambitions of "non-governmental organizations"—often linked to powerful governments—whose competition with each other for donations provides motivation for exaggeration of the abuses they specialize in denouncing. Yugoslavia, a country once known for its independent approach to socialism and international relations, the most prosperous country in Eastern

Central Europe, is being systematically reduced to an ungovernable chaos by Western support to secessionist movements. The emerging result is not a charming bouquet of independent little ethnic democracies, but rather a new type of joint colonial rule by the international community, enforced by NATO.

---

1. Diana Johnstone, "The Creeping Trend to Re-Balkanization," *In These Times*, 3-9 October 1994, p.9.
2. Diana Johnstone, "We Are All Serbo-Croats," *In These Times*, 3 May 1993, p.14.
3. "Ethnically defined" because, despite the argument accepted by the international community that it was the Republics that could invoke the right to secede, all the political arguments surrounding recognition of independent Slovenia and Croatia dwelt on the right of Slovenes and Croats as such to self-determination. Recognition of the internal administrative borders between the Republics as "inviolable" international borders was in effect a legal trick, contrary to international law, which turned the Yugoslav army into an "aggressor" within the boundaries its soldiers had sworn to defend, and which transformed the Serbs within Croatia and Bosnia, who opposed secession from their country, Yugoslavia, into secessionists.
4. This point is developed by Wolfgang Pohrt, "Entscheidung in Jugoslawien," in *Bei Andruck Mord: Die deutsche Propaganda und der Balkankrieg*, edited by Wolfgang Schneider, Konkret, Hamburg, 1997. A sort of climax was reached with the 8 July 1991 cover of the influential weekly *Der Spiegel*, depicting Yugoslavia as a "prison of peoples" with the title "Serb Terror."
5. The slogan was immortalized in the 1919 play by Austrian playwright Karl Kraus, "Die letzten Tage der Menschheit."
6. The role of the Washington public relations firm, Ruder Finn, has been widely celebrated. See especially: Jacques Merlino, *Les Vérités yougoslaves ne sont pas toutes bonnes à dire*, Albin Michel, Paris, 1993; and Peter Brock, "Dateline Yugoslavia: The Partisan Press," *Foreign Policy* #93, Winter 1993-94.

7. The 1993 Pulitzer Prize for international reporting was shared between the two authors of the most sensational "Serb atrocity stories" of the year: Roy Gutman of *Newsday* and John Burns of the *New York Times*. In both cases, the prize-winning articles were based on hearsay evidence of dubious credibility. Burns' story was no more than an interview with a mentally deranged prisoner in a Sarajevo jail, who confessed to crimes some of which have been since proved never to have been committed. See Peter Brock, op.cit.

8. Martin Lettmayer, "Da wurde einfach geglaubt, ohne nachzufragen," in *Serbien muss sterbien: Wahrheit und Lüge im jugoslawischen Bürgerkrieg*, edited by Klaus Bittermann, Tiamat, Berlin, 1994.

9. See: Barbara Delcourt & Olivier Corten, *Ex-Yougoslavie: Droit International, Politique et Idéologies*, Editions Bruylant, Editions de l'Université de Bruxelles, 1997. The authors, specialists in international law at the Free University of Brussels, point out that there was no basis under international law for the secession of the Yugoslav Republics. The principle of "self-determination" was totally inapplicable in those cases.

10. Within the European Parliament, leading champions of Croatian secession were, on the right, the heir to the defunct Austro-Hungarian Empire, Otto von Habsburg, and, on the left, the followers of Italian *Partito Radicale* leader Marco Pannella—both markedly "supranational" in their outlook.

11. No one denies that many rapes occurred during the civil wars in Croatia and Bosnia-Herzegovina, or that rape is a serious violation of human rights. The propaganda has consisted in focusing solely on Muslim and Croatian allegations against Serbs, accepting the most inflated figures without any evidence whatever, and worst of all, in accepting as fact the very questionable allegation that rape was a key part of "the Serb strategy of ethnic cleansing," designed to impregnate Muslim women. In addition to the internal contradictions of such a "strategy," which could logically only increase the population supposedly being "ethnically cleansed," no evidence has been produced either of its instigation in the form of commands or

of its results in the form of massive pregnancy. The late Nora Beloff, former chief political correspondent of the London *Observer*, described her own search for verification of the rape charges in a letter to *The Daily Telegraph* (January 19, 1993). The British Foreign Office conceded that the rape figures being bandied about were totally uncorroborated, and referred her to the Danish government, then chairing the European Union. Copenhagen agreed that the reports were unsubstantiated, but kept repeating them. Both said that the EU had taken up the "rape atrocity" issue at its December 1992 Edinburgh summit exclusively on the basis of a German initiative. In turn, Fran Wild, in charge of the Bosnian Desk in the German Foreign Ministry, told Ms. Beloff that the material on Serb rapes came partly from the Izetbegovič... government and partly from the Catholic charity Caritas in Croatia. No effort had been made to seek corroboration from more impartial sources.

Meanwhile, without further effort to establish the facts, a cottage industry has developed around the theme. See: Norma von Ragenfeld-Feldman, "The Victimization of Women: Rape and the Reporting of Rape in Bosnia-Herzegovina, 1992-1993," *Dialogue*, No 21, Paris, March 1997.

12. From his experience in Zagreb, British sociologist Paul Stubbs has written critically about "Humanitarian Organizations and the Myth of Civil Society" (*ArkŽin*, no 55, Zagreb, January 1996): "Particularly problematic is the assertion that NGOs are 'non-political' or 'neutral' and, hence, more progressive than governments which have vested interests and a political 'axe to grind'. [. . .] This 'myth of neutrality' might, in fact, hide the interests of a 'globalized new professional middle class' eager to assert its hegemony in the aid and social welfare market place. [. . .] The creation of a 'globalised new professional middle class' who, regardless of their country of origin, tend to speak a common language and share common assumptions, seems to be a key product of the 'aid industry'. In fact, professional power is reproduced through claims to progressive alliance with social movements and the civil society whereas, in fact, the shift towards NGOs is part of a new residualism in

social welfare which, under the auspices of financial institutions such as the World Bank and the International Monetary Fund, challenges the idea that states can meet the welfare needs of all. [. . .] A small number of Croatian psycho-socially oriented NGOs have attained a level of funding, and a degree of influence, which is far in excess of their level of service, number of beneficiaries, quality of staff, and so on, and places them in marked contrast to those providing services in the governmental sector. One Croatian NGO, linked to a U.S. partner organisation, has, for example, received a grant from USAID for over 2 million U.S. dollars to develop a training programme in trauma work. The organisation, the bulk of whose work [. . .] is undertaken by psychology and social work students, now has prime office space in Zagreb, large numbers of computers and other technical equipment, and is able to pay its staff more than double that which they would obtain in the state sector."

13. At the time, some 400 radio and television stations had been operating in Yugoslavia with temporary licenses or none at all. The vast majority are in Serbia, a country of less than ten million inhabitants on a small territory of only 88,361 square kilometers.

14. Figures from "State Media Circulation Slips," on page 3 of the June 8, 1998 issue of *The Belgrade Times*, an English-language weekly. There is no doubt that press diversity in Serbia has profited from the extremely acrimonious contest between government-backed media (which are not as bad or as uniform as alleged) and opposition media seeking foreign backing. Without this ongoing battle, the government would almost certainly have managed to reduce press pluralism considerably, but it is also fair to point out that the champions of independent media need to keep exaggerating the perils of their situation in order to attract ongoing financial backing from the West, notably from the European Union and the Soros Foundation. Private foreign capital is also present: the relatively mass circulation tabloid *Blic* is German-owned.

15. Serbia is constitutionally defined as the nation of all its citizens, and not "of the Serbs" (in contrast to constitutional provi-

sions of Croatia and Macedonia, for instance). In addition, the 1992 Constitution of the Federal Republic of Yugoslavia (Serbia and Macedonia) as well as the Serbian Constitution guarantee extensive rights to national minorities, notably the right to education in their own mother tongue, the right to information media in their own language and the right to use their own language in proceedings before a tribunal or other authority. These rights are not merely formal, but are effectively respected, as is shown by, for instance, the satisfaction of the 400,000-strong Hungarian minority and the large number of newspapers published by national minorities in Albanian, Hungarian and other languages. Romani (Gypsies) are by all accounts better treated in Yugoslavia than elsewhere in the Balkans. Serbia has a large Muslim population of varied nationalities, including refugees from Bosnia and a native Serb population of converts to Islam in Southern Kosovo, known as Goranci, whose religious rights are fully respected.

16. After obtaining support from Berlin and the Vatican for war against Serbia, Vienna on July 23, 1914, delivered a 48-hour ultimatum to Belgrade containing a list of ten demands, of which the Serbian government accepted all but one: participation of Austrian officials in suppressing anti-Austrian movements on Serbian territory. This refusal was the official reason for Austria's declaration of war on July 28, 1914, which began World War I. See Ralph Hartmann, *Die ehrlichen Makler*, Dietz, Berlin, 1998, pp.31-33.

17. The comparison between Jews in the Warsaw ghetto and Albanians in Kosovo is outrageous. The terms "ghetto" and "apartheid" are used to win international support by the very Albanian nationalist leaders who have created the separation between populations by leading their community to boycott all institutions of the state in order to strengthen their claims to secede and form an independent state on the way to merger with neighboring Albania. The Kosovo Albanians have kept Slobodan Milošević… and his party in office by refusing to use their electoral rights, which have never been denied, and which if exercised could have ensured them the balance of power in

the Serbian parliament. Ethnic Albanians who have dared to exercise those rights and have held office in Kosovo have been assassinated by armed Albanian separatists.

THE MEDIA AND SERBS IN A NEW EUROPEAN ARCHITECTURE

Modern Media — The Fourth Branch of NATO

ZORAN PETROVIC-PIROCANAC

> The Serbs are two dimensional people with a craving for simplicity and an ideology so basic it can be understood without effort. They need enemies, not friends, to focus their two-dimensional ideas. Life for them is a simple tune, never an orchestration, or even a pleasant harmony. Animals make use of their resources with far greater felicity than these retarded creatures, whose subscription to the human race is well in arrears.

This is, ladies and gentlemen, the dominant way world intellectuals and media describe my ugly, ethno-fundamentalist, murderous, baby-killer people, the Serbs. The world is really in a serious trouble if even a famous actor, novelist, columnist, film director, painter, singer-and ambassador of UNESCO, sees any people this way. This is how Sir Peter Ustinov described my people in his column in *The European* in June 1993. His words will join the shameful anthology of racist and fascist expressions in the world media at the end of the Millenium.

And this is only one of numerous examples of the activities of the modern media in exercising its profound role in the Balkan wars.

A new source of all evil, are these Serbs. Even in the children's magazines (such as the French *Les Journal des Enfants)* and school books, adults are teaching future generations how to recognize the evil Serbs. This journalism is no longer what I learned from the founder of *Le Monde*, Hubert Beuve-Mery, and other journalists of his stature. This was clear to me in Sarajevo, during the night between February 28th and March 1st, 1992—the "night of the barricades," when the Serbs, Muslims and Croats divided up their city with about 20 barricades, creating another Beirut, at least in the geographical sense of East-West, because at that moment the killing hadn't started yet.

The crowd of reporters that had come to the city in large numbers the week before in the anticipation of trouble, to pour oil on the flames in their reports, scattered when the first barricades went up. I set out alone in the company of English and French reporters from the major media in their respective countries to see the barricades. In the area of Bembasa, near Bas Carsija, around midnight, several of us saw some people distributing new, well-oiled AK-47 automatic rifles from a large truck to the Sarajevo radio-taxi drivers, Moslems from Sandzak. The scene was impressive, because from the center, calls were continually being sent out to the radio-taxi drivers to come to collect the weapons. On the night of February 28th, 1992, I did not see a more newsworthy event, clearly indicating that fighting would break out and turn into a real war.

Neither the English radio correspondent nor the French television correspondent in their noon (and evening) reports on the March 1st, 1992 mentioned a word of what we had all seen the previous night.

Journalistic ethics had been forgotten, because what they had seen did not fit in with the reporting cliches that were required of them. And one knew what kind of reports were required at the Sarajevo Literary Authors' Club later that evening, where reporters talked of Serb aggression and wild mountain people who were attacking the peaceful city of Sarajevo. It was the cafe preview of what one of the stars of the Bosnian war, Sir Martin Bell, recently defined as the journalism of attachment.

Today an MP in British Parliament and "one of the most even-handed journalists" (as wrote Christopher Dunkley in *Financial Times* on September 20, 1997), Martin Bell gives a name to the new style journalism in his essay in *The British Journalism Review* (vol.8, no 1,1997):

"By this I mean a journalism that cares as well as knows; that is aware of its responsibilities; and will not stand neutrally between good and evil, right and wrong, the victim and the oppressor."

Fellow colleague Dunkley says that "the worrying thing about 'the journalism of attachment' is that it is being preached—and, worse, practiced—by hard news reporters."

The event which most inspired "the journalism of attachment" was the war in Bosnia, says Dunkley, "with one side demonized, the other sanctified, and the public in other countries often encouraged to believe that Serbs alone were responsible for atrocities and all other parties were blameless. . . . It is bad enough that reporters are starting to believe that they should reflect their emotional involvement in what they report. From there it is only a step, and perhaps not a conscious one, to the selection and manipulation of the facts to favor one side. Worse is what appears to be the endorsement of this new 'Emotion is important-let's get involved' attitude among news executives at the highest level."

Dunkley concludes: "Television news reporters should continue to be passionately interested in events but wholly dispassionate about them. Indeed, they should, in the true meaning of the word, always be completely disinterested."

Within the mainstream media of the developed world, this principle has been discarded. In the process, the battle for a journalistic deontology has, I am afraid, been lost.

My analyses during the wars in the former Yugoslavia and the continuing secessionist war in the Serb province of Kosovo and Metohija indicate that the media played the role of a fourth branch of NATO's army, acting rather like an additional task force. In countless situations, the powerful, modern propaganda machine, like CNN's real-time global TV, "the new Coca-Cola at the end of the Millennium," and the other vast TV networks, forgot the basic ethics of our profession, the simple truth and facts. Sadly, most media outlets adopted the parrot-like manner of imitating the all-powerful CNN.

When CNN transmitted carefully formulated and precisely aimed news items, most of the other media outlets blindly followed with amazing uniformity. The "free world," through institutions like the American Foundation and the National Endowment for Democracy, "imposes democracy throughout the world," taking members of the old communist nomenclature in Russia and Serbia into its service.

The dominant journalism of America, which propagates a military concept of the American Way of War, is also applying the ideal of "new internationalism." The media are extremely important for successfully imprinting a view of the world as the Americans see it. Their new internationalism is modernized to accommodate an era of global TV, Internet and the multimedia, making it more digestible and more effective in its messages.

For such a media orientation, the war in Bosnia (and new war in Kosovo and Metohija) directly served (and serves) the U.S. State Department and the foreign ministries of its allies as a propaganda testing-ground, rather like the testing of new weapons.

This new doctrine propagated from Washington has been subsequently supported, without question, by the mainstream media, forming the basis for many newspaper articles beginning in 1991 and early 1992. For the first time in a long while, the media throughout the entire world functioned synergistically. Journalists from America and Iran, England and Libya, Turkey and Russia, France and Algeria, worked hand in glove. The target was "designed in the laboratory" long before the conflict—it was the Bosnian Serbs, the "bad guys"—who were to be the victims on the altar of New World journalism.

In order to clarify this statement, think for a moment of the possibility of the entire world media today openly rooting: for the independence of the Basque region of Spain; for the secession of Corsica from France; for the secession of Padania from Italy; or of Quebec from Canada. It's hard to imagine, isn't it?

The new world journalism brings a profile of journalistic stars like Christiane Amanpour, who goes to Tehran wearing a veil according to Islamic custom. This pays court, on behalf of the State Department and American business, to a sacred totalitarian principle, which is equally as dangerous to the future of our planet as the bloodthirsty multinational companies.

At the end of the millenium, the media have become the brutal means of propaganda for the so-called open society, which is simply the weapon of multinational capital that devastates everything in its way, often provoking wars in the process.

The majority of mainstream media in today's world, unfortunately, have simply become the instrument of the planet's media moguls, the political commissars of the insatiable global markets and multinational companies.

I remember the unsavory episode from the Belgrade "Hyatt," immediately before the beginning of Holbrooke's improvised press conference on the 7th floor. The Bosnian war had reached its culmination and an infinitely arrogant Holbrooke was furiously trying to measure up to his teacher, Henry Kissinger. We were all waiting for him in the Hyatt hallway, on the stairs of the 7th floor. Peter Arnett, "the star of Baghdad" (because Sadam Hussein had evidently permitted him to stay as part of a deal with CNN and the State Department) was beside me. Holbrooke saw him, and as Arnett came down the stairs they hugged and before the crowd of journalists, Holbrooke, as I remember, said: "Hi, Peter. I've just read your book. It is excellent!"

That is the new "open society journalism." Being on intimate terms with politicians has obviously become not only acceptable but also required, despite the fact that such an act spells the beginning of the end to serious journalism. I have not yet seen this fashion being accepted among European colleagues, but considering the McDonald-like speed with which everything the Americans launch spreads, it won't be long before it catches on in Europe as well.

Indeed, we should ask ourselves whether we are all going to be hugging and kissing ministers, special envoys and presidents, soon, and then presume to present credible, objective reports. Is this the future of our profession?

From the very first moment of the war in the former Yugoslavia, I never failed to be amazed at the measure of conviction with which these correspondents regularly and exclusively attributed the blame for all the events in the war to the Serbs, and compounded it with an "aggression from Serbia" catch-phrase. It is interesting to note that the so-called "aggression from Serbia" was successfully marketed, despite the fact that Serbia never sent troops to Bosnia while between 30,000 and 50,000 regular Croatian Army troops had been in operation on the territory of Bosnia-Herzegovina from the very outbreak of the war in 1992. This key military fact remains concealed to this day.

Silence is also an important concept in the collegial dance between the warmakers and the media. In the former Yugoslavia, this was the most frequent method used by journalists. Even the birds knew about the Islamic volunteers, the mujahedin, throughout the entire Bosnian war, but it was not until the American troops appeared after the Dayton Agreement that news about them began to emerge. American and western reporters had U.S. congressional documents at their disposal describing the activities of Islamic terrorists, whose numbers reached 30,000 in some periods of the war. These are murderous characters, against whom the western states and their media raise an outcry when American soldiers are killed in an explosion, such as the one in Dhahran in Saudi Arabia, or when a bomb is planted in the World Trade Center in New York.

When the terror is directed to Yugoslav territory, it does not bother the press. They did not write a single word about Clinton and his White House advisers turning a blind eye throughout the war to the continual Iranian shipment of weapons to the Muslims by way of the Adriatic Sea and through Zagreb and Tuzla airports. It was not until the U.S. intelligence services learned of Islamic terrorist plans to attack American

troops in Bosnia that tne media began to write about the mujahedin. Similarly the western media's inexplicable persistence
in promoting Izetbegovic's purely Islamic vision for Bosnia (he
was a member of the militant pro-Iranian Fedayin'e'Islami organization for over two decades) conflicts with the public story
of "the struggle for a multiethnic and civil state of Bosnia."

It is simply incredible that American and world media never
wrote about analyses of the Congressional Task Force for Terrorism and Unconventional Warfare, and not a word about
Yossef Bodansky's precise work on the activities of mujahedin
on the territory of the former Yugoslavia. Also, not a single
word on Bodansky's book—*Some Call It Peace*—a precious
document on this war, which could have changed many prejudices.

Professor Pierre Guislain of the Ecole Nationale d'Art de
Guerre speaks of modern Man being lost in a world that is pro-
gressing from skepticism into a form of "generalized cynicism." Essentially, the West no longer believes in the existence
of any reality beyond its political fiction, tirelessly generated to
cover the world. The show has never been so total. Even war
has become a show, seen in the warmth of one's own home,
from a distance, in a purified, dramatized, simplified version.

Today's media systematically resort to the historical analogy (Sadam-Hitler, Serbs-Nazis, Mauthausen-Omarska), "and
that has enabled western propaganda to reach its essential goal-
to legitimize war; to make it seem necessary, even rightful, in
the eyes of the public." (Guislain)

Another French author, Jacques Allul, confirms the truth of
the media-driven war in the former Yugoslavia, that this corporate journalism, this politically monitored media frequently
acted in accordance with the suggestions of the political establishment. The "journalisme austere," the rhetoric of objective
presentation, the journalism of objective intention, was tragically absent in war reports from the former Yugoslavia. Instead, we have received pure propaganda, a media totalitarian-
ism.

Jacques Allul says: "Propaganda is essentially totalitarian; not in the sense of being part of the totalitarian state, but because it has a tendency to absorb everything. Consequently, in the hands of democracy, it always becomes a weapon of self-destruction."

What else than propaganda were the writings of leading newspapers like the *New York Times* a few years ago. Early in the Bosnian conflict, these newspapers reported that 20,000 Moslem women had been raped in Bosnia. By the end of the conflict the figure had risen to 80,000. The Serbs, of course, were blamed for this. Indeed, an American actually won the Pulitzer Prize for spreading disinformation.

We still remember John Burns, the *New York Times* reporter who won this prestigious journalism award for his false accusations against a mentally disturbed, impotent and sick man, Herak, who had been certified as unfit for military service. Even today, this poor invalid, and some other Serbs, are rotting in a Sarajevo jail, through no fault of their own. Newsday reporter Roy Gutman used a devious, even impermissible method of hyperbolizing the stories about the prison camps, and Burns made use of an invalid to weave gruesome stories about murders which this poor unfortunate never committed. I believe that calling on the Pulitzer Foundation to restore the authentic principles of journalism is one of the most urgent tasks of our profession. We should approach the Pulitzer Foundation and request a public debate on confiscating the award that was presented to a person who degraded our profession.

The scandalous and immoral silence of the press continues, even though photographs were published of Herak's alleged victims grazing their sheep in the suburbs of Sarajevo. Apart from one article by Chris Hedges in the *Times,* no one writes about Herak anymore. Once upon a time, many people had exclusive reports on the Herak case. Today, even international organizations like the UNHCR, the UN, SFOR, and Westendorp are silent.

Esteemed colleagues, how do we view this drastic attack on the deontology of journalism, this annihilation of our profession, led by the powerful American media machine? Gutman and Burns are synonyms with the implosion and total erosion of our profession. Their manipulations were well-known to the media community, but everyone remained silent.

Pulitzer remained silent too. Let me remind you, in this regard, that we currently celebrate 100 years of so-called "tabloid journalism" or "yellow journalism." The American press is a progenitor of this corrupt form of journalism, and two celebrated names are synonymous with it: Joseph Pulitzer, publisher of the *New York World*, and William Randolph Hearst, publisher of the *New York Journal*. These are the pioneers of "yellow journalism."

Hearst dispatched the famous illustrator Frederic Remington to Cuba to cover the Cuban guerilla uprising against Spain. Remington wired to Hearst that "there will be no war. I wish to return." The answer from his boss was: "You furnish the pictures, and I will furnish the war." Which Hearst did, with screaming headlines and frequently inaccurate articles that fanned the U.S. conflict with Spain. But the final rush to war was orchestrated by Pulitzer's New York World, which used the explosion on the U.S.S Maine in 1898 to bring war with Spain within weeks.

William Randolph Hearst came to Bad Nauheim in September 1934 to bathe in its waters. Hitler sent his two most trusted Nazi propagandists, Hanfstangel and Rosenberg, to ask Hearst how nazism could present a better image in the U.S. Hearst agreed to travel to Berlin to meet with Hitler, and the result was a $400,000 a year deal signed between Hearst and Goebels. After that, Hearst completely changed the editorial policy of his nineteen daily newspapers. Effective the same month he got the money. Hearst also instructed all Hearst press correspondents in Germany, including those of INS (International News Service) to report happenings in Germany only in a "friendly" manner. (According to William Davis, author of *Shadow of Swastika*).

If we replace the word "friendly" with "unfrendly," we see exactly the same media orchestration with respect to Yugoslavia. The question is who today pays for this distorted picture and who colors Serbs as the worst kind of sub-humans?

This cliche of propaganda journalism is being repeated regarding Kosovo and Metohia today. The Serbs are again the target and, as Chancellor Helmut Kohl declared, "the whole international community has the task of restraining the Serbs." And the most powerful weapon for restraint, as we know, is the media.

From the very outset, the media have written supportively about the ethnic Albanians' liberation struggle, although this classic secessionist movement attempts to change the borders of a sovereign state. The fact that such analysis is considered inappropriate with respect to the British problem in Northern Ireland, the Spanish problem with the Basques, or the French problem in Corsica shows that a double standard is again being applied exclusively against the Serbs.

The media, reminiscent of the Hearst-era support for German expansionism, are helping to accelerate secession and change the borders of Serbia. All this in anticipation of the formation of the so-called new architecture of Europe.

The language of western journalists when describing the Balkan conflict has begun to take on an air of unreality. Irresponsibly, ignorantly, and rudely, the world media apply linguistic perversion to make the secessionist struggle in Kosovo more effective. Take the example of Laura Rosen of CBS News who informed her audience last March that "Serbia annexed Kosovo in 1989." How can a sovereign nation annex one of its provinces?

Today, defying all the laws of linguistics, the newly created term those living in Bosnia-Herzegovina is "Bosniak," and the imaginary Bosniaks have been recognized officially as a nation. Until the war in the former Yugoslavia, these terms did not exist. There is no Bosniak language in linguistic theory or practice. The language spoken in Bosnia is Serbo-Croatian or Croato-Serbian. And, it is only through the successful propaganda of the legendary PR company Ruder Finn, the true victor in the war in Bosnia, that the Islamic leaders in Bosnia have managed to impose this ridicule of all the basic laws of linguistics.

This "guerilla terminology" is continuing even today, in a very sophisticated manner, regarding Kosmet, the correct abbreviation for Kosovo and Metohia. Just as one often hears Bosnia and Herzegovina referred to as simply Bosnia, the name Kosovo is popularly used. But in official documents, the word Kosmet is obligatorily used in Serbia. Nonetheless, the world media never use this term, which, given the sensitivity of the region, is scandalous. The U.S. Congress has gone so far as to adopt legislation regarding this Serb region which officially uses the word KOSOVA instead of the correct Kosmet, or at least the popular term Kosovo. The bill in question, adopted December 15, 1997, says sanctions against Serbia and Montenegro are extended unless a "separate identity" is granted for "Kosova." Such incorrect language in official documents is a form of revisionist history.

Kosova is only a derivative from the Serbian name of Kosovo, and in the Albanian language it has no particular meaning. But it is important for the secessionists, because they have begun using it to build an artificial legitimacy. The media have irresponsibly encouraged that legitimacy and are slowly and artfully shifting their terminology to directly interfere with the sovereignty of a nation. The "Voice of America" is cunningly testing out the new media treatment of the KLA, ethnic rebellion's armed wing, and the mainstream media are moving toward open support for the KLA. How would it look, if we were to write sympathetically about the National Liberation Front of Corsica (FLNC), or Herri Batasuna's National Unity of Vascos (Basques), or the IRA in Ireland?

There is virtually no media analysis of the origins of the Kosmet violence. According to American analyst Yossef Bodansky, one of the world's top experts on terrorism and Islam, "the current escalation of sectarian violence in Kosovo is not a sudden event, but a result of thorough preparations in Albania and Bosnia-Herzegovina, as well as throughout the Muslim World."

He speaks of Iranian deep penetration of Albania, of the Albanian Arab Islamic Bank, (AAIB), which dominates the Albanian financial system and bolsters Kosovo Albanian secessionism. Iranians also continue to expand their training and recruitment in Albania, preparing more and better operatives for infiltration into both Kosovo and Western Europe. Iranians and other Arab Islamist allies (like Osama Bin Laden) have established training camps to prepare Albanian mujahedin from both sides of the border.

Tehran has transferred many groups of Arab and Albanian mujahedin from Bosnia and elsewhere. By late 1997, a large number had crossed into Kosovo, either directly or via the Former Yugoslav Republic of Macedonia. Tehran directly helps train and arm Ushtria Clirimtare e Kosoves (KLA). They even organize advanced military training for ethnic Albanian officers of KLA with Al Quds forces and in Iran with Pasdaran (Revolutionary Guards).

Iranian spiritual leader Ayatollah Khamenei gave instructions to his intelligence services about comprehensive military assistance to enable Muslims to achieve the independence of the province of Kosovo. Thanks to the Iranian influence (openly tolerated by Americans, Germans and Russians), the KLA became increasingly Islamist. Today, Iranian influence is predominant among ethnic Albanian KLA.

Western political leaders and the world media are silent on these problems, an incredible circumstance given the sensitivity of such matters.

Why is the danger from Iranian terrorists only a concern when American occupying forces are directly threatened in Bosnia? Why is media attention appropriate with respect to Dhahran anti-American terrorism, but inappropriate with respect to Islamists in Kosmet? Why do the media ignore such an important political trend?

The evidence suggests that the media's selective coverage of world events plays an essential role in extending American power.

As the Secretary of State and unofficial World Cop Madeleine Albright, said: "The United States stands ready in every region on every continent to strengthen the system of law, political and economic freedom and respect for human rights that enables nations not only to exist, but also to progress. In that effort, we will expect others to do their fair share, but we will not hesitate to lead."

Tell us which region and which continent, say the media, and we will prepare the way.

PART FOUR

CULTURAL IMPERIALISM:

THIRD WORLD PERSPECTIVE

THE MASS MEDIA AND THE MEDIA OF THE MASSES

JEAN-BERTRAND ARISTIDE

During the early part of this century, European scientists studying the nature of subatomic phenomena faced a deep and almost shattering intellectual challenge. They found that the concepts of classical physics on which they relied were inadequate to describe the phenomena they encountered. Einstein described the experience this way. "All my attempts to adapt the theoretical foundations of physics to this new type of knowledge failed completely. It is as if the ground had been pulled out from under us." In this new physics of relativity and quantum theory, space and time were not absolute. Matter did not behave consistently, cause and effect could no longer be definitely located. The physicists were forced to make a giant conceptual leap.

For the media to emerge from their Dark Age will require a leap of similar magnitude. Making this leap will require imagination and an opening of the mind. The dominant paradigms reproduced by the mass media regarding democracy, development, progress, and growth do not explain or even respond to the realities we face in our time. We must observe them from a new angle.

Today's media report that democracy has triumphed throughout Latin America. It is true that throughout the 1980s and '90s dictator after dictator fell, election after election was held and democratic governments were installed throughout the continent. But is this the whole story? What about the consequences of neoliberalism?

Objectively speaking, in the South transitions to democracy coincided with the most severe economic crisis of the century.

In Latin America, 240 million people live in utter poverty, an increase of more than 120 million since 1980; 1.6 billion people live in countries with shrinking or stagnating economies, where real wages are often lower than they were in 1970. However, the most staggering statistics of our time are those that represent the gap between the world's rich and the world's poor. In 1960, the richest twenty percent of the world's population had seventy percent of the world's wealth. Today they have eighty-five percent. In 1960 the poorest twenty percent of the world's people had 2.4% of the world's wealth, and today that has shrunk to just 1.1%. And it is likely to get worse, not better, in the coming years. From 1995 to the year 2001, during which global income is expected to increase by an estimated $212 to $510 billion, the less developed countries are expected to lose up to $600 million a year in income.

This is the great untold news story of the century. The poor are getting poorer; the rich are getting richer, at a pace unprecedented in history.

In many countries of the South, states are saddled with insurmountable debt. They are being forced to rapidly divest resources, abandon the economic field to market forces, and play a smaller and smaller role in the provision of basic human services. Neoliberal and structural adjustment policies mean that they have neither the money nor the will to invest in their people.

For the 46 countries of Sub Saharan Africa, foreign debt service is currently four times their combined governmental health and education budgets. The dire human consequences of structural adjustment policies is perhaps the biggest story of the 1980s and 1990s. Yet the toll of human suffering remains hidden from international view, except on those rare occasions when it explodes into view as it did in Indonesia two weeks ago.

Today, worship of the market and its invisible hand has become a world religion in which economic growth is the only measure of human progress. The dominant discourse regarding the meaning of progress is so constricted, so narrow as to represent a global crisis of imagination. Within this discourse the human being fades from view.

Consider this: Last year a newborn baby was found in a pile of garbage by one of our Haitian teachers. Ants had eaten part of the child's hand. The teacher, Rose, is a poor woman. She already has two children. Yet she spontaneously adopted the baby, naming him Ti Moise (little Moses). This woman teaches us that beyond market values there are human values. No child can be thrown away.

Study after study has shown that the burden of structural adjustment falls disproportionately on women. By the same token, it is no exaggeration to say that the survival of the people rests on the strength of women. If we look at worldwide income generated through the informal sector, that is income not counted in GDP, it is sixteen trillion dollars a year, and of this, eleven trillion is generated by women.

Studies around the world have shown that when household budgets are in the hands of women, they are more likely to be spent for primary needs (food, education, and health care). I would hazard to predict that when the budgets of nations are in the hands of women we will see the same result.

Democracy today risks being rapidly outpaced by the galloping global economy. We must take a giant leap forward. We must democratize democracy. The major media often equate democracy with the holding of elections every four or five years. The news cameras duly arrive to film the rite. But elections are only the exam, testing the health of our systems. Voter participation is the grade. School is in session every day. Only the day-to-day participation of the people at all levels of society and governance can breathe life into democracy and create the possibility for people to play a significant role in shaping the state and the society that they want. Media in all forms play a critical role in democratizing democracy. It is often the vehicle for communication between the governed and the governors.

Twelve years ago we founded Lafanmi Selavi, a center for street children in Port-au-Prince. Today there are over 400 boys and girls at Lafanmi Selavi. In 1996 they opened a radio station. Radyo Timoun (Little People's Radio) is their radio station. It broadcasts their music, their news, and their commentaries 14 hours a day. The station allows them to participate. And in a world in which a child dies of hunger every 3 seconds, children must speak out. I was recently listening to a commentary on democracy prepared by three eleven-year-old girls. They asked what was democracy? I thought I should share their answer with you. They defined democracy as food, school, and health care for everyone. Simplistic or visionary? For them democracy in Haiti doesn't mean a thing unless the people can eat.

When decisions are made for the people and without the people, they are most often made against the people. The voices of the huge majority of the poor are not echoed in the mass media. But they know what they want. Like Berthony, a very bright six-year old who is one of the co-directors of Radyo Timoun. One day he was learning English. The children repeated a simple phrase, "Give me water." When they said it correctly they got chocolate. But when it was Bertony's turn he said, "Give me Chocolate." They asked him, "Why don't you say water?" He answered, "I am not thirsty." A child speaking the truth.

Women, children and the poor must be the subjects, not the objects of history. Put in other words, they must make the news. Their voices can echo via their own media. Their participation will democratize democracy, bringing the word back to its full meaning: Demos meaning people, Cratei meaning to govern.

Within the Haitian context, journals like *Haïti Progrès* help to deepen understanding of economic issues. At the Aristide Foundation for Democracy in Haiti, through our bi-monthly newspaper *Diyite* (*Dignity*) we are creating a forum for written participation. The journal is in Creole, the language which everyone in Haiti understands, and sells for just one gourde (about 6 cents U.S.) with the slogan "Dignity is priceless, but the journal *Dignity* is a bargain." Our last issue carried a front-page editorial on structural adjustment. We quoted an IMF study completed in September 1997, which found that in developing countries undergoing structural adjustment programs from 1981-1995, per capita income stagnated. While in developing countries free of the IMF, per capita income rose. This simple and critical piece of information coming from the IMF itself needs to reach the poor.

The other great untold story of our day is the heroic survival of the people under the weight of neoliberalism. We invite you to Haiti where, in the poorest country in the Western Hemisphere, with 80% of the population living on less than $220 U.S. a year, suicide is practically unheard of. Warmth of character, wealth of humor, dignity, solidarity; in Haiti we are rich in these.

While the major media does not report on the richness of our culture, they do print story after story on the supposedly huge amounts of development aid that flow to the Third World. In fact, we know that global spending priorities remain grotesquely skewed. It is estimated that only 10% of development aid goes towards meeting primary human needs (education, health care, clean water, and sanitation). This amount represents less than what the industrialized world spends on athletic shoes each year. And it would take only six billion dollars a year, from now to the year 2000, in addition to what is already spent, to put every child in the world in school. Does this seem like a lot? It represents less than 1% of world military spending.

For us the seeds of hope, the seeds of change, lie with the people. That is why in 1994, in a true expression of Demos + Cratie, government and people together, we dismantled the Haitian army, bringing Haiti's military spending down to zero, an historic step in our struggle to eradicate poverty.

The United Nations Human Development Report for 1997 tells us that poverty is no longer inevitable. The world has the material and natural resources, the know-how and people to make a poverty-free world a reality in less than a generation. I quote, "The costs of eradicating poverty are less than people imagine: about 1% of global income and no more than 2-3% of national income in all but the poorest nations."

This is very good news. It ought to make headlines. The media in all its forms will likely play a critical role in mobilizing the international political will needed to meet this challenge.

Will this require a giant leap in thinking? Perhaps, but I believe we, like Einstein, are poised on the edge of a new era.

If creating the political will needed to eradicate poverty seems impossible, reflect on this: During the coup, while I was in exile, a member of our parliament who was fiercely opposed to our return declared on television that I would never return. The people should stop talking about Aristide, he said, for when did you ever see an egg laid by a chicken go back into the chicken? After my return, the people painted murals on walls throughout the country: a huge chicken, a huge egg, and a finger pushing the egg back into the chicken.

The impossible became possible.

PUBLIC ACCESS TO INFORMATION IN INDIA

MANIK MUKHERJEE

There can be no denial that since the 1980s the world has been experiencing a phenomenal change in the structure and content of media information. We can now envisage the Information Superhighway or Global Information Infrastructure (GII) bringing most individuals instantaneously in touch with any data or with any person from every corner of the globe, simply via a personal computer. It was claimed that this would help do away with the governmental bureaucratic clutch of censorship on media and information, making communication and the acquisition of knowledge more competitive and democratic. For instance, the Chairperson of the Telecom Regulatory Authority of India announced, "Competition leads to choice and in choice lies the best interests of consumers."

This reliance on competition raises two questions: How much access does the public have to the information being purveyed globally by the media, including the electronic network, and what kind of information is accessible to them? I propose to address these questions after considering the type of changes that have already taken place and will continue to do so in the future.

These changes involve the restructuring of national media and communication industries, and the overwhelming trend toward privatization, commercialization and globalization. The global commercial media market claims to be in tune with the spirit of competition in a free market economy, but it is dominated by a few dozens of TNCs (Transnational Corporations) of which U.S.-based conglomerates form a major portion. These firms produce films, books, recorded music, and TV programs. They own newspapers, magazines, radio stations, cable companies, and TV networks. They are often connected to electronics manufacturing firms and may have holdings in sports, amusement parks, retail outlets, and leisure enterprises. In short the market is oligopolistic and bars any newcomers.

In the U.S., the Telecommunications Act of 1996 has deregulated all communication industries; it permits the market, and not public policy, to determine the course of the system. We can also cite our own example from India, where during the last two decades there have been continuous and distinct efforts to privatize and deregulate broadcasting services under the slogan TINA (There Is No Alternative). Prasarbharati and the Broadcasting Authority of India (BAI) are the two brainchildren of the government, supposedly conceived to autonomously regulate the media. Prasarbharati was conceived as a broadcasting unit accountable to parliament, while BAI is planned not as a broadcasting unit itself, but as a coordinating body for many private broadcasting institutions.

Even before implementation of their scheme, which faces opposition from the people, the government had already allowed Indian private TV channels to use foreign satellites (ATN, AsiaNet, Sony, Sun etc.). Foreign channels like CNN, Star TV, MTV, and TNT of Time Warner have also been permitted to work via the Indian Satellite INSAT or have been allotted prime time in the Metro Channel of the government-owned DOORDARSHAN itself. The result is obvious: the Indian people can watch the World Cup being played anywhere in the world via the STAR SPORTS or ESPN or can watch films on SONY, a private Indian channel, but only on pay-per-view. They cannot see the victorious Indian team playing in their own city by switching on their normal DOORDARSHAN channels.

The new BJP-led union government in India insists that foreign and Indian private channels receive uplinking from Indian satellites and plans to issue a license system to control their programs; it harps on Hindutwa (Hindu ethos), BJP's vote-catching slogan. This move in no way opposes privatization. It only intends to exert pressure on the foreign and private channels to allow BJP to use them for their parliamentary ends.

The present growth of the global media market may be summarized by a few points. The info-communication sector (ICS) is now a major part of the global economy, with an output in 1994 of around 1.5 trillion dollars. But what is more important is that the ICS grows at twice the rate of the rest of the global economy. And in this global media market a few TNCs dominate and are naturally pitted against competition and democracy. Two of the largest global media firms, Time Warner and Disney, both doubled their annual revenues from 1994 to 1996, partly through internal growth, but mainly via acquisitions and mergers. Every such merger is accompanied by an increase in the strength of the bigger partner, therefore adding to further centralization and domination. This invariably leads to a massive reduction in the workforce.

Such are the structural changes. We must realize the real significance of them. The print media was brought under monopoly control long ago. The other forms of media and communication networks are now being privatized and deregulated. But privatization does not mean access to information.

Next we will look at the basic changes in content. But before that we must note the significantly changed political situation of the '80s and '90s that acts as the background on which these developments take place. I refer to the collapse of the socialist camp and the restoration of capitalism. With no socialist camp to interfere, the world capitalist-imperialist system headed by the U.S., has moved toward globalization, aimed at bringing the whole world within its clutch. This also leads to the phenomenal growth of the global media market, with a small corporate clique monitoring and, of course, controlling the global capitalist market.

At this crisis-ridden hour of the system the competition is cutthroat. "We are in an era of global marketing warfare," cites an expert on global corporate "positioning." He adds, "The number one tactical weapon of the age is advertising." This fundamental lies at the root of commercialization, intensifying every minute and, eventually, vitiating everything. From India comes this extreme and sad example. A child mimics an advertisement feat; he jumps from his bed, legs tied to the cot, head down, diving to snatch a bottle of soft-drink. The rope nooses around his neck and brings death. The soft drink company, the advertiser, merely apologizes.

Marketing infiltrates entertainment. Commercials are dished out as artwork. "Infomercials" are introduced by leading electronic and industrial houses—Microsoft, Ford, Kodak and others—with an interlacing of information and commercials. All these marketing measures, commercials and infomercials are punched with the hype of consumerism, emanating particularly from that fountainhead, U.S. imperialism. All these are guided by the motive of marrying entertainment with selling. So this boils down to deliberate promotion of a culture centered around commercialism-consumerism or to ultimately replace culture by sheer entertainment, which is again watered down to avoid any depth and seriousness that might interfere with the primary commercial or corporate message. It is further smeared with a self-centered careerist outlook on life, an apathy about social problems, a fascination with sex, violence and commodities that sell well but rob people of morality, ethics, zeal, and the determination to fight against injustice and exploitation. In reality, this prepares the base on which moribund capitalism-imperialism ensures its rule.

This menacing trend finds recognition even in the Second World Summit on TV for Children, held in London, March 1998. The Summit expressed concern about the "new gate-keepers," who make programs, manage channels and deliver them via cable and satellite to every doorstep. They are the media conglomerates who can deny access to local producers and rival programs; through them creativity is subjugated to commercial concerns. The participants in the Summit found this trend alarming, particularly with the TV for children. Whereas it is desirable that such TV programs should help children hear and see their own language and culture, the scene is otherwise. "In India we are allowing our children to grow up on 'borrowed' programs," expressed the Chairman of the Center of Media Studies in Delhi. He adds, "All that is being done is to dub foreign programs into regional languages. Children's programs of late have become synonymous with foreign cartoon films."

Thus, with privatization and globalization of the media and electronic network, the governmental bureaucratic censorship is replaced by a different kind of censorship. The corporations that control the network, also called "the new gatekeepers," are politically conservative. They are hostile to any criticism or measure that would seek to change the capitalist social setup and challenge the rule that presently allows capitalists-monopolists to reap the harvest. Therefore they prefer promotion of a culture of entertainment that stinks of consumerism, sex and violence rather than debate, discussion and controversy. They would prefer to present the news as briefly as possible, minimizing costly time for downloading rather than go in for analysis and polemics to search for and reach the truth.

The constant drumbeat of the age of teledemocracy is that individuals are able to collect information of their choice, to get in touch with their preferred political leaders and to express their opinions and exercise their franchise without any interference. But this user-friendly system is not really cost-friendly for the vast majority of the human population, who live on the threshold of bare sustenance. In addition, the right to express their opinions through elected representatives and therefore exert some influence on the politics of their country, a minimum right in a bourgeois parliamentary system, is lost. Each individual is directly connected with the system and the role of the elected body is gone.

In addition, there is another nefarious role of the media. The imperialist-capitalist rule, based on deception and exploitation, is fast leading to utter dissatisfaction and resentment among the toiling peoples of much of the world. As a result, popular democratic movements, often assuming a militant character, are also rising up. Here the information revolution with the corporations at the helm reveals its true nature. The corporations leave no stone unturned, even going against all ethics of journalism to suppress or distort the news of the anti-capitalist, anti-imperialist movements. The trick is old. When they cannot avoid presenting the news, they dish out selective information or even misinformation. The shrouded truth thus presented confuses the people, whose poverty and lack of education prevents them from seeing through the deception of the media.

The corporations have used the media throughout much of the world as a plea for privatization. This became evident from the role of media, print or visual, during the parliamentary election campaigns and processes in developing countries. In place of a real democratic process, the media launched a regimented campaign to mold public opinion. In India, the corporate effort is presently aimed at polarizing the political spectrum into a two-party system, with only the parties of bourgeois and petty bourgeois shades finding favor with the media. Any force that may represent a genuine popular opinion is gagged. When some nonconformist editor or journalist tries to provide news impartially, that individual is attacked and silenced. This is then a form of censorship in disguise, which is stronger and more penetrating than autocratic or prohibitive acts.

The present changes, truly gigantic in scale, thus corrode the relative importance of public broadcasting and applicability of public service standards. On the contrary, they pose threats to citizens' participation in public affairs, their understanding of social issues and to the effective functioning of democracy itself. The information is neither real nor universal to the public. Thus, we can conclude: 1) Deregulation will transfer many of the economic roles of government to corporations); 2) Since programming is market-oriented, only those who reap profit are benefited; and 3) The new media system will accelerate economic centralization.

The phenomenal growth of the media and electronics has taken place in an age when the capitalist-imperialist world system is plunged into a deep crisis characterized by extreme wealth alongside abject poverty. Fundamentally, the growth is a frantic bid to save the system and establish its firm grip over the world market, including natural and human resources. However frantic the bid may be, crisis casts its shadow here too. The "myths" are exploded; the whole business runs on a principle: "money is power and power earns more money"; it can thrive only by fomenting and generating a culture that dehumanizes mankind into "robots" with no morality, ethics, or any vision for humanity. But in these efforts too the crisis takes its toll. While the corporate conglomerates take the fruits of the infotech revolution, the sale of personal computers slumps in countries like the U.S.A.

The Internet is touted as the last word in human communication, even as a new wing of the underworld develops, with crime assuming a new shape in the hand of "hackers." Even the computer-kids become hackers through play. The Israeli police, worried and horrified, imposed house arrest on an Israeli youth who had broken into the Pentagon's computer system. Elsewhere, the U.S. attorney arrested a fourteen-year old boy for delinking and crippling an airport and a town for hours.

The stupendous technological growth and development are the harvest of human civilization itself. They are assets of the entire human society that open an ever widening horizon to mankind. But society gasps under the shackles of capitalist-imperialist exploitation and oppression. And so technology, owned by the rulers and their henchmen, is bridled to serve this system. We must realize that we have no choice but to do away with this system once and for all by a determined blow from the mighty and militant anti-capitalist, anti-imperialist struggle across the globe. Till then we will not only be unable to enjoy the fruits of technology, but we will be acting tacitly in support of an exploitative system that leads humankind to the chasm of disaster with a handful of privileged sitting on the brink and fiddling merrily at the cost of billions.

NEO-COLONIALISM AND MEDIA'S DARK AGE

NAWAL EL SAADAWI

Two phrases in an African-Jamaican song summarize the media's dark age in which we live:

> Raise the chains off the body.
> Put the chains on the mind.

On April 14, 1998, at Harvard University (U.S.), I was invited to give a lecture. Among the audience were women professors from Harvard and other institutions in Boston. Many of them had their faces covered in layers of make-up, their lips painted a deep red color, their ears pierced and weighted with heavy pieces of metal, with fashionable earrings, their feet arched on high heels. Some of them had old tired eyes, but the skin of their faces looked strangely smooth. They had undergone a face lift. Their breasts stood up small and rounded. They had removed part of the flesh and skin by plastic surgery.

This process is not specific to educated middle and upper class American women. It is universal, in the North and in the South, in the West and in the East. Sometimes I cannot differentiate between women. They look alike, walk and talk in the same way and flutter their eyelashes in the same way.

Men of the same class have recently entered this beauty race, with similar hair styles, similar perfumes, body deodorants, underwear, shoes and pants which emphasize the slow movement of their buttocks.

This is one aspect of the media's dark age. The media have developed a capacity to mold women and men in the same way as coins come out of a bank machine.

At Harvard University, during the discussion, one of the women professors stood up and said: "Nobody obliged me to put on make-up, it is my free choice." A veiled Moslem woman stood up and said: "I chose to wear the veil." A male professor stood up and supported women's freedom to wear the traditional religious veil or to put on make-up (in other words a post-modern veil).

Many of the women and men in the audience supported the idea of "free choice," to be veiled or to put on make-up, wear earrings, high heels, or whatever one can choose from the free market. In spite of their impressive educational status as university professors, they were not aware that the so-called free market is not really free, and that they are not free to choose.

But this is one of the functions of the media. To give you the illusion that you are free to choose what you like from the free market, that you are free to elect your representative in Congress or Parliament. But in media's dark age how can anyone be free?

Never before in history has there been such domination of people's minds by the mass media. Never before in history has there been such a concentration and centralization of media, capital, and of military power in the hands of so few people. The countries that form the group of seven (in the North) control almost all the technological, economic, media, information and military power in the world.

Five hundred multinational corporations (MNCs) account for 80% of world trade and 75% of global investment. Less than five hundred billionaires own more than half of the wealth of all the inhabitants of the globe. With such concentration of the economic and technological means of power, the mass media and electronic telecommunications have served to colonize the minds of men and women, to plunder the economic and intellectual wealth of the majority of the world's population, especially in our so-called Third World or South. The word "colonize" is no longer used by the post-modern media. More innocent words are used: Post-Colonial, Free Trade, Aid, Cooperation, Sustainable Development, Structural Adjustment and other post-modern terms with a double meaning.

To expand the global market, the media plays its role in developing certain values, patterns of behavior and perceptions of beauty, femininity, masculinity, success, love and sex. The media creates a global consumer with an increasing desire to buy what the transnational capitalists (TNCs) produce, thereby maximizing their profits. Neo-colonialism, like colonialism, cannot maximize its profits without exploiting others, and you cannot exploit women and men without deceiving them. Post-modern deception by the media and the broader information system is subtle. It works on the conscious and the unconscious levels. It gives you the impression that you are free to choose while it robs you of all the means of free choice.

But how can we be free to choose if the media injects us day and night with false information? The media has developed an ideology of individualism based on destroying the resistance of the individual. It glorifies the individual hero, the star. It destroys the idea of collective resistance. It propagates post-modern ideas such as the end of history, the end of ideology and the end of representation. It divides people by religion, ethnicity and race, under the idea of difference, diversity, and authentic identity, but it globalizes capital and profit under the idea of One World and One Humanity.

Post-modern capitalist writers and journalists provide the media with ideas which deceive the majority of men and women. Most of the writers and thinkers from our countries in the South adopt the ideas of capitalist thinkers in the North. Independent and original thought is not encouraged by our governments. You go to jail if you create new ideas for more justice and freedom. Most of the governments and dictators in Africa, Asia and Latin America are agents of the global economic powers and are protected by the U.S. army or police. Women and men are prevented from resisting locally or internationally. How can we organize ourselves under such oppressive systems? How can we unite the efforts of women and men if collective resistance is punished?

Our NGO group in Egypt was closed down by the government in 1991 because we opposed the Gulf War, because we had different views from the government and emphasized the need to oppose the policies of the multinationals and neo-colonial powers, and because we resisted discrimination between people by class, gender and religion.

Religious political groups (so-called fundamentalists), whether Christian, Moslem, Jewish, Buddhist or other, are the other face of neocolonialism, the legacy of the late capitalist patriarchal system. They separate the economy from culture, but in reality both their money and culture are limited. For example, the Gulf countries and Islamic fundamentalist groups have their money and political and information headquarters in Western financial centers, New York, London, Geneva, Frankfurt and Luxembourg. They are an integral part of the global economic and information system.

Most of the powerful media and TV satellites in our region are owned by the rich Gulf governments or billionaires in oil rich states, or the head of the state himself. They follow the American media. After the Gulf War (1991), the Gulf countries were exploited economically even more ferociously and used as military bases by the U.S. Ironically, they actually pay the U.S. to exploit them in return for so-called protection.

The media in Egypt are Americanized just like the media in Europe and other parts of the world. The mass media serve as agents of neocolonialism in the South. Information is considered to be the missing link in the so-called development chain. We, the underdeveloped in the Third World, have to be taught how to consume and how to be modern or post-modern. The cultural imperialism thesis explores the harmful influence of the U.S. media on countries in the South and in the North as well. Media and cultural imperialism is a logical accompaniment to economic imperialism. Through control of the mass media you create the conditions for conformity to the global market and limit the possibility of effective resistance to it.

The dominant global economic forces are the MNCs, especially those in communication, advertising and marketing.

They dominate local economic and political activities, including the election campaigns. The international and national groups which organize and control the MNCs constitute an elite class called the "Transnationalist Capitalist Class" (TCC). The dominant individuals in the TCC are the executives, the politicians, the media marketers. The theory of globalization suggests that the key to understanding how media and communications function in the global capitalist system lies in examining the ways in which the communication of information is being transformed into a global ideology of consumerism.

In Egypt, as in other parts of the world, many poor women and men obey the messages of the media and advertisements, even when these messages are against their health or general interests. In many circumstances this is the only economically rational option open to them. It is often a trap, but one that is entered not out of choice (as some may think) but out of a lack of viable alternatives. It is a trap similar to the one that poor working women enter when they wear high heels which hinder their movement on unpaved streets. But they have no alternative if female shoes in shops have high heels, if advertisements in the media connect high heels with femininity and beauty, if movie stars, TV stars, the wives of rulers and upper and middle class women wear high heels, and if media messages are subliminal, affecting the subconscious, exploiting the needs of deep instincts and depravations from which most women and men suffer. The media need only show the so-called "first lady" wearing earrings (as big as footballs) and many women will hurry to wear them.

The struggle over control of the electronic media is reflected in the growing number of TV satellites, cable TVs and video cassettes in our countries. The opportunities for domination are obvious and have been seized by hegemonistic groups, whether official organizations or rich individuals in the government or private sector. Today in Egypt the mass media are owned by the government, but with the process of privatization and hegemony of global capitalism, the mass media, including TV and cinema, will be handed over to rich individuals or groups.

As the result of the Nile Satellite launch, we will have several TV satellites owned by a few billionaires in Egypt. The rent of one TV satellite is about three million dollars, beyond the means of anyone other than the government or the billionaires.

Under government control, most dissenting ideas were censored, but under the new billionaires, the media will be controlled by the rich business class who are agents of the global neo-colonial powers. Mass media control can be exercised directly through the capitalist production process and indirectly through marketing and distribution. Commercial rather than intellectual goals are dominant and will continue to be so. The prospect that private satellite television in Egypt will create progress has been disputed. Sometimes governmental control of telecommunications is relatively preferable to private sector or individual control, under which only those rich enough to own the technology may speak to those who are rich enough to use it.

Alternative media which are less capital intensive may challenge the hegemony of the TNCs in the mass media, but they are still marginal in the North and unknown in the South. The Transnational Advertising Agencies (TNAAs) are increasingly active in the South, where they direct local agencies. Most advertisements in Egypt serve the distribution of American and TNC goods. The TNAAs build up admiration of American "heroes" who fight in the Gulf or in Somalia (or other parts of the world) for humanitarian goals, or who fight in Iraq or Libya or Somalia or other countries.

The mass media have become the superstructure of dictatorships, globally and locally. The football or baseball competitions, like the terror of sex and crime films, are designed as alternative channels of youth protest in repressive societies. The so-called "identity politics" which tend to glorify indigenous values, such as the veiling of women, is part of the postmodern media deception. Neocolonial powers are selective in their "identity" policies. They preserve local values that serve their interests and destroy the others that do not work in their favor. The veiling of women's faces or hair does not prevent the distribution of western goods. Many upper class women in Egypt and Gulf countries wear import veils from the U.S. or bought from the local market. The veil became a fashion, a commodity like earrings and face lifts. Indeed, veiled women often wear lipstick, complete make-up, fashionable earrings, high pointed heels, mascara, artificial eyelashes and perfumes.

An American scholar and expert on the Middle East produced a film about women in Egypt under the title *A Veil Revolution*, praising the veil as the "authentic identity of Egyptian Moslem non-westernized women." A British woman produced a film under the title "Hidden Faces," in which she distorted the views published in my books by ignoring the connection between global neo-colonial power and the increasing poverty, unemployment, and the discrimination against women.

Feminists are seen by the global media as women fighting against sexual harassment or rape. But in our countries we are fighting against both economic and sexual rape. This is not shown by the media. Indeed, when the media allows us to speak, the *economic* part of our statement is censored out. This has happened to me several times, especially in American and British media. In Egypt, my name is included in what they call "the gray list." I am virtually banned from TV, radio and major newspapers and the cinema.

In spite of all these obstacles, we have to continue the struggle locally and globally. Globalization from above by the TNCs and their media should be challenged by globalization from below by women and men who are the majority of the world. We have to create our own media and communicate with each other through the Internet, the e-mail and other electronic devices. With the continuous advance in communication technology, we will be able to reach each other with less money and less time. The decentralization of the media and communication technology is inevitable and it can be turned to our favor. Unveiling of the mind is our goal, to be accomplished by exercising political power through local and global organizations.

MEDIA AS A NATIONAL CLASS TOOL FOR OPPRESSION

ADEL SAMARA

The New World Order has created a media that hides social resistance, or in the words of Gramsci, "a censoring acceptance of capitalist society." The new industry rarely contributes information which will help human beings to oppose oppression and discrimination. For many writers, scientists, historians, journalists and economists, the world has become one "village," which they call the global village. In theory, if this were an accurate picture then every human being would have access to the means and tools of knowledge, allowing them to pursue liberty, freedom and happiness. Obviously there is something wrong with the concept of a global village when illiteracy is increasing around the world, and a whole generation of young people are denied a real education. The media writes about the great economic growth that is taking place while a few billion people face poverty every day.

When we examine the policy of those who control the media, we find that the media only represents one class of people. This class is made up of the wealthy establishment that actually owns the media. It is so in my country, Palestine, where the media are owned and controlled by the Israeli government. The Zionist media attempts to justify the destruction of the Palestinian land, culture and the physical existence of its people.

In the United States, the media function as a class machine, shaping and reshaping the mentality of the American citizen. The people are taught to support prohibitively expensive space wars despite the fact that 38 million Americans live under the poverty level. They are taught to accept aggression against Iraq, Cuba, Libya and the Sudan. They are taught to accept the colonization of Palestine by the Israelis. The media attempt to get U.S. citizens to adopt a passive attitude when it comes to foreign policy.

A striking feature of the capitalist media is its hegemony over people's ideas. Following the collapse of the Soviet Union, superficial press reports and propaganda, not real analysis, were used to distort what socialism was really about. Writers like Francis Fukuyama, who was supported by and linked to the U.S. State Department, jumped to inaccurate conclusions and generalizations. For Fukuyama, history itself ended when a victorious capitalism was given the right to define it.

With the collapse of the Soviet Union, the world media has become subject to control by the capitalist nations, whose agenda is to subjugate the socialist countries and to suffocate any factions that might oppose its power. This would include organizations, individuals and the broader socialist culture.

Media under Occupation

Since its beginning in June 1967, the Israeli colonial regime has imposed military control over all aspects of life in the West Bank and the Gaza Strip. All local radio stations, newspapers, magazines and publishing houses were closed or transferred to Amman, Jordan. The only radio and TV broadcasting for the area were those controlled and designed by the Israeli police, which helped play a role in the brain-washing or psychological war imposed on the people. *Al-Ayiam* was published daily under the supervision of the Israeli police.

By the beginning of the 1970s, some Palestinians received permits from the Israeli military administration to produce newspapers. These licenses were limited to Palestinians from occupied East Jerusalem, whose land was annexed by the Israeli occupation. The rest of the Palestinian population was considered on a lower status. They were given IDs that reflected this lower status, though no nationality was mentioned. These IDs were imposed over the West Bank and Gaza population. Those from Jerusalem, though lower in status than full

Israeli citizens, were relatively "privileged" when compared to the other Palestinians.

The papers of those who succeed in gaining a newspaper or magazine license had to be produced in Jerusalem, and distribution to the West Bank or Gaza requires a special permit. Under the strict control of the Israeli authorities, this permit can be cancelled at anytime. Newspapers and magazines must show all material (news, analysis, advertisements, even deaths), to the Israeli military censors in West Jerusalem, who can pass, edit or cancel the article. Licenses for producing a publication are decided arbitrarily on the basis of the Israeli security official's attitude toward the person applying, not according to law or civil rights.

Books are censored as well. The Israeli occupation produces an annual list of prohibited books which, when found, are confiscated and book store owners fined for marketing them. Even words and expressions are censored in the newspapers. Any terms that refer to Palestinian rights in Palestine, even in a metaphoric manner, are prohibited. In poetry, the words "lover" or "darling" have been removed by the Israeli military censors, who felt it might mean "Palestine."

Discussion of foreign affairs has also been closely monitored. Criticism of the Shah of Iran was prohibited, while criticism of the United States was not. In an attempt to give some political analysis, the Palestinian journalists had to delay their writings until Saturday night, a religious holiday, when the Israeli military left the office early. The military would quickly read over the material and "pass" it in their haste. Newspapers were often warned and punished later for publishing these "passed" articles. The Israelis argued that the Palestinian journalists "knew what was acceptable and what was not." For the Palestinians this meant that they had to censor their own writing. It was as if you had to put an Israeli censorship chip inside your brain. It was a call for Palestinians to colonize their own minds.

When the Israeli court decided, in a secret session, to close the *al-Shira* biweekly in 1983, the judge accused the editor of wrongful writings 60 times for 60 articles passed and stamped by the Israeli military censorship. Most of the articles were analyses critical of "moderate" Palestinian leaders in the PLO, the Jordanian regime, or local notables loyal to the Hashemite kingdom of Jordan.

Today, five years after the imperialist-designed Oslo "peace settlement," Israeli censorship still controls the Palestinian newspapers distributed in the West Bank and Gaza. My article, "The Palestinians of 1948 vs. a State of All Its Citizens," in the April 17, 1998, *Al-Quds* daily, was published only after cleansing all "radical/leftist" terms (i.e. imperialism, capitalism). The editor informed me that with these terms included, the article would be canceled. This is a destructive war against the basic right of expression by individuals, and it controls national expression as well. Despite this and the fact that the Jewish state is occupying all of Palestine, most of the U.S. public still supports Israel. A poll conducted by the *New York Times* showed that 58% of Americans still support the Israeli cause, while only 13% side with the Palestinians. In my opinion the media has caused this slanted opinion.

Media in Jail

In December 1967, I was arrested by the Israeli army. Seeking to read and write while incarcerated, I met with the prison leader to ask for books, paper, and pens for myself and the prisoners. The request was denied. We were forced to steal pens from the prison guards and use the small sheets of paper inside cigarette boxes. After inspecting our rooms, the military administration confiscated these simple pieces of paper, on which we had written Arabic-Hebrew vocabularies. I applied to the prison administration to continue my studies by correspondence in the Lebanese University. The response was negative. I applied to the British Council to study by correspondence, and again the jail administration refused. In desperation I went on my first hunger strike for the Palestinian cause, demanding books. After seven days I received the first book in the jails under Israeli occupation. It was Maurice Duverger's book *The Political Parties*.

But this was not the end. Even when books were permitted, they had to pass through the jail's censorship administration. All Marxist or nationalist books were prohibited. We told our families to change the books covers and replace them with poetry or literature titles. To pass into the prison, the cover of Lenin's book, *What's to Be Done*, was changed to *Alf Lila wa Lila*.

Even letters from our families were tightly controlled. The officer in Beit Leed (Kfar Yona) jail called me in for investigation after reading a letter to my family. I was asked why I wrote that "by forbidding us from reading, they were trying to make us zeros."

Despite all of this repression, we could produce one hundred handwritten monthly magazines, translate books, and write articles. After my release from prison in 1978, I applied for a permit to publish a theoretical journal in Ramallah, but I was refused. After being arrested for the second time in November 1978, the Israeli army confiscated 80 books from my private library. Despite all of my lawyer's protests, the books were never returned.

The Palestinian Media under the PLO

During the "semi-formal" resistance movement in 1967-1993, the Palestinian media was never a creative revolutionary force. It was a media related to the PLO's political and ideological stance. The writers, who were both intellectuals and academics, were tied to the formal position of the PLO in Lebanon where they formed a small Palestinian government. This political leadership was a source of income and helped to rechannel the intellectuals, mainly refugees, and find them jobs within its bureaucracy. Those who worked in the media sector became similar to their Arab counterparts in other Arab regimes.

The Palestinian media in most Arab countries worked according to the political relationship of their organizations with the Arab regimes. As a result, the PLO was maintained as a resistance movement, not as a revolutionary one. Palestinian intellectuals were regarded as formal employees by the PLO, but they were prevented from organizing a revolutionary movement. While the popular and grass roots organizations (writers, journalist unions, theater groups, volunteer work groups, etc.) developed from within the Occupied Territories, the PLO leadership decided to bureaucratize these "naturally" developed groups by controlling the flow of money to them. This terminated their self reliance and integrated them into the bureaucratic structure of the formal PLO organizations.

The resultant policy of the PLO to make the Palestinian media similar to media within the Arab regimes has produced the same unfortunate consequences that can be seen in the Arab regimes, where collaboration by Arab intellectuals has supported repression, harmed democracy and hindered development. In fact, the bureaucratization of the Palestinian intellectuals has been even more damaging to Palestinian society. For example, the Palestinian intellectuals have terminated their people's historical rights and memories by supporting the Oslo agreement. All the Palestinian intellectuals, writers, media workers, etc. who were part of the formal PLO institution before the Oslo agreement continued to work for the same leadership afterwards. They came to the West Bank and Gaza encouraging "normalization with the occupation," either by defending Oslo or by keeping their silence.

Under PA (Palestinian Authority)

After Oslo, the PA established its own radio and TV in sections of the West Bank and Gaza, placing other newspapers, magazines, radio and TV stations in jeopardy. All of them were supervised by PA authorities. Many of them were closed when they broadcast pieces of news that the PA opposed. The media acted as the mouth of the regime. They spoke of independence, development and self reliance on the one hand but called for Israel to absorb more Palestinian workers into its economy on the other. There was also a significant increase in corruption.

The Palestinian media was, of course, reluctant to talk about the PA's corruption. When they did, it was in an off-handed manner.

The most dangerous role of the Palestinian media is its co-operation with programs introduced by the United States, Israeli, foreign NGOs and the World Bank that plan to "reeducate" the Palestinian people. These are plans designed to vanquish the deeply rooted traditions of the Palestinians (e.g. community cohesiveness, support for revolution and readiness for resistance) and replace them with individualism, free market ideology and competition, and private sector support for the regime.

The areas controlled by the PA were the first to follow the lead of the World Bank and IMF by subscribing to a policy that puts all economic power in the hands of the private sector. Most of the activities pursued by these dependent private sectors are under subcontracts with Israeli factories. The Palestinian formal and private media are fully committed to this program of reeducation. They are supported by the well-financed foreign and local NGOs, UNDP and the World Bank. In a work shop called "Financing Development in Palestine" at the University of Beir Seit, the speakers of the UNDP (Thomas Baunsgaard) and of the World Bank (Timothy S. Rothermel) presented an optimistic picture of the PA's economy regarding its potential to compete on the world scale and its highly skilled work force. In contrast, all the Palestinians who shared in the workshop emphasized that the situation was catastrophic.

While separating the Palestinian youth from their revolutionary traditions, the media is increasing the nihilist, consumerist and anarchist trends among them. The youth are unable to build a connection between their recent role of resistance during the Intifada and their current situation as idle and careless people. Nor can they reconcile their struggle against the occupation with its legitimization by the so-called peace agreement.

Cooperation between Formal Medias

The role of the Palestinian formal media is varied according to the PA's political and class interests. On the national level, the PA radio and TV began referring to just the West Bank and Gaza as "Palestine," in an attempt to reeducate the Palestinian people in compliance with the terms of the imperialist Zionist peace agreement. This is not a mere recognition of Israel. It is a destruction of the people's memory and historical rights in Palestine, especially their right of return.

On the class level, the Palestinian media is supporting the private sector, a market ideology and an open door policy. All of these are for the sake of the peripheral capitalist comprador and dependent capitalist class in the West Bank and Gaza.

On the pan-Arab nationalist level, the PA media is reeducating the Palestinian people against Arab unity, cooperation and economic integration. Arab regimes are deliberately fostering the current situation of unequal development between Arab countries in an attempt to terminate the necessity of Arab unity. These regimes are maintaining little more than cooperation between Interior ministries and police, as evidenced by the recent agreement to fight "terrorism," as demanded by the U.S. and Israel.

Following the collapse of the radical regimes in the late 1960s, the Arab regimes decided to seek a joint reconciliation. Their media continued to support the revolutionary popular movements, but under the control of Arab regimes that had no democracy, no free press and which were integrated into the world order in a subservient position, media coordination became a requirement of self defense. The PA became part of this Arab bourgeois monopoly.

A recent example of this formal bourgeois alliance comes from Jordan. The government told the newspapers that they should not criticize the Palestinian Authority and its president Mr. Arafat. In addition, the prime minister took the necessary measures to introduce a new law prohibiting any media expression that might damage Jordan's relationships with other Arab countries. (*Al-Quds*, 4-16-98) None of the TV channels could criticize other Arab regimes, except for Iraq. This exception shows the strong influence of the United States. The only area of media that is still not controlled by Arab regimes is the internet. Unfortunately, even if this media stays free it will take a long time to become a popular phenomenon in the area.

PART FIVE

INTERNATIONAL ALTERNATIVES

TO THE

MEDIA MONOPOLY

Do Media Alternatives Exist Outside the 'West'?

Barbara Nimri Aziz

As the West becomes more and more dominated by a handful of media behemoths, and the public voice is stifled or pushed far to the fringe, do we tend to lose sight of the rest of the world? If the Western media's credibility in the free world is shrinking and its subscribers dwindling, can things be any better in the Third World press? Surprising at it may seem, we in the lagging, indebted, barefoot and war-torn Third World may be better off than the journalists in the West. For us, this is a time of expansion and new possibilities.

It is an axiom in the West that the Third World is backward. This is applied to our media as well as our weaponry and our human rights. What this charge implies is that any problem or adversity the West experiences will:

a) be soon extended to the rest of the world;
b) be more severe and more damaging elsewhere in the world; and
c) eventually be solved within the West, which will lead the rest of the world out of the dilemma.

I am aware that U.S. companies like Disney and Gulf which control media are global, not simply American. Thus their dominance extends globally, and if they have not yet bought up newspaper syndicates and TV stations across the world, they will certainly try. However, you may be glad to learn that their reach and impact may be limited. These limits are not those gallantly won by human rights advocates for Third World victims. They are the age old limits of culture, set by language, by reading habits, by local educational standards, and, believe it or not, by cultural pride. We also cannot discount geographical limits, even in this era of satellite communication.

Despite satellite transmission technology and the globalization of American culture that it facilitates, elsewhere much information still travels overland. (One would have thought the U.S. war in South East Asia would have taught Americans this.) We forget that by comparison to the U.S., most countries in the world are rather small. They have fewer people, and are far smaller in geographical size. These are cultures where effective interpersonal communication happens through neighborhoods, from town to town, even across nearby international borders.

Proximity and personal exchange here are significant even in the media, indeed these provide real alternatives to global high tech transmission. Because two countries are close to each other—sometimes the cities of one are hardly two hours from the capital of another—information flows (or seeps) over their borders. These conditions affect how a public is informed. It means it is impossible, even for a repressive government, to screen out critical comments and alternative views. They cannot keep their public completely ignorant of developments.

In the West, to avoid being pushed farther and farther into the margin, journalists are desperately seeking new means of access, to impact public opinion through a bigger role or through forceful alternatives. I'm going to discuss alternatives in another part of the world—the Arab Middle East. This may seem odd. Considering the public perception of the Middle East and press freedom, the Arab states would be the last place to expect anything in the way of media sophistication. On the other hand, perhaps it is a good example, because people here are sometimes forced by circumstances different from those of the West to work in alternative realms.

I have come to appreciate "alternative" systems in the Middle East during 10 years observing a number of Arab countries at close hand. During this time, working as a freelance journalist, I brought my 18-year career in anthropology to my observations in journalism. Ethnographers, you may know, are the masters of discovering and working with often obscure and informal systems that cultures create for themselves. Anthropologists rely heavily on below-the-surface dynamics that are often the engine of a society.

Alternatives to Hosni Mubarak or King Hassan?

In the course of work in Syria, Kuwait, Egypt, Lebanon, Iraq and elsewhere, I have been astonished by how well-informed Arab people keep themselves, and how they develop and use alternatives to their state-owned media. Outsiders, and even Arab people, speak little about these alternatives, but I think they will recognize them once we point them out.

So, what are the alternatives in media for the Arab people? The majority of Arab countries, like many Third World nations, have a fairly high standard of literacy. All children go to school, and many finish high school and attend college, which, in most cases, is free to all citizens. This is relevant in our discussion because a faulty education system, I believe, lies at the heart of media's dark age in the West.

The Arab lands have something else that keeps their media viable, namely an active and legitimate intellectual elite. In any Arab city one finds a community of teachers, artists and writers. Many of their colleagues have chosen to leave because of political difficulties and low income, yet the men and women who remain are able to function. They are well regarded by the society as a whole and they enjoy some respect from their governments. And they are highly productive, even creative!

Journalism itself is an old and established profession in the Middle East. Arab journalists and newspapers are remembered for their role in the early 20th century independence struggles. But perhaps journalists are more respected because, unlike in the U.S.A., they are associated with the intellectual professions and are accepted into the intellectual elite. This is not insignificant to their survival and their function in society.

You will surely be wondering about our censorship, which you hear so much about in the West. No one would deny the existence of censorship in the Arab countries, although it would be helpful to the wider discussion to also acknowledge and understand how censorship also persists in the "free" West. Our censorship is sometimes frightening, because it is directly related to the totalitarian nature of our leaders, men who seem unable to tolerate open criticism. So, yes, as a result, little open political discussion takes place. I stress the word "open" because, however difficult it may be for outsiders to understand, this censorship does not completely stifle the press. It limits it, yes. But independent journalism exists in the Arab countries, and it is even expanding today with the growth of TV journalism and the universality of TV in everyday life.

Another point to bear in mind is that in the Middle East too, there is more to life than politics. Western observers tend to conclude that if there is no open discussion about the leader and national policies, everyone is gagged and terrified to express any opinion. This is far from the truth. Arab people are very opinionated, and critical about political developments, but not in public. That's where censorship is so strong. By force and law, we pretend to be observers only. This contrasts with the West, where people may be informed, yet by various kinds of manipulations or cultural factors, they have no role in policy planning. Although the western media offers its own versions of both sides of an issue, the U.S. public remains effectively ill-informed. The causes are not the same as in the Arab world, but, you too find yourselves only observers. Your common phrase "infotainment" captures the growing reality that Western "news" is not intended to inform, but to entertain.

When speaking about the impact of news, we also have to distinguish between domestic and international politics. In the West, you have a vigorous, fairly open debate on domestic issues. But when the subject is international politics, the area where Americans are so poorly informed, debate is limited. This is very different from our experience.

Few outsiders appreciate how well-informed Arab women and men are about the world, their neighbors and their own country, but visitors to the Middle East witness an active public discussion of international, economic, social and political issues. People clearly enjoy these discussions and no one is excluded. This is where basic education comes into play, as well as our history.

"We are in a state of constant turmoil and instability, and we have been for decades," noted one commentator. "This makes us think about the world around us and how changes elsewhere may impact on our lives. If we were stable, we might not be so interested."

We should also remember that even in the Middle East, politics—domestic or international—is not everything. Limits certainly apply to domestic political matters, but the issues of environment, minority rights, preservation of culture, some aspects of economics, health, sports, education and even some areas of corruption remain open to debate. Look at the Western press, alternative or otherwise. What percent of TV or radio hours or print space in newspapers or magazines is devoted to political discussion? Except during times of political scandal, very little. And one really learns little about fraud in the American government or the corruption-riddled United Nations.

Our analysis would benefit from considering some simple logistics like size and shape. Even today, the small size of most Arab states has a real impact on information and debate. A lot of news can and does travel by word of mouth. From the centers of power, the military councils, and the diplomatic corps, news travels through family and school networks and beyond to the wider public. It is not difficult to find a source close to the center of power who can verify a story. A policy change, or a military concern, or an arrest, may not be in the papers, but before long, everyone will know. This is vital when political censorship is in place. So, while the Iraqi or Moroccan public may not be aware of all the details of a debate, many people are able to follow developments by their access to the inner circles of government and military. Gossip from those circles is a significant means for the public to find out what's really going on among their leaders. Such gossip is usually more than rumor. It is news.

While this kind of informal knowledge is not generally converted into direct participatory activity in government, it is nevertheless valued knowledge. It adds to a nation's sophistication on government matters. At some point, the accumulated knowledge from these sources may translate into various forms of opposition—the creation of new parties, underground movements, even uprisings or threats.

Is Knowledge Power?

Anyone who has talked at any length with an Arab man or woman on the street will be astonished at their grasp and interest in both local and international politics. Their general knowledge is far deeper and wider than that of Americans. Often, I find an average Arab observer can offer a better analysis on international matters than even a so-called western expert. This is due, at least in part, to the high standard of education in these countries. Young Arab people are taught world history with a far more critical approach than the American college graduate.

Recently, satellite TV has transformed the media business in the Middle East just as it has across the world. Before we discuss this, let's take a closer look at other media through which Arab men and women get their news. Given press restrictions, where do they get such up-to-date knowledge and opinions of world events, including policies of their own country?

First, take a look at a map. Note the proximity of neighboring countries. In Iraq for example, news filters in from Jordan, Iran, Kuwait, Turkey, Syria; in Jordan it comes in from the neighboring states. Their capitals are less than an hour's flight away, or a short drive by car. In Saudi Arabia, news comes in from the small Gulf states—The Emirates and Bahrain, where there is extensive contact with the wider world.

Sister Arab states are real alternative sources. The dialogue and exchange among Arab states is so strong that their intellectuals and journalists are experts in each other's affairs. For many years, Lebanon was a major education, media and publishing center in the Middle East. Their graduates and professors came from throughout the world, and they produced fine thinkers. Lebanon became a major publishing center in the Arabic language, and their newspapers reached every corner of the Arab world. Even where some of those publications are not sold commercially, people have ways of finding them.

Again, information flows across borders via newspapers. Oddly, Arab governments do not seem willing or able to restrict news from those sources. It appears that they are willing to treat foreign Arab journalists more liberally than their own, and the local population takes advantage of this. Doubtless, the power of the Arab language comes into play here; people from Rabat to Baghdad, Jerusalem to Dubai, all use the same written language. Arabic is a powerful psychological force for all Arabs; it unites their intelligentsia and perhaps in that process it links their news channels and professions. Women and men— whether they are teachers, bankers or taxi-drivers—want to know what fellow Arabs outside are thinking. So reports from the international Arabic dailies will be widely discussed in any Arab community. A Kuwaiti paper may quote *Al-Hayat* (Lebanese, from London) or *Al-Ahram* (from Egypt).

Don't Forget about Radio

Radio is another means of news distribution between Arab populations. Since radio transmission is in classical Arabic, it is understood in all 22 Arab states. Radio in the Middle East, unlike the U.S.A., is a major source of alternate information to the public, in part because of geography. We often forget how close Damascus is to Beirut, Tel Aviv, and Amman. So Syrians regularly tune in to radio news (often targeting their population) from Tel Aviv, Ankara and other nearby capitals. Traveling by taxi in the capital, one will find that the car radio is tuned in to Israel for example. The driver explains, "I listen to the news; I know they lie; but my government also exaggerates; so does Voice of America; I don't believe any one of them; I listen to them all and I decide. Besides, the music is good."

Like the BBC, Voice of America, Monte Carlo from France and Turkish radio, Israel too produces special Arabic language radio programs for export. All include a lot of good Arabic music in their broadcasts. Radio is still a major propaganda tool in the region, with stations set up to target specific populations in enemy states. Before their restoration of relations, the Syrians had a station beamed to Iraq; the Iranians also had one directed to Iraq during their war, and vice versa.

From One Open Door, Many Friends Can Benefit

Among the Arab states, until this decade, Lebanon played a special role in journalism in the region. Lebanon has a highly heterogeneous population, good technicians and designers and a long history of interaction with Europe. With its unique laisez-faire culture and policy in the Arab world and considerable support from France, the UK and the U.S., Lebanon assumed a special role in the area's journalism. Arabs everywhere regard the Lebanese as the best in the news business. So there is a large market for books and papers originating in Beirut.

Inside Lebanon one finds a plethora of media sources— over 60 radio stations and dozens of TV stations—although its population is barely 3 million. The Hizbollah Party has its own TV station; each of the major parties, including Christian and communist, also have their outlets. In addition, purely commercial companies add to the Lebanese mix. Until 1992 when Damascus' influence in Lebanon put some restrictions on its media, none of Lebanon's media outlets were subject to close government control. Vigorous competition among them made for a wide range of news sources and opinions and a high level of professionalism.

The Lebanese press became even more central as an Arabic news service in the '80s. With the outbreak of its civil war, many of its trained journalists had to leave their homeland. Some found work as journalists in the Gulf states, while others moved to Paris and London where they joined in the development of new Arabic language dailies and magazines.

Today London is a major center for the Arab language press, the home of *Al-Hayat, Sharq al Awsat,* and *Al Quds Al-Arabi,* among other respected Arabic dailies. With modern technology, they print editions in several countries simultaneously. They can reach readers from Detroit to Brooklyn, Amman to Abu Dhabi. Each paper has its distinct editorial line, related to its ownership. This is really no different from the British or American press. Everyone knows for example, that *Sharq al Awsat* is Saudi owned. But this does not eliminate it from the competition; whatever respect it enjoys is based on its superior journalism. Arab readers are looking for up-to-date world news and informed commentary. The same applies to the Palestinian-run *Al Quds Al-Arabi* or the Egyptian press. Readers are aware that on matters close to Saudi policy, or Palestinian concerns, or Egypt's national interest, each has its bias. Traditionally, Arab readers do not depend on only one paper, just as they do not rely on one radio source, so for them, these editorial limitations are not bothersome. Again, these kinds of alternatives depend on a sophisticated, critical public.

In the U.S.A., papers have biases and limits too. But it's not the custom for a reader to subscribe to several in order to arrive at their own conclusion. Few Americans would think of buying a "foreign" paper in order to gain a wider perspective on U.S. policy or know more about the world. And that's a source of the problems faced by the alternative press in the U.S. The American public is not really looking for alternative views, whereas in the Middle East, people are.

To understand the dilemma facing American journalism, we need to look more critically at the American education system. What makes Americans feel so certain that their news sources are uncensored and without bias? As long as a community denies that it needs alternatives, its intellectual scope will continue to shrink.

Expansion Is Not Necessarily Globalization

In recent years Arab dailies and other news media have expanded immensely to offer even better international coverage than in the past. Relying less on western news agencies or on telephone research, these companies have their own correspondents around the world. Arab journalists in Washington, Toronto, Tokyo, Jerusalem, Vienna, or Sao Paulo report and comment on any range of international events. Surely this is an improvement in terms of new alternatives available to American and European news sources.

The best example of the growing media possibilities open to Arab people is to be found in television. Before widespread satellite transmission arrived, domestic TV in each Arab country was rather mediocre and parochial. Arab TV companies were purely local until the end of the Gulf War of 1991. Many depended on Egyptian films to fill air time, and some aired an occasional French or American film in their late night schedule.

In the early 1990s, with the American push to "globalize" national economies and extend American culture, I noticed that many of those state-controlled TV companies started to carry more American serials like the Bill Cosby Show, BayWatch, and a lot of violent American crime films. With the widespread access to satellite, more Arab families, but also local journalists, were turning to CNN for their world news. The Arab people joined the rest of the world, watching live coverage of international events with the rise of CNN. They also had access to Turkish and European TV. Meanwhile French and Italian satellite transmissions bombarded North Africa.

These developments were unchallenged for a short time. But anti-American feeling was growing in the region, and that demanded alternatives. Rising Muslim pride also called for changes. Meanwhile, Arab journalists learned to master the new technology, and financiers came forward to build larger and better regional TV companies. The best known of these is MBC (Middle East Broadcasting), again a Saudi financed company based in London.

MBC stressed quality news coverage, and built a network of correspondents worldwide to gather their own news and produce features directly relevant to their public. MBC was an immediate success among Arab viewers. They naturally prefer Arab language programs; they are also choosing their own familiar regional prejudices over the American ones that are so evident in networks like CNN. A major issue for Arab viewers is sensitive coverage on Muslim issues, special programming for Ramadan, and the Haj pilgrimage.

Soon after MBC was underway, Dubai TV (from the Gulf Emirates) jumped into the market. It claims that it reaches a wider audience than MBC. Recently another new company, ANN (Arab Network News), based in London, joined the companies providing Arab news services worldwide, and more than one satellite company from Egypt is now transmitting globally. All have correspondents not only in the Arab states, but around the world. Most give timely attention to the affairs of Muslims globally and also produce quality children's programming.

These companies now compete with CNN and other large western networks as well as with local stations that broadcast American serials and cartoons. Arab viewers generally believe that the world coverage provided by their own regional Arab stations is less biased than the American networks. They may be right.

In addition to these international Arab networks, citizens of any state still have their local TV stations. Jordan TV, which broadcasts in Arabic, English and French, has remained relatively stagnant and seems to rely increasingly on U.S. films for diversity. The same applies to the North African states, but instead of U.S. films, they rely on French imports. The new Palestinian TV company is beset with problems and is still in infancy. Iraq cannot compete because it is held back by the sanctions.

By contrast, Syrian TV has moved in leaps and bounds with wide international coverage and top quality drama. Many Syrian dramatic series are produced for export to other Arab states. Syrian TV (state-run) has also upgraded its news and commentary programs, which are gaining respect in the region. It too has its correspondents based over a large part of the world. Many Arab viewers agree that Syria's news programs are outstanding. This will surprise many outsiders who unfortunately have no opportunity to evaluate these productions for themselves.

The most recent member of the Arab international news club is the Qatar company Al-Jazeera, launched two years ago. Within months of its appearance, this all-news channel has stirred up controversy and interest by moving to the next stage of development in a competitive market—introducing more aggressive on-air political debates. The company has featured interviews with exiled opposition figures, and a hard-hitting interview with Yasser Arafat received wide attention. The company also airs debates on issues such as "who is a Jordanian?" Besides broadcasting controversial questions about other Arab countries, this state-funded company also includes criticism of local government. According to observers, al-Jazeera's appearance has already prompted other regional satellite channels to air livelier debates.

The emergence of these companies has been possible with the availability of satellite dishes, now common across the Arab world. A strength of these companies is undoubtedly their large overseas staff. With competent correspondents throughout the world, they offer wide coverage and up-to-date news on current issues. On international issues, according to viewers, these channels compete with CNN and other western companies. Because of their use of Arabic, they are naturally preferred. But they are also free of the anti-Muslim bias and pro-American views that characterize the American networks. Of course, their commentators are better informed on Middle East history and politics as well.

On the other hand, a great deal of low quality productions are also reaching a wider public. One young producer in Lebanon wants to produce features on local issues such as environment, refugee matters, problems of ex-prisoners, abuse of women, etc, in order to stimulate citizen awareness and debate on local social and economic issues. Thus far he has had a hard time convincing his company to take on these subjects. Meanwhile, they produce increasing numbers of light audience game shows and music programs which, he says, bring in the commercial sponsors.

Twenty-two States Make Good Competition & Diversity

In their education system and in their media, the Arab states have as an advantage a pool of shareable resources. Twenty-two states, if we include the Palestinian state, make up the Arab world. Each has its interests, its traditions, and its pool of talent. A newspaper and TV company in one nation is of interest to others whose concerns and politics may be very different. One state may be critical of another; but at the same time, using their common language, they feed one another.

Within this dynamic are the personnel, the men and women who ultimately make it work. There again, the region has the advantage of a pool of skills from many backgrounds. In Dubai TV one can find Iraqi cameramen, a Lebanese host, an Egyptian producer and a Syrian writer. MBC TV and *Sharq al Awsat* daily will have a similarly diverse mixture of staff.

Finally, the growth of these industries in the Arab world and the popularity of the new kinds of programs is attracting bright, talented young women and men. This, in turn, will probably give rise to even more diversity.

This review is not a comparison between Arab and Western media alternatives and should not be taken as such. I offer these examples as a reminder of the vitality of the human mind itself. These are examples of how hungry people can use the diversity around them to enrich themselves, however limited their possibility of changing government policies may be.

It is rather ironic that someone should go to a part of the world notorious for its restricted press to find solutions to the problems that now beset western journalists. We condemn the limits imposed on the Arab public with regard to their political rights. Yet their unrepressed love of knowledge and their critical nature is a reminder of how precious that human capacity is. We need also to appreciate what I see as so evident in the Middle East—the alternative information that people receive from their neighbors. They listen to what their neighbors say.

Perhaps we need to ask new questions of the American public which is experiencing its information crisis. For example, why is the Western public losing its appetite for the kind of information that journalists make available? Why do they uncritically accept the narrow coverage of international issues? Why do they appear satisfied with a single source? Why don't they seek out the interpretations of others beyond their national boundaries?

Perhaps Western citizens can also begin to face the question of their own censorship. Relatively little Western censorship is legislated, but censorship exists in many other subtle yet effective ways. Perhaps western people cannot face this, and have therefore not completely defined their own problem. We hear repeatedly about the media giants who work with government to stifle all opposing views. Maybe there is more to this than rampant capitalism. This would not be the first time corporate wealth and government power functioned as comrades. Perhaps if we look deeper at the issue of censorship or intolerance, we will find some new answers.

ALTERNATIVE RADIO—AUDIO COMBAT

DAVID BARSAMIAN

To create a new culture does not only mean to make original discoveries on an individual basis. It also and especially means to critically popularize already existing truths, make them so to speak social, therefore, give them the consistency of basis for vital actions, make them coordinating elements of intellectual and social relevance.

Antonio Gramsci from *Prison Letters*

Why radio? Edward Said calls it "the oppositional form." Whereas with television there is the constant drive for the sound bite, with radio, he says, "You have to think in a different way, you have to think consecutively, you have to think with reason rather than with pictures. The fact is that radio is open to intervention." (Personal letter to me, 1993)

I have been a radio interventionist, doing combat on the airwaves, since 1978. Alternative Radio, my "organization," is part of a burgeoning movement of community-based, non-commercial stations in alliance with independent producers. I produce and distribute a weekly one-hour public affairs program that is broadcast on more than one hundred stations in the United States and Canada as well as to over seventy countries via shortwave. The technical aspect is not very complicated and the cost is quite modest. The U.S., with all its media problems, has by far the most developed and evolved network of community radio stations in the world. There are about 100 such stations in the country. For example, Pacifica, established in 1949, has five stations: New York, Houston, Berkeley, Los Angeles and Washington, DC.

A little background first. I moved to Boulder, Colorado in July, 1978. A friend who picked me up at the airport told me that KGNU had recently gone on the air and was looking for people to do radio. I quickly submitted a proposal, and before I knew it I was doing a weekly one-hour program which later expanded into 2-1/2 hours. Mind you I had no background in the medium. KGNU was open and supportive, but actual training in radio arts and crafts was perforce limited due to the usual formula: too few staff doing too much work. Much of what I learned about "doing" radio came on and off the air in an auto-didactic fashion. I gradually developed my editing, production, interviewing and other skills. Some grants and awards followed, which were all very gratifying. But I was still very much a local voice.

A significant turn in my audio evolution came in 1986. I was appointed program director of KRZA, a new bilingual station in Alamosa, in the San Luis Valley in southern Colorado. During my tenure there I learned the intricacies and mysteries of the satellite system. I began Alternative Radio in late 1986 in a bizarre way. I did something unheard of: I put up on the satellite in one block, three and a half hours of Noam Chomsky, a ninety-minute lecture followed by four 30-minute interviews. It was my first national broadcast. No one told me that most stations usually only have half-hour or one-hour slots. It was the proverbial learning experience. However, the Pacifica network did pick up the programs and listener response was tremendous. AR was on its way.

How do I do a program? First of all I use professional equipment; a SONY TC-D5M portable tape recorder that costs about $600, an Electrovoice RE-50 microphone which runs about $150, SONY MDR-V600 headphones, $70, and an AKG mic stand, $30. There are of course other configurations. Some producers prefer a SONY Walkman-PRO or a Marantz tape recorder. Others are advocating DAT machines. Whatever you get, don't chintz. Get good reliable equipment. Forget K-Mart bargains and completely forget using cheap tape. Always record with chrome cassettes from name manufacturers. I use Maxell, but the others, TDK, Fuji, etc., are comparable. And it is best for recording purposes to have 90-or 100-minute length cassettes. Know your equipment well and have full confidence in it and yourself before you venture out into the field. If the financial aspect is daunting, then most stations, with conditions, will permit you to borrow equipment.

Secondly, I tape and edit a lecture or interview. Let's say Winona LaDuke is giving a talk in Boulder at the University of Colorado. Her topic is "Social Justice, Racism and the Environmental Movement." I get her permission to record before she speaks. I record her presentation. It is brilliant. I decide to turn it into an AR national program. My associate Sandy Adler transcribes the tape. The transcript helps me enormously for I can see the tape. I time all the paragraphs and then start the actual editing process. I boil the program down to some fifty-odd minutes, tack on my music theme on both ends, add an introduction and closing and it is ready to go up on "the bird," the satellite.

Another example. I want to do an interview with Marilyn Young, the historian who teaches at New York University. Her book *The Vietnam Wars* is impressive. I contact her to see if she would like to be interviewed. She agrees. I go to New York and interview her. I then go through the same procedure as with LaDuke although this time I have expended much more time and money in the collection process. Some of my programs are locally generated but frequently I have to travel to find what I am looking for. I often feel that I am a hunter and gatherer. I go out and get tape and then bring it back to be cooked! A heartening development in the last couple of years is that I have established a coterie of field producers in various parts of the U.S. and Canada who send me tapes which I then turn into programs.

Thirdly, most of the cooking is done at KGNU studios where I continue to do local political and world music programs. I was station office manager in 1981 and then from 1987 to 1991 I was the News and Public Affairs Director. There is a healthy give-and-take between me and the station. I give them tapes to offer to listeners who become members during their fundraisers and I help with on-air pledge rapping, i.e., asking listeners to send in money, as well as in a variety of other ways.

Finally, I reserve in advance a regular time, day and channel on the satellite. I express the completed program to the uplink. I use the one in Ames, Iowa. The satellite system is the electronic umbilical cord linking hundreds of stations. It is run by National Public Radio. But fear not. All they want is your money. I have never heard a peep from them about the content of any of my programs. Some 400-plus stations have dishes or downlinks, i.e. they are capable of receiving programs. There are some 20 uplinks through which programs are distributed. Working with satellite deadlines is a constant stimulation. It is like having a Damocles sword of tape over your head at all times. The program has to be at the uplink before the scheduled uplink time. Stations record the program off the satellite and air it during a designated time. It is possible to broadcast live off the satellite and that is the case for news and breaking events, hearings, marches, etc. You can find out all about the satellite system and how you as an independent producer can use it by contacting NPR, 635 Massachusetts Ave, NW, Washington, DC 20001. Tel: (202) 414-3329. If at some point you decide to produce and distribute your own programs then NPR charges a one-time only $25 registration fee.

Of all the electronic media there is no question that radio is the least expensive. And as far as I am concerned it is the most satisfying. There is something very intimate about radio. It doesn't rob or preempt the listener's imagination. And for spoken word, which is what I do, it is the best. An hour is a decent amount of time to cover a subject. Alternative Radio programs focus on the media, U.S. foreign policy, racism, the environment, indigenous rights, NAFTA/GATT and economic issues and other topics. Recent programs have included Elaine Bernard on Creating a New Party; Juliet Schor on The Overworked American; Ali Mazrui on Afrocentricity and Multiculturalism; Edward Said on the Israel/PLO Accord; Helena Norberg-Hodge on Rethinking Development, a two-part debate on NAFTA; and Michael Parenti on The Struggle for Democracy.

I distribute via satellite. Fees run about $100 per program. The fee also gets me into the DACS (Direct Access Communications System). It is a device somewhat akin to a news wire. Every station that has a satellite dish has one. The DACS is the eyes and ears of the satellite. Program and news directors check it to find out what's up! The DACS tells them for example that on Tuesday, November 9 at 1400 eastern time on channel 6, Alternative Radio is offering a program on GATT featuring Herbert Chao Gunther. The DACS is a direct way to reach all the stations that are interconnected to the satellite system. I mail, fax and phone stations to nudge them further. Unfortunately, the satellite system is limited to the U.S. That means I have to send tapes via mail to Canada, Australia and elsewhere. Clearly an expensive, inefficient and not as good audio method. I look forward to the day when we'll be globally connected.

How do I support my "operation?" Directly through the sale of printed transcripts and audio cassettes to listeners. I don't charge the stations. It is important that the programs be broadcast so I make it as simple and as painless as possible for stations. My goal is to disseminate diverse perspectives and views. It does me little good to produce a program and then have it sit on a shelf.

There are stations and there are stations. Some of them won't go any where near my work. Most of these stations are NPR-types. Their licenses are mostly controlled by colleges and universities. And their schedules consist of lots of NPR news and other network produced programs with a good dollop of classical music and/or jazz. Sometimes stations like WGBH in Boston, KCFR in Denver or WHYY in Philadelphia are not institutional-based but nevertheless have very narrow politics. NPR-type program directors and managers worship at the chimerical icons of balance and objectivity, the kind exemplified by *Morning Edition* and *All Things Considered.* AR represents to them a bias. It is advocacy radio and hence anathema to their ears. Listeners must be protected from ideas outside the framework of received wisdom.

However, scattered around the country there are a handful of NPR-type stations that are willing to take risks and explore. They need to be encouraged and their numbers need to increase. A two-prong strategy seems appropriate. We need to create our own media as well as to penetrate existing structures. One of my goals is getting beyond the choir. Certainly our friends need information, news and analyses but simply preaching to the converted is neither intellectually nor emotionally satisfying. It is not easy but I can attest from my own experience that breakthroughs do happen. A sustainable media movement cannot abandon these possibilities.

The other category is community-run stations where there is a pluralism in programming and certainly more diversity in terms of gender and race among staff and volunteers. Community-run stations have been growing in steady numbers since the mid-1970s. Noam Chomsky has observed that when he visits a town or city that has a station that people tend to be more informed and aware of what is going on. Radio provides a means of intellectual self-defense and a vehicle for connecting with others. One of the things I love to do is to visit stations like KMUD in Garberville, California or KMUN in Astoria, Oregon or WERU in E. Orland, Maine or Co-op Radio in Vancouver, British Columbia. Though lacking in resources, the vitality, energy and sense of commitment at these stations is inspiring. And yes, there is political infighting and there are struggles but the positives far outweigh the negatives. The overwhelming number of on-air programmers are volunteers. It is the exact opposite of the NPR group where virtually only paid-staff are on-air and volunteers are fine for answering the phone during fundraisers.

What do community stations sound like? Their formats vary. KGNU, for example, has a news mix of the BBC and Pacifica that provides it with national and international coverage. Local news is tough to do. It is very labor and capital intensive. Its quality can range from excellent to fair. KGNU has a number of interview programs. Guests are either in the studio live, pre-taped or on the phone. Call-in programs are popular and get people interactive and talking. The station has a diverse music format with a good amount of international music. The fare is definitely not top-40. Much attention and emphasis is given to small, independent labels. The music to spoken word ratio during the week is about 70-30. On the weekend it is 85-15. KGNU has five paid staff, 230 volunteers, 3,000-plus members and a budget of $325,000.

If you are interested in more information and/or would like to establish a community radio station, then contact: National Federation of Community Broadcasters, Ft. Mason Center, Bldg. D, San Francisco, CA., tel: (415) 771-1160. NFCB is a national service and representation organization for community broadcasters. *Audio Craft*, a useful how-to book on production techniques written by audio wizard Randy Thom, can be ordered from NFCB. The annual community radio conference, sponsored by NFCB is a good opportunity to network.

Outside the U.S. you can contact AMARC, the World Association of Community Broadcasters, 3575 Blvd. St. Laurent, Suite 704, Montreal, Que., H2X 2T7, Canada. AMARC's seventh global radio conference is set for Milan in late August 1998. Bruce Girard of AMARC has edited *A Passion for Radio*, an informative book about what is happening in community radio in various countries. Traditional state control of radio is somewhat breaking down and radio activists are making inroads. AMARC has literature available in English, Spanish and French.

If you don't have a good local station and have a shortwave receiver you can hear a number of progressive programs on Radio for Peace International. It operates out of Santa Ana, Costa Rica. For a free schedule and frequency information write to: RPI, P.O. Box 20728, Portland, OR 97294.

Right-wing talk shows dominate the airwaves. A progressive response to the toxic emissions spewed forth by the Rush Limbaughs, Howard Sterns, Paul Harveys, and Tom Valentines is urgently needed. Now is the time to launch a daily national call-in talk show that will address issues and concerns of our communities. An 800-number as well as a fax are requisites. Such a program or programs—let's get one going but think of doing more—would be most valuable in creating an audio dialogue among ourselves as well as reaching out to a much wider audience and building new constituencies. The money required is not huge. The project will be supported by listener memberships. Additional income could come from tape and transcript sales.

Another critically needed program is a national morning news service that will challenge NPR's *Morning Edition*. Currently Pacifica offers a daily half-hour late afternoon newscast. In my view that program should be expanded to an hour and shift to the morning where radio use is at its maximum. If money is available the late afternoon news should be retained but the priority is the morning. Funding for this program will come directly from stations subscribing to the service. This project will involve much higher costs than the call-in show. If Pacifica is unable to do a daily morning news program then other sources must be identified.

A new development with potential is low-watt micro radio. It's sometimes referred to as pirate radio. It is a mechanism that does an end-run around the stations which are the gate-keepers of the airwaves. There are scores of micro radio stations popping up all over the U.S. M'banna Kantako in Springfield, IL is a pioneer in this field as is Steven Dunifer in Berkeley. Micro radio has the virtue of being low cost. However its narrow signal range limits its audience.

William Barlow of Howard University writes that community radio "has more democratic potential than any other form of mass media operating in the United States." Activists should seriously consider radio as a medium for action and engagement. There are more and more signs that that is happening. Matt Rothschild of *The Progressive* has *Second Opinion*, an interview show. *Fairness and Accuracy in Reporting*, the New York-based media watch group, has *CounterSpin*. It is hosted by Janine Jackson. *Making Contact* is produced by the National

Radio Project in the SF Bay Area. All of these are weekly half hour programs that are distributed via satellite to connected stations and by mail. Pacifica's *Democracy Now* is a daily one-hour program hosted by Amy Goodman. *The Nation* has launched a weekly one-hour program hosted by Marc Cooper. *In These Times,* the Institute for Policy Studies and others are contemplating radio. All these efforts are to be encouraged but they must locate themselves in a larger context. Edward Herman in the very first *Z Papers* wrote, "A full fledged democratization of the media can only occur in connection with a thoroughgoing political revolution."

The trend toward greater media concentration will continue. The amount of literature documenting corporate control and domination of media is staggering. We have done our homework and while that critique is ongoing I believe it is essential for psychological as well as political reasons to project and produce positive alternatives. It is vital that it happen. And radio offers just such an opportunity.

Broadcasting, the Constitution and Democracy

Louis Hiken, Alan Kom, Allen Hopper, Peter Franck

Media Regimes Based on Private Profit Constitutional?

In his classic testimony before the House Judiciary Committee in 1954, the late Alexander Meiklejohn said: "To find the meaning of the First Amendment we must dig down to the very foundations of the self-governing process. And what we shall there find is the fact that when men govern themselves, it is they—and no one else—who must pass judgement on public policies. And that means that in our popular discussions, unwise ideas must have a hearing as well as wise ones, dangerous ideas as well as safe, un-American as well as American. Just so far as, at any point, the citizens who are to decide the issues are denied acquaintance with information or opinion or doubt or disbelief or criticism which is relevant to those issues, just so far the result must be ill-considered, ill-balanced planning for the general good. It is that mutilation of the thinking process of the community against which the First Amendment is directed."[1]

The First Amendment had to be added to the Constitution before it could be ratified to insure that the United States would have a robust democracy. As Meiklejohn pointed out, a robust democracy requires broad channels of discussion and debate on all of society's issues and concerns. It requires a media system which is open to the broadest possible range of views and in which all citizens can effectively express and communicate their ideals, thoughts and concerns, as well as receive and consider the thoughts, ideas and concerns of their fellow citizens.

The Communications Act of 1934 says that it is enacted "so as to make available, so far as possible, to all the people of the United States, without discrimination on the basis of race, color, religion, national origin, or sex, a rapid, efficient, Nation-wide, and worldwide wire and radio communication service with adequate facilities at reasonable charges. . . ."[2]

Does the present media system, in which broadcasting is the primary channel of communications, meet this Constitutional and legislative mandate? Let's look at radio, the media sector most thoroughly affected by the Telecommunications Act of 1996. The Act relaxed ownership restrictions so that one company can own up to eight stations in a single market. In the twenty months since the law came into effect, 4,000 of the nation's 11,000 radio stations have changed hands, and there have been over 1,000 radio company mergers.[3] Small chains have been acquired by middle-sized chains, and the middle-sized chains have been gobbled up by the few massive companies which have come to dominate the industry. This sort of consolidation permits the giant chains to reduce costs by downsizing their editorial and sales staffs and running programming out of national headquarters. According to *Advertising Age*, by September 1997 in each of the fifty largest markets, three firms controlled over 50 percent of radio advertising revenue (and programming).[4] In twenty-three of the top fifty, three companies controlled more than 80 percent of the ad revenues. CBS alone has 175 stations, mostly in the fifteen largest markets.[5]

As the *Wall Street Journal* puts it, these deals "have given a handful of companies a lock on the airwaves in the nation's big cities."[6] Relative to television and other media, radio is inexpensive for both broadcasters and consumers. It is ideally suited for local control and community service. Yet radio has become nothing but a profit engine for a handful of firms so that they can convert radio broadcasting into the most efficient conduit possible for advertising. Across the nation, these giant chains use their market power to slash costs, providing the same handful of formats with barely a token nod to the communities in which the stations broadcast. On Wall Street, the corporate consolidation of radio may be praised as a smash success, but by any other standard this brave new world is an abject failure.[7]

Access to the Airwaves

Since 1979, the Federal Communications Commission, by regulation, has decreed that no radio station can be licensed at a broadcast power of less than 100 watts, and the FCC requires all potential licensees to conduct expensive engineering studies, which with associated legal and hardware expenses for a typical new station amounts to over $250,000.

It is as if a "Federal Newspaper Commission," in the name of efficiency, has said that to conserve paper and ink, only newspapers of at least 1 million general circulation would be legal. All church newsletters, PTA bulletins, and community weeklies would be banned. The situation in broadcasting is quite analogous.

Whether valid or not at the time, the ban on low power radio today fails constitutional muster. In *Federal Communications Commission* v. *League* of *Women Voters of California,* 468 U.S. 364, 380-381 (1984) the United States Supreme Court enunciated the test for restrictions on broadcasting. ". . . [A]lthough the broadcasting industry plainly operates under restraints not imposed upon other media, the thrust of these restrictions has generally been to secure the public's First Amendment interest in receiving a balanced presentation of views on diverse matters of public concern . . .. But, as our cases attest, these restrictions have been upheld only when we were satisfied that the restriction is *narrowly tailored to further a substantial governmental interest.*" [emphasis added]

The rationale, i.e., the "government interest," for the restriction put in place in 1979, was the enhancement and strengthening of public radio stations. This was done at a time when the Corporation for Public Broadcasting and the National Federation of Community Broadcasters wanted to "professionalize" public stations by driving out of existence a large number of small 10 watt, mostly college stations, and consolidating that energy and the money into a smaller number of more powerful stations. Today, public radio is fighting for its life, is underfunded, caters to an elite audience, and is being forced to drift into commercialization. It provides no real alternative and no access for the community.

Whatever the case may have been in 1979, banning low power radio is no longer the least restrictive means of accomplishing a legitimate government interest. The arbitrariness, and, in fact, the content relatedness of the ban on low power radio is made very clear by the FCC's current policies with respect to translators. The Commission will license a ten watt translator sitting on top of a mountain, retransmitting into a small town in a rural valley a signal from a 50,000 watt station in a city 50 to 100 miles away. Yet, it will not permit that small town to have this translator/transmitter send any local news, information or entertainment down to the same town over the same transmitter.

The Response of the Grass Roots

Starting in 1989, with M'banna Kantako, an unemployed black man living in a housing project in southern Illinois, the Microradio Movement has grown as an indigenous grass roots response to the terrible and unconstitutional vacuum on the airways. Spurred on by the efforts of Stephen Dunifer, an engineer and philosophical anarchist, and by the recognition of United States District Court Judge Claudia Wilken[8] that the constitutional challenge to the present regulatory regime was a serious one meriting a very close look by the FCC and the courts, the Microradio Movement has grown to the point that there are probably 1,000 such stations on the air in the United States.

In Southern California "Esscellent Radio" broadcasts the local city council meeting every week. The council was concerned about the "legality" of allowing a non-licensed station to broadcast its proceedings, but it was advised by its attorney that it would be violating the law by preventing the broadcast. This non-licensed station replaced a service abandoned by a local commercial station in search of greater profits and more advertising revenue. In the Northwestern United States, Korean communities who were not served in their own language by commercial broadcasters have set up their own non-licensed Korean service.

The micro radio movement is international. Steven Dunifer was consulted by then president of Haiti Jean-Bertrand Aristide on the feasibility of setting up low-power transmitters in Haiti. In fact, he has assisted Haiti several times and has taught local community groups to assemble and operate their own community based stations. Several years ago, during the same week that Steven Dunifer received a Notice of Apparent Liability in the sum of $20,000 from the Federal Communications Commission, he received by fax from the United Nations Educational Scientific and Cultural organization (UNESCO) an order for $5,000 worth of micro-radio transmitters for their community development project in the Philippines.

Since Dunifer's Free Radio Berkeley went on the air in 1991, there have been five conferences of micro broadcasters, each larger than the last. In April, 1998, several hundred micro broadcasters met in Philadelphia to consolidate their plans and continue growing the movement. In May 1998, several hundred more micro broadcasters met in Las Vegas with the same purpose.

Official Response

The FCC has released a Notice of Inquiry with respect to the question of whether it should open a formal rule-making proceeding to review the ban on low power radio. FCC Chair William Kennard has conceded that micro-broadcasters have a point when they complain that it is hard for community broadcasters to get on the air. He has said that he thinks that micro-broadcasting has exploded in popularity in the last few years as a backlash against the consolidation of station ownership spurred by the 1966 federal communications law.[9]

When the National Association of Broadcasters assembled on April 6, 1998, they had a historic opportunity to show the world that their organization was committed to the Constitution and democracy, and to the sharing of the electronic spectrum between the commercial broadcast industry and grass roots stations. The Micro Radio community came forward at that meeting to present a simple, practical and democratic proposal for a low power radio regime. We in the Micro Radio community continue to urge the National Association of Broadcasters to join in this inevitable and necessary democratization of the airwaves.

Proposal for Low Power FM Service
We propose:

a. A micropower station may be established on any unused frequency within the FM broadcast band and extending down to 87.6.12 where there is no TV on channel 6. A second adjacent channel would be the closest spacing allowed. A micro station shall fill out a simple registration form, sending one copy with an appropriate registration fee to the FCC and a second copy to the voluntary body set up by the micropower broadcast community to oversee the micro power stations. Such modes of self-regulation already exist within the ham radio community and the commercial broadcast arena.

b. Maximum power shall be 50 watts urban and 100 watts rural. In the event of interference due to power level, a station shall have the option to reduce power to remedy the situation or else be shut down.

c. Equipment shall meet basic technical criteria with respect to stability, filtering, modulation control, etc.

d. Only one station per organization. The organization must be based in the local community and not be a profit-making organization. Local origination of programming is encouraged as much as possible.

e. No commercial sponsorship shall be allowed.

f. There shall be no content requirements. Stations shall deal with "community standards" issues on an individual basis and in accordance with their own particular mission statements.

g. When television broadcast stations go digital, leaving Channel 6 free, it shall be allocated as an extension to the bottom of the FM band strictly for low power community FM service. This would add thirty new channels, since TV channel 6 is 6 MHz wide and an FM broadcast is only 200 kHz wide. Radio receivers manufactured or entering the country after that allocation must meet this band extension.

h. Registration shall be valid for four years.

i. Problems, whether technical or otherwise, shall be resolved, if at all possible, at the community level, first by technical assistance or voluntary mediation. The FCC shall be the court of last resort.

j. Micro broadcasting of special events (demonstrations, rallies, festivals, etc.) do not need to be registered but are encouraged to meet all technical specifications. One frequency could be set aside for this.[10]

---

1. Alexander Meiklejohn, *Political Freedom: the Constitutional Powers of the People.* New York: Oxford Press, 1965.
2. 47 U.S.C. Section 151 as amended in August 1996.
3. David Johnston, "U.S. Acts to Bar Chancellor Media's L.I. Radio Deal," *New York Times*, November 7, 1997, p. C10.
4. Ira Teinowitz, "Westinghouse Deal Fuels Consolidation in Radio," *Advertising Age*, September 29, 1997, p. 61.
5. Timothy Aepel and William N. Bulkeley, "Westinghouse to Buy American Radio," *Wall Street Journal*, September 22, 1997, p. A3.
6. Eben Shapiro, "A Wave of Buyouts Has Radio Industry Beaming with Success," *Wall Street Journal*, September 22, 1997, p.A3.
7. *Wall Street Journal*, September 18, 1997, p. A1
8. U.S. v. Dunifer, No.C94-03542, Memorandum Decision of January 30,1995 (N.D. CA 1995)
9. Mary Curtis, "Defiant Pirates [sic] Ply the Radio Airwaves," *LA Times*, March 5, 1998, p. 1.
10. For example, in the San Francisco Bay Area, 87.9 serves this purpose.

INFORMATION ON THE INTERNET: THE PROSPECTS OF A DEMOCRATIC MEDIUM

MANSE JACOBI

In this paper, I shall address the extent to which the Internet can serve as an alternative medium, showcasing some of the work we do at Free Speech Internet Television. But before I speak about this new technology, I would like to digress a bit and provide a brief history of the cable project we grew out of. This will serve as an introductory anecdote to the topic of the overwhelming corporate ownership of media operating in the "freest country in the world."

Free Speech Internet TV was first launched in 1995 by the 90s Channel and became the largest cable network in the U.S. dedicated to progressive and activist-based programming. Telecommunications Incorporated (TCI), the world's largest cable operator, had dropped the 90s Channel in 1995, while it provided support for conservative networks such as Newt Gingrich's National Empowerment Television.[1] TCI's decision and its continuing television monopoly offer an excellent illustration of why free markets can never guarantee a democratic media system. The danger posed here is not an exact parallel with an oil or steel monopoly, since TCI's objective is not just profit, but the invaluable ability to "control the public mind."[2]

The Telecommunications Act passed by the U.S. Congress in 1996 crippled safeguards meant to protect the American public and ushered in a new era of media robber barons by permitting already powerful companies to acquire ownership of even more telecom production, programming and distribution operations. The 1996 Act may have been one of the most significant pieces of legislation in this century, referred to by some as "the biggest public giveaway," yet it was covered in mainstream media merely as a business story. The goal of Free Speech Internet TV's founding was to find a way for progressive media to survive—and even thrive—in this hostile environment.

The seemingly inexorable trend toward media centralization, which is addressed extensively elsewhere in this book, is also extending to the Internet, the most recent hope for a "truly democratic medium." Free Speech Internet TV was launched in 1995 in hopes of utilizing newly developed video streaming technologies to effect social change. We are also currently attempting to start a full-time progressive television network. In November 1998, the FCC issued rules requiring Direct Broadcast Satellite (DBS) operators to set aside four percent of their channel capacity for non-commercial, educational and informational programmers. Free Speech Internet TV (along with Internews, Deep Dish TV and a number of other independent networks) has been working to get a DBS channel, and this goal is within reach.

This paper's discussion will focus on this medium and its prospects for changing the way people gather and disseminate information.

The Internet as a Viable Democratic Medium

My interest in the Internet as a communications tool was fueled by the early enthusiasts who were enchanted by its seemingly open and democratic structure. There were good reasons to believe that it had the potential of revolutionizing the techniques of human communication. With a mild inclination towards technological determinism, the new technology resembled Raymond Williams' early conception of a democratic medium of communication. Its disordered many-to-many topology had the promise of overriding the centralized traditional media outlets.

Much has been said and written about the revolutionary prospects of the new technology. Conservative author George

Gilder summed up this euphoria when he described the new technology as one which moved intelligence and control "from a few national broadcast networks to millions of programmers around the globe."[3] In the first edition of *Wired*, publisher Louis Rosetto wrote that the digital revolution will bring "social changes so profound their only parallel is the discovery of fire."[4] And recently *The Wall Street Journal*, writing on the new webcasting technology, cited our project director as one of many "basement media moguls" who are leading the "big entertainment conglomerates."[5]

There is broad agreement that the Internet acquires features not found in any other medium. The Internet is endowed with an adaptability to multiple methods of distributing information. Internet users are no longer restricted to traditional text and still graphics, and are rapidly utilizing new audio and video streaming technologies. Nothing prohibits the online version of a newspaper from including video clips in its articles. In cyberspace, the physical boundaries between text, radio, and television no longer exist, but a more important distinction is the relatively low cost of making information available to a large audience.

Unfortunately, the democratic elements in the new technology are rapidly disappearing. Streamed media, for instance, requires higher—and more expensive—bandwidth (data transfer speed). New connectivity technologies such as wireless and cable modems offer much higher download speed than upload, virtually minimizing user interactivity. The many-to-many architecture of the net is being replaced with technologies resembling the traditional centralized and commercial media outlets. This is why corporate interest has pushed for analogies that replace interactivity with concepts like 'Internet channels' and 'netcast stations.' The business press covering the new technology is quite frank in its description of future Internet users as "passive consumers."

This rapid movement towards commercialization should be understood in the context of the existing economic system and not the immunity of any new technology. While the Internet has been subsidized by taxpayers for more than two decades, the possibility of using it to serve very narrow interests was understood from its inception.[6] U.S. Vice-President Al Gore's adaptation of the term 'information superhighway' serves as a useful analogy to his grandfather's initiative in the 1950s to build a national highway system which would serve the military-industrial complex. "The main beneficiaries of the new capabilities in information [technology]," writes Herbert Schiller, are "the new transnational corporations, the intelligence, military, and policing agencies."[7]

But the fundamental factor which keeps progressive voices from being heard is not embedded in the technology itself. It's not that these voices don't exist. Browsing the member listings of APC (Association for Progressive Communication) or Znet demonstrates that activism and noncommercial media is alive and well in cyberspace. In fact, public virtual communities have existed in the periphery since the 1980s and constituted much of the news distributed globally. This was before the big giants logged on.

Before the Internet was commercialized in 1995, Howard Rheingold wrote about the remarkable potential of the emerging technology in his 1993 book *The Virtual Community*. His early warnings are particularly relevant today: "[T]he technology will not in itself fulfil [the potential of bringing enormous leverage to ordinary citizens at relatively low cost]; this latent technical power must be used intelligently and deliberately by an informed population. More people must learn about that leverage and learn to use it, while we still have the freedom to do so, if it is to live up to its potential. The odds are always good that big power and big money always found ways to control new communications media when they emerged in the past."[8]

The landscape of the Internet has since changed dramatically. While there has been growing participation from grassroots organizations, their ability to attract an audience is increasingly overshadowed by large conglomerates who are investing heavily in the new medium. These are companies like

Disney and USA Networks who seek to extend their domination into the new medium. Portal sites and start-pages exert a strong influence on the medium and what Internet users see and don't see. Search engines, a focal starting point for many users, are beginning to solicit money from those willing to pay for "top placement." Amazon, the largest online bookseller, charges publishers for added visibility on their site. Jeff Bezos, Amazon's chief executive, suggested that "retailers [are] pioneering a new medium that shouldn't be held to the same standards as, say, the book-review sections of newspapers and magazines, which strive for independence from advertising concerns."[9]

The challenges we face are therefore no different from those that progressives face within the television, radio, and print world. There is too much corporate control of information distribution. The task at hand is for progressives and advocates of democracy worldwide to pool their resources and utilize a medium that could serve the interests of people instead of corporations. Certainly, my work at Free Speech Internet TV during the last two years offers persuasive evidence that this goal is within reach.

Webcasting and the Free Speech Internet Project

The terms 'webcasting' or 'streamed video' simply refer to the method by which digital video is continuously streamed over the Internet. By way of metaphor, it works the same way a cable channel is 'streamed' through the cable wires to your home. This technology grew out of the need to offer live audio and video content to Internet users who had been confined to text and still graphics. The challenge has been the ability to compress digital video to the point were it could be streamed over regular phone lines. The pioneer behind RealVideo, the ubiquitous video-streaming player with over 50 million users worldwide, is Foundation for National Progress board member Rob Glaser. As early as 1994, Glaser envisioned the prospects of using the new medium to create and distribute 'progressive' media. He started a company called Progressive Networks, which was to become a multi-million software company and renamed RealNetworks.

Free Speech Internet TV was one of the first to utilize RealNetworks' software, and we began offering streamed audio and video as early as 1996. Our programming ranges from video magazines like the New York-based People's Video Network and the London-based Undercurrents, to grass-roots media such as Food Not Bombs and the Chiapas Media Project. We also feature interviews and lectures, short experimental films, video poetry, radio shows, and a wide range of documentaries. While we try to maintain a professional standard, we are committed to the idea that ordinary people are capable of producing meaningful media reflecting their daily issues. In 1997, we launched Do-It-Yourself Television (DIY-TV), on which we provided outlets for people to create their own content and stream it through our servers. It may sound like America's Funniest Home Videos, and in fact the video quality was a close resemblance, but the material we continue to receive reflects the wide range of issues people are really interested in.

Our Challenges Ahead

As mentioned earlier, our biggest challenge now—and my objective in this paper—is to let people know that there exists a place where they can not only watch meaningful media, but where they can create their own programming. Unfortunately, the discrepancy between those who are connected and those who aren't conforms to the prevailing class division and the disparity between industrialized nations and the Third World. There also exists a problem of estrangement to new technologies like video streaming in particular and the Internet in general. But it is our optimistic belief that this can only improve through the important work of activists and social organizations which seek to transfer the ownership of communication outlets from corporations back to the people. For this movement to be effective, it has to be part of a broader movement for democracy, equality, and social justice. As Robert

McChesney puts it, the "extent to which there is non-elite participation into communication policymaking may be a barometer for the level of democracy in a society." [10]

This movement has to be a global one, since media conglomeration is principally a global trend. Cyber activism is endowed with the remarkable feature that it lacks geographic boundaries. With increased globalization and concentration of power, the struggles of people are more and more the same all over the world. The Internet could serve as a place of convergence; where progressive voices are heard from different parts of the globe. This is what Egyptian writer Nawal El Saadawi has described in this book as "globalization from below." While our audience is mostly concentrated in North America and Europe, we have had viewers from almost every Internet-wired country in the world. We are committed to increasing viewer participation and content creation from all parts of the world, specifically the underdeveloped and under represented countries of the South. I am proposing this endeavor in the context of the Civil Society Convergence Project, in the hopes of constructing a solid stepping stone to "building alternative media outlets."

Civil Society Convergence Project

The Convergence Project is put together as a collaborate initiative of AMARC, APC and Videazimut.[11] This initiative involves creation of a world-wide network of journalists, writers, and activists who share information freely and democratically. This would be a kind of alternative, non-commercial news wire service. Currently, alternative news sources look like tiny islands scattered in a vast sea of disinformation. What is needed in this era of corporate media conglomeration are ways of bringing these voices together. This would require a physical distribution infrastructure in addition to a network of dedicated contributors from all parts of the world. This domain of convergence would take advantage of the Internet's portability and provide text, audio and video distribution for media specialists, concerned groups and citizens all over the world.

The possibilities are endless, but they are only possibilities. Real systems—both human and technical—are necessary to turn these opportunities into reality. While small pieces of this picture are starting to fall into place to deliver content for specific projects, a more integrated collection of production, distribution and communications resources needs to evolve. Existing and new media projects need to connect to create a "shared convergence platform." This should be the goal of every participant at this unique gathering of journalists, activists and writers from all over the world.

---

1. For more on TCI's decision to drop the '90s Channel, read "S.F.'s Cable Censor," *San Francisco Bay Guardian,* November 22, 1995.
2. Term borrowed from Noam Chomsky and Edward Herman, *Manufacturing Consent: The Political Economy of Mass Media* (New York: Pantheon, 1988). The use of new media technologies for propaganda has been a topic of study since the 1960s, most notable are the works of communication economist Herbert I. Schiller and sociologist Jacques Ellul.
3. George Gilder, *Life After Television* (New York: Norton, 1992).
4. Quoted in "Wired Words: Utopia, Revolution and the History of Electronic Highways" by Mark Surman, <kows.web.net/wiredwords/default.html>
5. Debra Jo Immergut, "Webcast News," *Wall Street Journal,* May 28 1998.
6. The Internet's origin was ARPANET, an experimental project created in 1969 and funded by the U.S. Department of Defense.
7. Gretchen Bender and Timothy Druckrey, ed., *Cultures on the Brink: Ideologies of Technology* (Seattle: Bay Press, 1994).
8. Howard Rheingold, *The Virtual Community* (New York: Harper Perennial: 1994).
9. David Bank and George Anders, *Wall Street Journal,* Tuesday 9, 1998.
10. Robert McChesney, *Corporate Media and the Threat to Democracy* (New York: Seven Stories Press, 1997)

11. AMARC is an international coalition of over 2,000 community radio stations and producers <www.amarc.org>. Association for Progressive Communications is a global meta-network of Internet providers serving over 50,000 organizations in 25 countries <www.apc.org>.

12. Videazimut is an international NGO promoting audiovisual communications for development and democracy <www.tao.ca/videazimut>. The description here is borrowed from a proposal prepared by Mark Surman of Web Networks <mark@web.net>.

CAN THE MARKETPLACE PROTECT FREE SPEECH?

CHARLES LEVENDOSKY

I want to begin by giving some good news about print journalism, news that we have not yet heard at the conference—and are not likely to hear. There are over a thousand small newspapers across America, with circulations of 25,000 to 75,000, whose aggregate circulation far exceeds that of the *Washington Post, New York Times, LA Times,* and even the number of viewers of major television network news programs. It is at these smaller daily newspapers that some of the best hard-nosed, workaday journalism goes on—which is not bent out of shape by the forces of commercialism.

In our newspaper, for instance, I cannot go across to the advertising side and ask the simple question about what ads are going to run in tomorrow's paper. Neither can someone from the ad department come to the news side and ask whether we're running a story concerning some business shenanigans in our community. That's verboten.

The reason is simple: We want to keep a clear line of demarcation so that the advertising side doesn't interfere with or alter the gathering of the news. That's an old and honorable journalistic ethic, and it survives today in America's smaller newspapers.

Now I'll get to the topic: "Censorship and Control of the Media."

Direct Censorship

There are a number of forces that are involved in trying to control and censor the media. The government is the largest and most powerful of these forces. The government interferes with news-gathering and news dissemination by withholding information regarding public policy or by presidential directives. Sometimes the federal government purposely disseminates misinformation—called trial balloons—by leaks to the press, or by slants from the administration, or spins from members of Congress.

I've read and written a great deal about public lands issues, which in Wyoming is a major concern—public lands meaning federally administered lands that belong to the entire populace of the United States. Nearly 50 percent of Wyoming is owned by the federal government and managed for the citizens of the United States. Therefore, public lands management and control is a major issue in the state.

I received a call from a senator's office late one Friday night. The voice asked, "Are you Charles Levendosky?" When I affirmed that, he said, "You know, you're on a list of journalists who are going to be used"—he used the word "used" repeatedly—"by the Forest Service to disseminate their point of view. How do you like being used?"

I interrupted him for a moment and asked in what senatorial office he works. He's an aide to Sen. Frank Murkowski, R-Alaska. Murkowski has a reputation for never seeing a tree he didn't want to cut down. I replied, "Look, everybody likes to use the press; nearly every call I get, someone wants to use me or the newspaper for some reason. As a journalist with 16 years experience, I know that, every working journalist knows that. The point is—we work through it, or around it, or we gather many viewpoints. So what's your point?"

And then, out of curiosity, I asked him, "Who else is on that list?" It turned out that reporters from the *New York Times*, *Washington Post*, and many of the major news media outlets were included.

Yes, I do contact and talk to people at the U.S. Forest Service concerning many issues, and I do listen to their points of view. However, I also try get Sen. Murkowski's perspective— if it's appropriate—or the view of another member of Congress. And I chase down the viewpoints of special-interest groups which either want more timber to be cut or less timber to be cut, and I try to weave through all of that, like any journalist should, to present my perspective.

Murkowski's assistant was playing a not-so-subtle game in an attempt to skew my thinking about the U.S. Forest Service—to make me suspicious of the motives of the people in that agency to whom I talk. I've been a columnist and editorial page editor long enough to ask hard questions of any potential news source—including members of Sen. Murkowski's office.

Government agencies interfere with Freedom of Information Act requests. They stall; they misdirect you. They may send reporters a box full of the requested information with nine-tenths of the pages totally blacked out. Or they'll tell you that you didn't aim your directive carefully enough and you should be more specific in requesting what it is you want. This kind of dallying around can take six months, a year, two years before a reporter sees what he or she has been requesting. The idea is to frustrate the person requesting the information so that the FOIA request is finally dropped, or the story for which the information was needed is no longer an issue.

Twelve states have passed food disparagement laws, laughingly called "veggie libel laws"—which means that the media can be sued for libel if they criticize an agricultural product or how an agricultural product is treated. Many other states are considering such food disparagement laws.

There are seven or eight cattle barons who control most of the cattle sold in the United States. Oprah Winfrey was sued by three of these cattle feedlot magnates under the Texas food disparagement law. On her TV show, Winfrey had suggested that mad cow disease might exist in U.S. cattle. The cattlemen sued. They lost the case badly—the jury not only ruled against them, but the judge, in an unusual move, sent down an opinion saying there was no way that the beef industry could have won this according to the law.

Even so, the beef barons have filed an appeal. In other words, they think they have more money than Oprah. It takes a lot of money to protect yourself against such lawsuits. The beef barons want to send a message to the public—you can't afford to criticize beef. If you're a small newspaper in a state that has a food disparagement law, you'd better be careful what you say about the hog farm that's polluting the groundwater in your neighborhood.

During the Vietnam War, reporters from the United States and other countries were all over that war, just as they were in the Second World War. However, with the beginning of the Grenada invasion and continuing throughout the Persian Gulf War, members of the press were forced to remain with escort military officers at all times. And—this is the most pernicious part—all news reports were subject to review by military officials.

The American public only received news from the battle-front that the military allowed. The generals and the White House don't want the public to know what is really happening to our men in these or future military actions. They don't want public pressure to end a war.

Section 14 of the Helms-Burton Act of 1996 authorizes the federal government to decide which news organizations are allowed to travel to so-called enemy countries, like Cuba, to report the news. In effect, the legislation set up a licensing system for the press and other media.

In 1997, the Clinton administration licensed 10 news organizations to operate in Cuba for one year. I mention the one-year license because it means that if a news organization is not reporting the news the way the Clinton administration would like it reported, the organization may not get its license renewed. That's the threat.

The government may attempt to halt a story relying upon government documents by using the courts and gag orders. The gag order in the Pentagon Papers case was lost by the government when the government couldn't persuade the United States Supreme Court that, indeed, publishing these papers would jeopardize the national safety.

However, in the CNN/Noriega case, when CNN attempted to broadcast tapes made of Manuel Noriega's conversations with friends and his attorney, the government, which had secretly made those tapes, brought a lawsuit to stop CNN. CNN aired the tapes anyway, but they were fined for doing so.

The new Anti-Terrorism Act allows secret court proceedings against foreign nationals and legal immigrants who are believed to be involved in terrorist activities. These secret proceedings are a first in American jurisprudence and in American history. Under the new law, the defendant's own attorney cannot learn the evidence against the defendant, preventing him or her from refuting or combating the charge. The Anti-Terrorism Act applies to immigrants who may only have given humanitarian aid (donations to hospitals, refugee camps or orphanages) to organizations labeled as terrorist by the United States Secretary of State.

A more subtle move is the privatization of government records and databases, not only at the federal level but at state levels. Government entities contract with private enterprise to maintain and store government records. These private companies turn around and charge for the information they hold—even though the information belongs to the public, which has already paid for it in tax dollars.

These private companies may claim to offer enhanced services. That is, if you're a journalist and you want some data held by the company, you may want to get more than what is being offered for a minimum charge. It may cost a news organization $250 or $500, to receive the enhanced service. This is beyond the means of most citizens of the United States, yet these are supposedly public documents.

260

Censorship by and for Profit

Another kind of force that warps news coverage is what I call censorship by omission. Small newspapers often do not fairly represent the views of minority groups. Ethnic, sexual, religious, and cultural viewpoints or perspectives on the news are lacking. And, unfortunately, the news and commentary about these minority groups are often negative.

For instance two years ago, if you picked up a story about Palestinians, it was mostly negative. If you pick up stories about gays, whether national or local stories, they are nearly always negative. This is true around the world about different minority groups or political dissidents.

In the United States, international news and views reflect the perspective found in New York City and Washington, D.C., not the views from the nations involved. Smaller newspapers cannot afford to subscribe to Associated Press, *New York Times*, Scripps-Howard and Reuters, all at the same time. Therefore, they do not receive news reports and perspectives written by responsible journalists in other nations. Smaller newspapers, with limited resources, only reflect news and views given to them by national wire services.

That is a major problem, and one that grows ever larger. And I hope it will be discussed in greater detail. Alternative media may be a way to deal with this problem. Every newspaper, from small to medium-sized, would like to have international perspectives on international news.

You've already heard a great deal about corporate ownership of major networks—and the corporate bottom line. We cannot really expect an in-depth investigative piece on nuclear energy by a major player in the news market if they are owned by an electric company that uses nuclear energy. The public will have to go somewhere else to hear or read that investigative piece.

But there's a more subtle trend that is a corrosive force in print journalism—features. Being a news junkie, as I travel around the country I pick up newspapers everywhere I go. What used to be proud, hard-news newspapers—like the *Atlanta Constitution*, the *LA Times* and the *Chicago Tribune*—are turning flabby as they have begun running feature pieces on their front pages as well as in the middle of the paper—features that focus on foods and cosmetics and consumerism in general.

How does that translate into a corrosive force? I know a reporter who used to work for a major East Coast newspaper who would receive expensive gifts from cosmetic companies—like $150 cosmetic sets—while or after writing a feature story on the company,

When newspaper editors allow feature reporters to accept gifts from those they cover, journalistic ethics begin to die. These gifts may not be a quid pro quo, that is, writing in order to receive such gifts; nevertheless, it means the next time around, that feature reporter is likely to be more friendly in the coverage. A feature reporter who accepts gifts and who writes about Nike sports products is unlikely to report on wage scales and treatment of workers—even if the story is staring the reporter in the face.

Feature news stories are a part of the trend to trivialize the news. And this is perhaps one of the most dangerous trends in the American media. When newspapers and TV networks spend weeks of time and scarce reporter resources following sex scandals instead of tracking the impact of poverty or the likely impact of congressional legislation, the people lose—all the people.

Libel and defamation lawsuits aimed at punishing the media cause those newspapers with smaller resources to shy away from important news stories. Lawsuits that punish major news organizations send a message to small news organizations. The Food Lion grocery chain recently won a fraud and trespassing case against ABC News, which used hidden cameras and false identities to investigate unsanitary food practices at Food Lion. These and other lawsuits are an attempt to muzzle reporters.

Such multi-million dollar lawsuits can create havoc in most newspapers.

When courts allow secret settlements in civil lawsuits regarding defective products, those products continue to be sold to an uninformed public. The settlements withhold important documents. The Ford Pinto had defective gas tanks. For something like six years, settlements were hidden, and it wasn't until a real disaster happened that people began to learn about the problem. The same kind of time lag was permitted by secret lawsuit settlements before the public was informed about problems with silicone breast implants, exploding Bic cigarette lighters, and defective Zenith TV sets that started fires. There were 100 cases settled quietly, secretly, and the public was kept in the dark.

Alternatives to the Corporate Media

On the positive side, there is the Internet. And before you rag on me for being a high-tech elitist, let me say that the radio was considered high-tech elitist at one time. The Internet is a major source of news in the United States, as well as most other developed countries. It was used by students in Indonesia to bring down President Suharto. The Internet is being used to battle the dictatorship in Burma.

The Internet—as the U.S. Supreme Court said recently in ruling the Communications Decency Act unconstitutional—has the potential of the street pamphleteer of pre-revolutionary America. The man on the street, regardless of wealth or lack of it, can enter a public library and use one of the library's computers with Internet access and send thousands of email messages around the world in a short period of time—for free. The Internet also provides hope for the dissemination of minority views, and for the views of dissidents.

Joe Shea, creator and editor of one of the major online newspapers, the *American Reporter*, makes his news stories available to other news outlets at a small charge per story used. Shea's formula earns money for his reporters and gives other newspapers the opportunity to diversify their coverage—at a small price. This model could be used internationally. An on-line newspaper, let us call it the *World Reporter*, could make its news stories available to smaller newspapers via the Internet at a reasonable price. This could give an international flavor to those newspapers which can only afford one or two wire services for their national and international news.

Let me end by urging that we look at alternatives for the distribution of news and views—in order to promote a balance, an alternative to major media outlets that are controlled by large corporate monopolies. The potential for alternative news media that reaches millions of readers does exist now—with the Internet. And good journalistic ethics survive despite the forces that would bend news coverage to their advantage. Look to your smaller newspapers and see that such ethics still exist.

There are other alternative news sources, such as those low-frequency, low-power radio stations, micropower radio, that are working in communities. They provide local voices outside the control of the global media corporations. Our hope for the future lies with such alternative media.

Author Biographies

JEAN-BERTRAND ARISTIDE (Haiti)

A world-famous "liberation theologian" and grass roots leader in Haiti, Dr. Aristide received 67 percent of the Haitian vote on Dec. 16, 1990, and took office February 18, 1991, to become Haiti's first democratically elected president. After less than 8 months in power, the CIA working with the Duvalierists overthrew Aristide on September 30, 1991.

After three years in exile, Aristide was allowed to return to Haiti only after he signed a U.S.-brokered agreement not to reclaim his "lost" three years. He is widely expected to win the next election for Haiti's president.

His books in English include: *In the Parish of the Poor* (1990); *Aristide: an autobiography* (1993); *Dignity* (1996).

SCOTT ARMSTRONG (U.S.A.)

Mr. Armstrong is an investigative journalist and scholar whose career has been distinguished by an unswerving commitment to open government. From 1976 to 1985, Armstrong was a staff writer for the *Washington Post*. He and Bob Woodward co-authored *The Brethren*, an account of the inner workings of the Supreme Court from 1969 through 1976. Armstrong also served as a senior investigator for the Senate Watergate Committee, and his interviews revealed the Nixon White House taping system, which eventually led to Nixon's demise.

In 1985, Armstrong founded the National Security Archive, a nonprofit research institute. He served as the Archive's executive director from 1985 to 1989 and oversaw its public opening in January 1987.

BARBARA NIMRI AZIZ (U.S.A.)

Dr. Aziz is an anthropologist and well known journalist specializing in Middle East issues. She travels extensively throughout the Middle East and visited Iraq both before and after the Gulf War to monitor social and economic developments. She specializes in analyzing the impact of the war and sanctions on Iraqi agriculture. Dr. Aziz produces a Saturday afternoon radio program on Pacifica WBAI in New York.

BEN H. BAGDIKIAN (U.S.A.)

A prize-winning journalist, Mr. Bagdikian is the former editor of the *Washington Post* and the former dean of the Graduate School of Journalism at the University of California, Berkeley. Ralph Nader described Bagdikian's book *The Media Monopoly* as "the most penetrating specific and reflective book on both the electronic and print media in many a year."

DAVID BARSAMIAN (U.S.A.)

Mr. Barsamian is a radio producer, journalist, author and lecturer, as well as Founder and Director of Alternative Radio. He is National Producer of "Making Contact." He has been "doing" radio since 1978. His interviews and articles appear in *Harper's*, *The Progressive* and numerous other magazines. He is the author of six books, including *Keeping the Rabble in Line* and *Class Warfare* with Noam Chomsky and *The Pen and the Sword* with Edward Said. His new book with Chomsky is *The Common Good*. He was featured in the award-winning documentary film *Manufacturing Consent*.

BRIAN BECKER (U.S.A.)

Brian Becker is co-director of the International Action Center. He was a spokesperson for the National Coalition to Stop the War Against Yugoslavia. Becker is a frequent commentator on Fox Network News. He is a contributor and co-author of several books including *War Crimes: A Report on*

United States War Crimes Against Iraq, as well as *The Truth Behind the U.S. Invasion of Panama* and *Challenge to Genocide.* He was a producer of the award winning video *Genocide by Sanctions,* and the TV documentary film *Muhammad Ali— The Whole Story.* Becker is a regular contributor to *Workers World* newspaper.

RAMSEY CLARK (U.S.A.)

Ramsey Clark is an internationally known lawyer and human rights activist. He was one of the most prominent opponents of the U.S. war against Iraq and the NATO bombing of Yugoslavia. He traveled to both countries during the height of the U.S. bombing campaigns. He has been outspoken in his opposition to every U.S. intervention, bombing or CIA organized coup of the past thirty years, from Vietnam and Central America to the Middle East and Africa. He initiated the International Action Center to help broaden this work. As a lawyer he has taken ground-breaking cases for the PLO, Indian Nations in Alaska and political prisoners such as Leonard Peltier and prisoners on Texas Death Row.

As Assistant Attorney General and then as Attorney General, in the Kennedy and Johnson administrations, he helped to draft the historic 1965 Voting Rights Act. Clark is the author of the best selling book, *Crime in America* and of *The Fire This Time: U.S. War Crimes in the Gulf.* He is a contributing author in numerous books.

MICHEL COLLON (Belgium)

Mr. Collon is a journalist for the weekly paper *Solidaire.* He is the author of *Attention, Medias!* (1992). He analyzes the manufacture of the "media-lies" during the Gulf War and the manipulation of Western public opinion. He also examines the whole of the "media system," including property, advertising, links with the establishment, and dominant ideology. Mr. Collon is also author of *Poker menteur* (1998), in which he analyzes the media lies and hidden strategies of the great powers during the Yugoslavian war.

THOMAS DEICHMANN (Germany)

Mr. Deichmann is co-editor of the bi-monthly German magazine *Novo* published in Frankfurt. Since 1993, he has worked as a freelance journalist and researcher for more than 20 European papers, including *Suedeutsche Zeitung*, *Der Standard* (Austria), *Weltwoche* (Switzerland), *De Groene Arristerdammer* (Netherlands), *De Morgen* (Belgium), and *Helsingborgs Dagblad* (Sweden). More recently, he has received international recognition for his article "The Picture that Fooled the World," which exposed the fraudulent ITN video of the Trnopolje camp.

Deichmann can be contacted at
Thomas.Deichmann@t-online.de.

BENJAMIN DUPUY (Haiti)

Mr. Dupuy was former ambassador-at-large for the government of President Jean-Bertrand Aristide in Haiti. He is the co-director of *Haïti Progrès* newspaper. He is also the founder of Haiti Films, which has produced documentaries such as *Haiti: Reason to Flee* and the award-winning *Bitter Cane*. Currently, he is spokesperson for the PPN, the National Peoples Party, one of the largest popular organizations in Haiti.

LAURA FLANDERS (U.S.A.)

Laura Flanders is executive producer and host of *CounterSpin*, the nationally-syndicated radio program heard on 100 stations in the U.S. and Canada, and director of the Women's Desk at FAIR (Fairness and Accuracy in Reporting), the ten-year old media watch group. She is a long-time author and journalist and currently writes a column on women and media for the magazine *EXTRA* and contributes regularly to such publications as *The Nation, The Progressive, On the Issues* and

The Village Voice. She's been an international correspondent for the TV series *Rights and Wrongs* (aired on PBS) and a national anchor for Pacifica Radio. The Institute for Alternative Journalism named her one of ten "Media Heroes of 1994."

SARA FLOUNDERS (U.S.A.)

Sara Flounders is a founder and co-director of the International Action Center. In 1992 she coordinated the International War Crimes Tribunal on U.S. war crimes in the Gulf. The Tribunal held mass hearings in thirty U.S. cities and twenty other countries. She helped initiate the international movement to oppose the sanctions on Iraq. She is an editor and contributing author of several books exposing U.S. wars of this decade including: *War Crimes* (1992), *The Children Are Dying: The Impact of Sanctions* (1996), *Metal of Dishonor: Depleted Uranium* (1997), *Challenge to Genocide: Let Iraq Live* (1998) and *NATO in the Balkans* (1998). She has mobilized opposition to U.S. military intervention from Panama, Iraq and Somalia to the Sudan. She is currently focusing on NATO's role in dismembering Yugoslavia.

LENORA FOERSTEL (U.S.A)

Lenora Foerstel has been the North American Coordinator of Women for Mutual Security since 1990 and a member of the board of Women Strike for Peace.

She is a cultural historian whose research in the South Pacific included extended field work with Margaret Mead. She has published extensively in that area, including the book *Confronting the Margaret Mead Legacy: Scholarship, Empire and the South Pacific.* Foerstel has also edited and co-authored several other books, written numerous articles and produced several films. Her most recent publication is *Creating Surplus Populations: The Effects of Military and Corporate Policies on Indigenous People.*

LOUIS N. HIKEN (U.S.A)

As an attorney in San Francisco, Louis Hiken represents microradio broadcasters, like Free Radio Berkeley, who are challenging the FCC's ban on low power transmissions. He is a member of the National Lawyers Guild Committee on Democratic Communications.

MANSE JACOBI (U.S.A.)

Mr. Jacobi serves as webmaster for Free Speech Internet Television, which hosts hundreds of activists and community-based video and audio programming. The site recently won the Progressive Networks' Excellence in Streaming Media award. Jacobi has been involved with the United States Student Association, Student Environmental Action Coalition, Amnesty International and other student activist groups. He studies computer science and history of technology and occasionally writes about Middle Eastern issues. He is currently working on a digital video biography titled "Think Differently."

DIANA JOHNSTONE (U.S.A.)

Ms. Johnstone is the former European editor of *In These Times* (1979-1990), and former information officer of the Green Group in the European Parliament (1990-1996). She is the author of *The Politics of Euromissiles: Europe in America's World.* Her well researched articles in *Covert Action Quarterly* and in several French publications have exposed the role of Germany and the U.S. in the dismemberment of Yugoslavia.

CHARLES LEVENDOSKY (U.S.A.)

Mr. Levendosky is editorial page editor, columnist, creator and editor of the Caspar Star Tribune's First Amendment Website. He has received numerous journalistic awards, including the National Society of Newspaper Columnists, and the Silver Gavel Award, the American Bar Association's highest media award for columns.

MANIK MUKHERJEE (India)

An author and journalist, Mr. Mukherjee is also the editor-in-chief of *The Golden Book of Saratchandra* (multilingual compendium) and *The Golden Book of Vidvasagar* (English compendium). He is editor of *Trend* (English magazine), *Pathikrit* (Bengali magazine), and *Banglar Manisha* (Geniuses of Bengal) in Bengali.

MICHAEL PARENTI (U.S.A.)

Mr. Parenti is a major voice among political progressives. He received his Ph.D. from Yale University in 1962 and has taught at the University of Canterbury in New Zealand and California State University-Northridge. He is the author of *Democracy for the Few; Inventing Reality: the Politics of the Mass Media;* and *The Sword and the Dollar: Imperialism, Revolution and the Arms Race.* He appears regularly on radio and television and lectures frequently at college campuses across the country.

PETER PHILLIPS (U.S.A.)

Mr. Phillips is Assistant Professor of Sociology at Sonoma State University. He is the editor of the annual publication *Censored: The News that Didn't Make the News* (Winner of the First Firecracker alternative book award). As supervisor and coordinator of Project Censored, he has been a guest on national radio shows including NPR's *On the Media* and *Talk of the Nation*, Pacifica Radio's *Democracy Now, Talk America* and numerous other programs.

ZORAN PETROVIC PIROCANAC (Yugoslavia)

Mr. Pirocanac is a freelance reporter covering events in Israel, France, England and Poland. From 1990-1994 he served as editor-in-chief of the weekly newspapers *Independent* and

Bina. He is co-author of the publication *The Media Happened to Be There.*

NAWAL EL SAADAWI (Egypt)

Dr. Nawal El Saadawi is a novelist, psychiatrist and journalist who is known worldwide. Her novels and books on the situation of women in Egyptian and Arab societies have had a deep effect on successive generations of young women. Because of her outspoken writings in Egypt she has been imprisoned, censored and several times forced into exile.

She founded and edited the magazine *Health* as well as the magazine *Noon,* which was published by the Arab Women's Solidarity Association. She has been awarded several national and international literary prizes.

ADEL SAMARA (Palestine)

Mr. Samara is an economist, editor of *Ma'an Review,* and founder of Al Mashrig/Al-A'amil Research Center. As a political activist, he was jailed by the Jordanian regime in 1963,1965, and 1966 and in the Israeli occupied territories in 1967 and 1978. He is the author of several books: *Palestinian Capitalism* (Arabic), *Woman: Poverty and Work against Woman* (Arabic), *Democracy, Political Islam and the Left* (Arabic), *Industrialization in the West Bank* (English), and *Women vs. Capital in the Socio/Economic Formation in Palestine* (English).

DANNY SCHECHTER (U.S.A.)

Danny Schechter is a founder and the Vice President and Executive Producer of Globalvision, Inc., a media company formed in 1987. At Globalvision, he created the award-winning series "South Africa Now," which aired for three years. He co-created and co-produces "Rights and Wrongs: Human Rights Television," anchored by Charlayne Hunter-Gault, an award-winning globally distributed, weekly television news magazine series. Mr. Schechter has also produced and directed seven independent films including "Timothy Leary Lives" (1997), "Seeds of Peace" (1996), "Beyond JFK" for Warner Brothers, "Give Peace a Chance" for Polygram, "Countdown to Freedom," and Prisoners of Hope" with Distant Horizon/ Videovision," "Mandela in America" for A-Vision Entertainment Time-Warner), "The Making of Sun City" and several others. He filmed the Dalai Lama's visit to South Africa in 1996.

INDEX

Books & Videos from International Action Center

War, Lies & Videotape: how media monopoly stifles truth
What passes for the news today has been predigested by a handful of
media mega-corporations. Media critics, journalists and activists examine
the emerging global media systems. Topics include:
* growing concentration of media that stifles dissent and information
* links between the government, the media and the military
* war propaganda and NATO's expanding role in Yugoslavia
* the role of Big Oil, the Pentagon and the media in the Gulf
* how new technologies can help break through the media monopoly.

Edited by Lenora Foerstel, Chapters by: Jean-Bertrand Aristide, Scott
Armstrong, Ben Bagdikian, Brian Becker, Ramsey Clark, Thomas
Deichmann, Nawal El Saadawi, Sara Flounders, Diana Johnstone,
Michael Parenti and others.
International Action Center, 288pp, index, January 2000, $15.95

NATO in the Balkans: Voices of Opposition
The truth about what NATO is doing in the Balkans is not being told. For
an understanding of the deals behind the U.S.-imposed Dayton Accords
and the implication of a U.S.-controlled War Crimes Tribunal, *NATO in
the Balkans* fills in what's missing. Selections from Ramsey Clark, Sean
Gervasi, Sara Flounders, Nadja Tesich, Thomas Deichmann and others.
International Action Center, 236 pp., index, 1998, $15.95

NATO's Targets (1999 video)
NATO's systematic destruction of civilian targets in Yugoslavia during
the 1999 NATO bombing. Footage of bombed hospitals and schools and
national resistance. Shot by videographer Gloria LaRiva in the war zone
while traveling with former U.S. Attorney General Ramsey Clark.
VHS, 1999, 29 Minutes, $20 individuals $50 institutions

Challenge to Genocide: Let Iraq Live
Detailed reports on the devastating effects of economic sanctions on Iraq
since the Gulf War. Features "Fire and Ice," a chapter on the history of
the U.S. war against Iraq by former U.S. Attorney General Ramsey Clark.
Also personal memoirs from the May 1998 Iraq Sanctions Challenge.
Contributors include Ramsey Clark, Bishop Thomas Gumbleton, Rania
Masri, Sara Flounders, Ahmed El-Sherif, Brian Becker, Barbara Nimri
Aziz, Kathy Kelly, Monica Moorehead, and Manzoor Ghori.
International Action Center, 1998, 264 pp., photos, index, $12.95

Genocide by Sanctions (video)
Excellent for libraries, schools, and community groups and for cable-access television programs. This video documents on a human level how sanctions kill. An important educational tool in Medicine for Iraq campaign to collect medicine while educating people to change U.S. policy.
VHS, 1998, 28 minutes. $20 individuals, $50 institutions

Eyewitness Sudan (video)
An expose of the August 1998 U.S. bombing of the El Shifa, the small factory that produced more than half the medicine for Sudan. The smoking ruins are skillfully juxtaposed to footage of Clinton, Albright and Berger's charges. This documentary by Ellen Andors connects the years of sanctions to the cruise missiles sent against an African country.
VHS, 1998, 28 minutes, $20 individuals, $50 institutions

Metal of Dishonor: Depleted Uranium Second Edition New 1999
Learn about the criminal use of depleted uranium to poison Iraq's people and U.S. soldiers. Scientists, Gulf War veterans, environmentalists discuss a new generation of radioactive conventional weapons. The connection to the Gulf War Syndrome is discussed. Includes a new section on DU use in the Balkans. Sections by Rosalie Bertell, Helen Caldicott, Ramsey Clark, Jay M. Gould, Michio Kaku, Anna Rondon, and others.
International Action Center, 260 pp. with photos and index. $12.95

Metal of Dishonor (companion video, 1998)
Interviews with noted scientists, doctors, and community activists explaining dangers of radioactive DU weapons. Videographer Ellen Andors explores the consequences of DU.
People's Video Network, 45 min, VHS $20, PAL version for Europe $35

To order:
To place credit card orders, use the web: www.leftbooks.com . All mail orders must be pre-paid. Bookstore and university invoice orders, call **800 247-6553** (24-hour) or fax purchase order to **419-281-6883.**
- Bulk orders of 20 or more items at 50% off cover price.
- Shipping and handling: $4 for first item, $1 each additional item.
- International shipping $10 for first item, $2 each additional item.

International Action Center 39 W. 14th St., Rm. 206 New York, NY 10011